POWER
Praying

Hearing Jesus' Spirit by Praying Jesus' Prayer

DAVID CHOTKA

FOREWORD BY MAXIE DUNNAM

PRAYERSHOP
PUBLISHING

Terre Haute, Indiana

Prayer Shop Publishing is the publishing arm of Harvest Prayer Ministries and the Church Prayer Leaders Network. Harvest Prayer Ministries exists to transform lives through teaching prayer. Its online prayer store, www.prayershop.org, has more than 600 prayer resources available for purchase.

Scripture quotations labeled "NIV" are taken from the HOLY BIBLE, NEW INTERNATIONAL VERSION®. NIV®. Copyright © 1973, 1978, 1984 by International Bible Society. Used by permission of Zondervan. All rights reserved.
Scripture labeled "NASB" is taken from the New American Standard Bible®. © Copyright The Lockman Foundation 1960, 1962, 1963, 1968, 1971, 1973, 1975, 1977, 1995. Used by permission (www.Lockman.org).
Scripture labeled "NKJV" is taken from the New King James Version®. Copyright © 1982 by Thomas Nelson, Inc. Used by permission. All rights reserved.
Scripture labeled "GNT" is taken from the Good News Translation—Second Edition. Copyright © 1992 by the American Bible Society. Used by permission.
Scripture labeled "KJV" is taken from the Holy Bible, King James Version.
Scripture labeled "CEV" is taken from the Contemporary English Version. Copyright © 1991, 1992, 1995 by the American Bible Society. Used by permission.
Scripture labeled "RSV" is taken from the Revised Standard Version of the Bible, copyright © 1952 [2nd edition, 1971] by the Division of Christian Education of the National Council of the Churches of Christ in the USA. Used by permission. All rights reserved.
Scripture labeled "NEB" is taken from the New English Bible. Copyright © 1961, 1970 by the Delegates of the Oxford University Press and the Syndics of the Cambridge University Press.
Scripture labeled "TNIV" is taken from the Holy Bible, Today's New International® Version TNIV©. Copyright 2001, 2005 by the International Bible Society®. Used by permission of International Bible Society®. All rights reserved worldwide. "TNIV" and "Today's New International Version" are trademarks registered in the United States Patent and Trademark Office by International Bible Society®.
Scripture labeled: "ESV" is taken from The Holy Bible, English Standard Version. Copyright © 2001 by Crossway Bibles, a division of Good News Publishers. Used by permission, all rights reserved.

ISBN: 978-1-9350120-6-1

Library of Congress Control Number: 2009904211
3 4 5 6 7 | 2015 2014 2013 2012

Dedication

Dedicated to Gordon Fee who taught me to "think Greek" under the anointing of the Holy Spirit, to John White (in heaven now), who, with his wife, Lorrie, came at his own expense to my little church to teach us to understand the power of the kingdom of God, to Maxie Dunnam, who took an unknown under his wing and encouraged his heart, and most especially to my wife, Elizabeth, whose utterly commonsense approach to life is my greatest inspiration. She puts up with my idiosyncrasies and loves me just the same.

Table of Contents

Foreword

Another book on prayer? Yes, and I'm grateful. Prayer is at the center of the Christian life, and certainly we are not without great books on prayer. When we survey Christian writing through the ages, prayer has been at the forefront of reflection. The fact that the reflection continues underscores the importance of this privileged practice.

Many years ago I was called to lead a ministry of prayer for *The Upper Room*. I told those responsible for choosing a leader for this ministry that the fact they were even considering me showed how desperate the church was. I was such a novice in the practice. Their response was, "In the school of prayer, we are all beginners." There is truth in that.

I accepted the assignment, despite my glaring deficiency in the practice of prayer, because I felt "called." I surveyed the great literature on prayer and read countless books. Though many of the classics of the ages teach us about prayer, I discovered that I could read and read and read about prayer, but not pray.

That's one of the primary reasons I am excited about this book. You will find it difficult to **read/use** this book without praying. It is designed as an eight-week *interactive prayer journal/resource*. David Chotka believes that though we may continue to be "beginners" in the school of prayer, we can be bold kingdom-focused pray-ers.

Jesus' prayer, commonly called "the Lord's Prayer" is the model for our praying. Chotka does an imaginative and effective job using that model as a tool for teaching us to pray. He keeps as the center, the core of Jesus teaching about the kingdom of God. There is abundant scriptural reflection and commentary because the truth is we can't be people of prayer without being people of the Word. ? *Is this true?*

Chotka provides challenging and reflective commentary on Scripture. He does not quote it casually or in a proof-texting way. The core meaning is sought and expressed.

One thinks of Jesus' experience of prayer and fasting for forty days in the wilderness. A reality, much like a Global Positioning System, emerged as

Satan tempted and enticed Jesus at every turn. At every opportunity to make a wrong turn, which would have been fatal to His mission of salvation, Jesus recalled God's story (Scripture) which was deeply etched in His memory: "It is written." So Jesus prayed the Word.

It is this immersion in Scripture and centering on the kingdom that give us a much needed perspective on prayer. Many of our notions of prayer are far too individualistic in scope. Prayer, by nature, is personal, but Christian prayer is never individualistic. When we pray, "Our Father," we express personal intimacy and yet a radical inclusiveness of others. Too often we reduce prayer to a coping device to help us appropriate the peace of God in our warring circumstances, and to be sure, praying is often a "battle." But the "battle" must never be a matter of exercising the *power of prayer*; rather, it is always depending upon and claiming the *power of God.*

In my teaching conferences on prayer, I often ask the question, "What if there are some things God either cannot or will not do until and unless people pray?" Some folks immediately think I am challenging the sovereignty of God. Not so. I immediately follow up by asking, "Why is it such a long leap in our minds to think that God is as dependent upon our praying as He is upon our acting?" Rather than a challenge, this is an affirmation of God's sovereignty. He has ordered His economy in a way to involve us in His kingdom enterprise. That involves praying as it does acting.

David Chotka knows this. For more than a decade, his life has been intensely involved with this prayer and the teaching of our Lord. He writes out of his own experience of personal prayer and, as pastor, leading his congregations in being centers of prayer. The material in this book has been refined in the fire of group sharing, teaching, preaching, and experience. So this is not just a reading/intellectual exercise. It is a resource that will assist the reader in confidently claiming the calling that is ours to be co-laborers with Christ in the Kingdom, and, as Jesus said about Mary, prayer may be the *"most necessary thing"* in the total enterprise.

It is my prayer that this resource will reach thousands, so that the army of Kingdom-focused pray-ers will increase. Prayer is God's idea. He calls us to this practice as our partnership with Him. What an opportunity, and here is a resource that will assist us in responding more effectively to the call.

Maxie Dunnam

Preface

What is "Power Praying"? Perhaps the best way to get at this is to tell a story.

It was Sunday, September 2, 2007. The crowd numbered around 50,000 people. These people were dirt poor—some were destitute. Many had traveled on foot for as long as two weeks. Some had come from the war zones of South Sudan and the Democratic Republic of Congo, some had traveled from Kenya, and some had been the victims of the madness of Joseph Kone's "Lord's Resistance Army"—gang rape victims, widowed or orphaned. They were victims of violence, kidnapping, and despair. Some were the children of AIDS parents who had died—and they carried the HIV virus. But they were all hungry for the Word of God.

They stood in a field in Arua, Uganda, tucked up in the northern corner of that nation. The crowd would stand in the field from 3:00 in the afternoon to as late as 10:00 at night, just to hear stories of God's power, to see what God would do, and to hear the simple gospel of Christ presented to them.

And then it happened. A strange kind of cloud began to form above the area in which the choir sang. It was a cloud unlike clouds that formed during the rainy season and that produced the torrents that came in that time of the year in Northern Uganda. It swirled around only the stage and response area of the revival. Suddenly I realized that thousands of souls would have their last chance to respond to the gospel of Christ that night. They would have no other options. They would return to the war zones, having traveled to hear of Christ, but they would not have heard due to a downpour that would soak the field and ruin the third world electronic equipment that belonged to the evangelist.

Pastor Dennis, the worship leader from Kenya, began to pray against the rain. Suddenly, Lisa Plunkett, a member of our training team, also sensed God's call to come against the storm. She begain marching across the field. The worship team on the rickety platform did the same—and like true Ugandan tribal people, they began to dance their prayers and sing. And yet the rain began to fall—and the evening threatened to be a washout—as flooding had already decimated parts of Uganda and Kenya as well.

Suddenly I found myself overwhelmed with the awareness that this storm was no ordinary storm and that it must not be allowed to stop the destitute from hearing of the love of God.

I turned to Professor Mike Plunkett (one of the presenters in our prayer seminar—a pastor and professor at Nyack College in Nyack, New York) and told him that God had called me to rebuke the storm, as it was demonic in nature. Before my Canadian logic could stop me, I found myself standing in the middle of the field, before a crowd of thousands, shouting at the top of my lungs that the storm must stop in the name of our Lord Jesus. And then the most amazing thing happened.

The cloud stood still.

Before I could think of what to do, the compassion of Christ for the thousands of souls overwhelmed my spirit. In Jesus' name, I commanded the storm cloud to move, against the direction of the wind so that no one longing to hear of Christ would have that taken away from them. And as I pointed, the cloud changed direction and left the field. After twenty minutes or so I left the field and sat down.

A Ugandan woman named Teddi turned to me and said, "Pastor David, you need to return to the field. The cloud is trying to return."

I went again. The same thing occurred. The cloud left the field and I sat down. The same woman noticed the cloud return again, and told me once more.

This time, Fred Hartley (the founder of the College of Prayer International) and Mike joined me on the field. Together we agreed that the destitute would hear of the love of God and that the rain would not come. We rebuked that cloud and once again it moved against the flow of the wind, and away from the field, following the direction that we pointed.

Alone and together, over a two-and-a-half- to three-hour window, we did this five times.

By this time the evangelist was preaching, testimonies were being proclaimed, God's grace was explained.

Something like three thousand souls were saved that night, giving their lives to the Lord Jesus Christ. I had never seen anything like it. Multitudes literally ran to receive God's grace, renouncing witchcraft, throwing their amulets and charms to be burned. They renounced animism and, in some cases, they turned from Islam to Christianity, because they saw the power of God revealed in an incredible way.

Fred and Mike and I stood on that field and watched it happen. Mike then prayed a barrier around the field so that any storm cloud that crossed the perimeter would turn from a dark storm cloud to a fluffy white one. That is exactly what happened.

I believed in Christ's power of nature before. After this event, I truly believe in it even more profoundly.

That was "power praying." This was a case of God's kingdom coming on earth just as it did in heaven.

This resource is designed to help you learn to enter into the Presence and the power of God—to teach you day by day, seven days a week for eight weeks, how to access the incredible riches of God's goodness. It is designed to help you learn how to advance God's rule and to remove the powers of darkness wherever despair has the upper hand. Jesus' prayer is the key to unlocking the power of God. Use this resource to learn of His power as you submit yourself to obey the simple words of Christ's command: "When you pray, pray this way . . . Our Father . . ."

It is my hope and prayer that God will use this prayer journal to help you in your journey to know Christ and make Him known. May God grant you His leadership as you take up the calling to partner with God in seeing earth itself bow down to His glory, until all the world is "handed over to God that He might be all in all."

Getting Our Bearings

In the fall of 1983, I was given a copy of *The Workbook of Living Prayer* by Maxie Dunnam, never realizing that this resource would fundamentally revolutionize my life. You see, no one had taught me how to pray. I was aware that Jesus prayed much, both in public and private. I was equally aware that He commanded that we should seek God, even as He did. I had memorized what most believers call "the Lord's Prayer" and would often repeat it, knowing that Jesus pray that way. Yet there wasn't a clear understanding that the content of that prayer was profound. Though praying those words would grant a measure of comfort, it wasn't clear just why Jesus taught us to use that approach.

Then I was given Dunnam's book.

It was a day by day workbook, with weekly sections, designed to teach the learner to become a disciplined intercessor. Starting from scratch, anyone using that resource would learn a new prayer principle on every consecutive day, for seven days a week, for six (and up to nine) weeks. Each day included a significant theme, Scripture texts, some teaching related to that passage, a section to record one's learning or praying, and then a challenge for each day.

This was new—a daily guide to teach me to pray. So began a journey of joyful learning that has lasted to this very day, a discovery of innovative prayer principles, fresh approaches, different prayer authors, new understandings of texts, until all of these became a part of a life of "living prayer."

One of those weeks required that we take apart the key words and phrases of the Lord's Prayer, and paraphrase each line to better get at Jesus' intention in asking us to pray that line.

There was a second defining moment.

In 1994 Dr. Carl George came to teach my congregation. On the last day of his teaching, he told us of how he was processing an event that had disturbed him. A Korean prayer leader had confronted him with his complete inability to understand the key words and phrases of Jesus' prayer. That leader looked him in the eye and said, "Dr. George, do you know what Jesus meant by the term 'Father' when He used it in the Lord's Prayer?"

George answered "No. I have never done that study."

Then the fellow said, "Then how can you obey Jesus' command, 'When you pray, pray this way!' if you don't even know what He meant? And how about the word 'heaven'? Have you ever studied what the Lord meant by the word 'heaven'?

This was followed by "name," "will," "kingdom," etc. You can see where the conversation went. That leader encouraged George to learn exactly what each key word meant, to discover Jesus' intention in the thought concepts and principles in the prayer, and then to use the Lord's Prayer as a highway into Jesus teaching. The prayer then served as a tool to "pray Jesus' thoughts/ teaching after Him" concerning whatever we were seeking God about.

As George told the story of his visit with this prayer leader, the words of gentle correction spoken to George began to have an effect on my inner being. They started to take up residence in the deepest part of my soul and to stir up my thinking. What *did* Jesus mean by "Father" or "the kingdom" or "the will"? What did Christ understand heaven to be like? How did the "kingdom come" in heaven? How was God's will done in heaven? Was it even possible for His will to be done on earth, just as it is in heaven? What does it mean to "hallow" the name of God? These questions and many more began to flood over my thinking and more importantly, my praying, until it became abundantly clear that my praying was not at all in harmony with the instructions of our Lord.

And so began the journey that has led to this workbook. My method was simple. Take each word of the prayer and follow it through the teaching of Christ. What I didn't realize was just how broad this prayer truly is. Following the one word "Father" with reference to God took the next three months! That one-word study fundamentally changed the way I understood God in his nature and being. This affected every prayer I offered to Him, forever.

Now, just about fourteen years after this study began, I find that it is still a journey and not a completed work. There is still very much to learn about the Fatherhood of God, let alone, the kingdom of God and the will of God, the nature of temptation and evil, the power and the glory. And so, this workbook is offered as a starting point rather than as a finished work. None of us will ever plumb the depths of Jesus' teaching until He returns at the end of time and we can ask Him personally. But until then we have His teaching, we have His example, and we have His prayer. It rests with us to use whatever skills and abilities we have to discover what He meant and to "think His thoughts after Him."

OUR APPROACH TO LEARNING THE PRAYER

The format of this book is simple to follow. It is intended to be a seven-day-per-week workbook; it is not merely a book to read, but a journal to use. It is broken up into eight weeks: one week to begin with the basics of prayer, and then one week for each section of the Lord's Prayer. (The exception is the second movement. Even though the phrase "your kingdom come, your will be done" is focused on a single thought, the topic of the kingdom and the will is so large that each needs a separate week.) Each week has seven sessions, one for each day of the week. Each day begins with a theme for the day and some teaching based on the biblical material related to the themes of the Lord's Prayer to reflect on. Then there are a series of questions for your own use.

It is intended that you commit to writing what you are praying. This way you can follow your progress and remember what you have prayed during your time of living with this guide. No one else need see your writings except you. (In fact, if your thoughts disturb you, you can shred the document!) However, if you wish to journey together with other travelers on this exploration through the prayer of Christ, you may find yourself wanting to remember what you prayed, what you were wondering, and what others discovered as they prayed on the same day. Much learning comes through listening to the prayers and yearnings of others as they seek out God with the same Bible passages as you.

At the end of each day, a daily prayer challenge is given to you as part of the discipline of learning the prayer of Jesus. What Jesus teaches, we should do, and do at once! You are encouraged to start to pray, and to do so with each session. If you have not had success developing a meaningful prayer life, this guide is intended to help you begin the process. The universal testimony of all who have learned to pray fluently is that the only way to learn to pray is to pray! Perhaps it will seem unnatural at first. You may find that you write your prayers better than you speak them. Perhaps you will speak them better than you write them! Regardless, the most important thing that will occur out of using this resource will be that you will pray both on your own and (God willing) with others. This brings us to the final component of *Power Praying*.

A study/sharing guide for a small group, Bible study leader or Sunday school teacher is available for **free download at www.prayershop.org**. Go to the book's product page to find this guide. The best learning is learning that becomes so strong within you that you offer it to others. It is one thing to understand a concept or to receive some new insight. It is another to have that fire your imagination to such an extent that you want others to know about it. It is even better to discover that what you have learned is in fact what others are also learning, and that through the filter of their experience you discover some new application of the teaching you have just begun to apprehend.

There are two presuppositions intrinsic to this workbook. The first is that God speaks through the clear teaching of the Bible. In some way that defies human comprehension and imagination, human language was transformed when it was uttered or penned by the prophets, apostles, and writers of Holy Writ. As they spoke to human contexts of sin or misery, hope and celebration, sacred memory or horrific pain, their human words became the very words of God himself. As God spoke through them to their day and generation, so God speaks through their words to us in ours. It takes work to understand their context, and more work yet to understand how the word spoken then speaks to our time now.

This leads us to the second presupposition. It is that the Holy Spirit is the ultimate and best teacher. The Holy Spirit assists us in hearing the Word for our time. He takes those transformed words of Scripture, and by His very presence moving on the Word, "transfigures" them so that they are infused with indelible power that leaves us fundamentally changed into the image of Jesus Christ the Lord. We can do no better than to let the Word of God be "stamped" into our souls, so that the Holy Spirit can transform us from within by the renewing of our minds.

The Word of God and the Spirit of God are not independent of each other, but rather are joined together in accomplishing the purposes of God within us and through us. It is my prayer that this workbook will assist you in "becoming," and that you find through its use that you are being "conformed to the image of his Son" (Romans 8:29, KJV).

Week One

BEGINNINGS

DAY 1

We need to decide to pray.

"It was Napoleon Bonaparte . . . who said: 'There are only two forces in the world—spiritual force and material force, and spiritual force always wins.' Napoleon died a prisoner on the island of St. Helena. His dreams of world conquest died with him, mute testimony to the fact that he had used the wrong weapons."[1]

There comes a moment when a person has to make a decision about prayer. First of all, you have to conclude that prayer is helpful, meaningful, and a means to an end—knowing God and accomplishing God's purposes in and through us. Then you have to decide to actually pray. After this, with the decision made, you just have to do it.

This decision shouldn't be taken lightly, for prayer is life-transforming. If you want to remain as you are, don't start to pray, for prayer will change you forever.

All of life consists of and is shaped by the decisions that we make, whether those decisions seem major or minor. Today you will make a series of decisions—from the time that you will rise, to the clothes you will wear, to the interactions you will have with people. Each decision will, in some sense, direct the course of your life, and leave you slightly (or radically) different than you were before. Life consists of decisions made, and each decision changes us.

Sometimes decisions that are seemingly inconsequential lead to big changes. You may decide to enjoy a drink at the coffee shop and meet your new employer at the next table. On the other hand, decisions that we agonize over sometimes lead only to minor changes in the way we actually live. You may need to buy a new vehicle, think that you are in way over your head, and blissfully discover that your monthly payment schedule is just about the same as the previous month's—only now there is warranty with the vehicle.

To live is to choose, and to choose is to change. The only question that must be answered is whether you want to change one way or another. Our ability to choose is part of what makes us distinctively human.

To pray, or even to want to pray, is to choose. If you are just starting a life of prayer, then to pray is to make a choice to take a chance on a relationship with God (for to pray is to relate). If you are seasoned in praying, then to pray again is to choose as well. You are choosing to deepen your bond with the Author of time and space, enter into deep counsel with the Father of the Lord Jesus Christ about the eternal destiny of others, and forge new bonds of intimacy between yourself and the Almighty. But whether you are just starting or are far along in the journey, you are choosing.

This choice to pray (or not) involves some presuppositions. Before proceeding any further, take a few minutes to consider this imperative from Scripture: "Anyone who comes to God must believe that he exists and that he rewards those who earnestly seek him" (Hebrews 11:6, NIV).

Ponder this text for a few minutes. Saying it aloud a few times will reinforce the point and help get it clearly in your thinking. Consider this as a beginning point. Ask yourself what it means and record your impressions here.

You wouldn't reach out to something that you didn't believe was real so praying indicates a belief in God, and those who truly / earnestly seek him will be rewarded with his presence / relationship.

I once heard someone describe prayer as "the bridge we throw across the space between our weakness and God's strength—a bridge over which He can walk into the human heart." Prayer requires the recognition that there is distance between us and God and that the distance needs to be bridged. If we do not decide to pray, there will be no progress at all.

PEN TO PAPER

1) Has there been a time in your life when a "small" choice turned out to be life-changing? If so, record that incident here.

   The way I met Jim: driving past the dark house then stopping to help friends out of gas on the side of the road — all seemingly inconsequential decisions with a huge impact!

2) To live is to choose. To choose is to change. What was the last choice you

intentionally made to change something for the better (a habit, a direction, a job, a course of study, a friendship)?

The choice this morning to forego other things to sit down and start this study, and the recent decision to join the gym then start the Whole 30.

3) It is one thing to believe that God *exists* (many do). It is another altogether to believe that He *rewards* those who earnestly seek Him (sadly, many don't). Think for a moment about rewards from God. What kind of rewards are you seeking from this prayer adventure? *- interesting word*

closer intimacy with God again
hear His voice in decisions
know His power in this world of evil

4) The condition for the reward from God is to *earnestly* seek Him. That requires a decision. One can seek God for a season and not be in earnest. Another can earnestly seek rewards from God but not seek God Himself. God rewards neither. To seek God Himself (and to do so for God's sake) in earnest is the first decision needed to begin a life of prayer. Will you decide to make that commitment today?

Yes. Father, Jesus, Holy Spirit - please help me.

PRAYER CHALLENGE

Author and theologian Richard Foster said:

> To pray is to change. That is a great grace. How good of God to provide a path whereby our lives can be taken over by love and joy and peace and patience and kindness and goodness and faithfulness and gentleness and self-control.[2]

Begin praying today. Give God a few minutes of your time as you get started. Simply tell Him, "Lord God, I want to learn to pray. Teach me how to communicate with You. I want the greatest reward, and that is to know You and Jesus Christ, whom You have sent."

DAY 2

Focused prayer needs a dedicated time and place.

*"Those who do not pray at stated times in a direct and earnest
manner are not likely to pray at other times."*
—*Dr. John Henry Newman* [3]

The first part of praying is deciding to get started. The harder part of praying is to continue after beginning! Even the Lord found that He had no choice except to retreat from everything and everyone in order to fellowship with His Father. "In the early morning, while it was still dark, Jesus got up, left the house, and went away to a secluded place, and was praying there" (Mark 1:35, NASB).

Examine the prayer life of the Lord, and it soon becomes clear that He had a routine of prayer. Though He prayed with others, it is clear that He prayed alone frequently, often when it was dark and quiet. The significant events of the life of Christ were regularly found to occur while He was at prayer:

> Now while He was praying, heaven was opened, and the Holy Spirit descended upon Him in bodily form like a dove. (Luke 3:21-22, NASB)

> It was at this time that He went off to the mountain to pray, and He spent the whole night in prayer to God. And when day came, He called his disciples to Him and chose twelve of them, whom He also named as apostles. (Luke 6:12-13, NASB)

> And while He was praying, the appearance of His face became different, and His clothing became white and gleaming. (Luke 9:29, NASB)

Even a quick look at a few texts is sufficient to make the case that prayer was a regular part of Jesus' life. It is also clear that prayer was a significant element in the major events of His life. We can see that even God, the Son of God, needed prayer in His life. Think of it. This was God at prayer! It may seem obvious, but the first secret of prayer is to pray. Put it in your day planner.

Plan to pray.

Choose a place.

Choose a time.

Clear your calendar.

Go where no one will interrupt.

Then pray.

Do this regularly.

The *habit* of praying is more important than the amount of time spent in prayer. Some years ago a seminary student in his twenties told me that he wanted to develop his prayer life. He had just read a biography of a great intercessor and was inspired. He rose the next day at 5:00 (though he didn't need to be at class until 9:00). It was his plan to pray three hours a day, and so become one used by God for His work. He prayed for every classmate, every pastor or Christian worker, every uncle, aunt, friend, and even foe. He even prayed for the scrawny cat who lived in his university residence. Convinced he had stormed the gates of heaven and sacrificed for his Lord, he ended his prayers. Then he noticed his watch read 5:07.

He managed to rise two more days that way; on the fourth day he crawled back into bed, miserable and defeated. While both of us were speaking of another matter, his self-disappointment came into the center of our conversation. As he spoke of his discouragement, a thought popped into my mind.

"Can you give God five minutes a day?" I said.

"Five minutes? Is that enough?" he answered.

"How much time does God get now?" I asked.

"Nothing," he answered.

"Then five minutes is better than nothing."

The man agreed.

Together, we picked the best five minutes—the time when he was most awake, most aware, and most able to concentrate.

We picked the best place, a place where no one would interrupt him, and where people would leave him alone for as long as a half hour should he want to pray longer (which he very much doubted at the time).

We picked a time and place that he could use seven days a week, so that he could make a routine of being still before God (for being still can be prayer just as well as speaking).

We picked a book of the Bible, so that if he ran out of things to say, he could focus on the Lord by reading or studying Scripture.

We picked a time to talk with each other again to make sure he followed through.

Then he made a solemn vow, that if any unforeseen circumstance should interrupt his five minutes he would immediately choose another five-minute window and complete his prayers the same day. In the presence of God he committed to never violate that promise, but to pray a minimum of five minutes a day, every day, for the rest of his life.

And he did—for about two weeks.

Then five minutes just wasn't enough.

Within a year, he was praying on average twenty-five to thirty minutes a day in a dedicated time and was in fellowship with God all through the day, turning his life into an example of "living prayer." Sometimes his dedicated time went as long as an hour; sometimes he was back down to five minutes (though by then, dropping down to five minutes left him utterly unsatisfied). But he had established a prayer habit that continues to this present day.

PEN TO PAPER

1) Have you ever tried to develop a prayer life and been unable to get started? Perhaps you were inspired to pray and found that you could not sustain the habit. Record that time here.

2) Can you give God five minutes a day for sixty consecutive days? If so, will you promise that you will not violate that commitment? What five minutes will you give to Him? Plan to make it your best five minutes. Write the specific time down in this workbook as an act of commitment.

3) Can you find a time and a place where you can commit to this for seven days a week, and with the possibility of going longer than five minutes? As an act of commitment, name the place where you will pray.

4) Finally, select an alternate prayer time, in case you find you are unable to pray well during your time. Do the same for the place. Sometimes a chosen location cannot be used well. Have a Bible with you. Pick a gospel to read (Luke has a special prayer emphasis, as does the Acts of the Apostles), or work your way through the Psalms and pray them out loud. As a final act of commitment, indicate in writing what you will do with your time to ensure it is God's time should you find you are unable to sustain a prayer focus for the time (i.e., read, reflect on a Scripture text, commit to acts of service that "appear" in your thinking, etc.).

PRAYER CHALLENGE

Simple prayer is the best prayer. Most of the prayers in the Bible were not elevated, lofty pieces of literary achievement. They were a sharing of the heart between God and the one praying, often concerning some need or desire. As you begin with a commitment to five minutes a day, plan to tell the Lord about your hopes, ask Him to direct your decisions to make you more like Him. Should you run out of words, simply wait in His presence with an open Bible in hand. This also is prayer. Prayer is nothing more than relating to God as God relates to you.

If others are sharing this resource with you, tell them of your commitment to five minutes a day. If you are doing this journey on your own, perhaps there is someone you could tell who would hold you accountable for those five minutes. Prayer shared is prayer multiplied: "If two of you agree on earth about anything that they may ask, it shall be done for them by my Father who is in heaven" (Matthew 18:19, NASB).

DAY 3

The goal of prayer is to know God.

What do I pray about? That is a common question. Most who begin the journey of prayer assume that prayer consists of a series of requests (coming from us to God) followed by a series of answers (coming from God to us). With this view in mind, we turn prayer into a sort of "achievement" orientation. Prayer becomes a means to an end, and the end is God's direct intervention into human affairs along the lines of the fulfilling of our legitimate needs (most know that to pray according to a purely selfish desire is not pleasing to God).

We must be careful here. It is right to communicate with God about anything (even to tell Him when we are being selfish). And God does intervene in human affairs as a direct response to the prayers of His people. One of the important ends of prayer is for God to hear and to answer. However, the main point of prayer is to enter into the fullness of life itself. Jesus said it best when He prayed about the nature of eternal life itself, and the goal of our very existence: "Now this is eternal life: that they may know you, the only true God, and Jesus Christ whom you have sent" (John 17:3, NIV).

When eternity arrives, we won't have any "things" to pray about, or any situations that will require a special intervention of the divine presence—God will be manifestly and directly present to everything and everyone at once. But we will find ourselves joyfully confronted with and be in intimate communication with the radiant presence of the living God and the risen Lord beyond the close of time and forever. Prayer is an anticipation of that ultimate reality, a starting point in the journey to that goal.

Two days ago we took a beginning look at the concept of receiving a reward from God in response to prayer. Author Philip Ryken makes the point well when he speaks of the ultimate reward:

The reward for secret prayer is the prayer itself, the blessing of resting in the presence of God. <u>Prayer</u> does not simply *maintain* the Christian life; it *is* the Christian life, reduced to its barest essence. Can there be any greater joy—in this world or the next—than to commune in the secret place with the living God?[4]

The text from John 17:3 quoted above is just the beginning of the main point of that chapter—that the goal of Jesus' coming to earth was that we might know God intimately. The supreme aim of prayer is utter union and complete participation in the very nature of God Himself—in all three persons of the Godhead. It is to be joined to the Father, the Son, and Holy Spirit in the same way as Christ Himself was joined to His Father.

Holy Father, keep them in Your name, the name which You have given Me, that they may be one even as We are . . . that they may all be one; even as You, Father are in Me and I in You, that they also may be in Us, so that the world may believe that You sent Me. (John 17:11, 21, NASB)

There is much to consider in these texts—too much for a single day's reflection. Take some time now to consider the union of Christ and His Father. Take some time to consider what it might mean for you personally to enter into that kind of relationship with God.

PEN TO PAPER

1) What came of your time of reflection on John 17 above? Jot your thoughts down for future reflection.

2) Have you ever found yourself in need and praying for God to intervene? Did you experience a sense of the direct intervention of God? If so, record an incident here to remind you that the Lord does in fact do this.

Leaving Elmhurst
Coming to MI

3) There are differences between knowing someone (and being able to greet them on the street), knowing someone well enough to determine how she will react to a certain set of circumstances (maybe she despises tuna casserole), and truly knowing someone at the deepest level. *The goal of prayer is to pass through all the levels of knowing until absolute intimacy is achieved with God Himself.* What does this thought mean to you? Attempt to put it into words. *I'm not totally comfortable with prayer having a "goal". Prayer is, though, relationship/ conversation with God. Being intimately known and accepted is, I believe, what every spirit was made for and longs for. This is the miracle of Christ, and prayer is one way it can be achieved.*

4) Think of the intimacy between God the Father and God the Son. What is clear from the Bible is that there was constant communication between them, and that their communication was perfect, clear, and sinless. Jesus was utterly and totally safe in knowing and being known. The Father was utterly safe in knowing and being known. Nothing was hidden between them. Jesus defines this "knowing" as "eternal life." God wants that kind of intimacy between Himself and you. If you knew that anything you said or thought was "safe," what would you say to God? Reflect on this for a few moments and record that here. *Thank you. Help me to grow in my intimacy with you so that every area of my life reflects You.*

PRAYER CHALLENGE

Decide today that you will give God the "unsafe" stuff of life—the nasty thoughts, the greedy inclinations, the lustful moments, the hard-to-explain yearnings that have no words. Give these to God's safekeeping and thank Him that they are safe there forever.

DAY 4

God initiates, we respond.

There was a long season in my life when I thought that prayer was to tell God what needed to be done. The profound impression I had was that if one just prayed longer and more intensely, God would be persuaded to alter the stream of events in my life (or in those for whom I was praying). Phrases like "we must pray this one through" or "we need to storm the gates of heaven" picked up from well-meaning people in prayer meetings contributed to the thought that all the initiative belonged on the human side. The heroes were Jacob, who wrestled with the angel and "had his way with God," even though it meant having his hip taken out of joint (a poor understanding of Genesis 32:22-32), and the widow who wore down the unrighteous judge (Luke 18:1-8). For the record, Jacob was a deceitful schemer who wouldn't let God bless him until he was broken and helpless. The parable of the widow and the wicked judge is a *contrast*, not a comparison. God is *not* a wicked judge, but a loving God who answers quickly—so don't give up praying (the point of Luke 18:1). Surely if a scoundrel could hear a persistent whiner, then a loving God will immediately pay attention to the needs of His people!

Just the same, these were the models, and long were the prayer meetings. We would agonize and have no sense of relief should the prayer not be answered, because it was *our* responsibility. The trouble is that praying like this leaves the believer's walk with God as disjointed as if he were wrestling with Jacob and the angel! We will find ourselves as weary as the widow of Luke 18 pestering a corrupt power-monger to get his attention!

It was a great relief to discover somewhere along the way that all true prayer arises not from us, but from God Himself. John White says it succinctly:

> Prayer is not *you* trying to move *God*. Prayer is among other things being caught up into God's directions and activities. He orders the

affairs of the universe, and he invites you to participate by prayer. Intercession is God and you in partnership, bringing his perfect plans into being.[5]

Here the heroes in our praying are the Lord (who did nothing unless the Father told Him [John 5:19-20]) and the apostles and prophets (who, when praying, obeyed the prompting of the Spirit to accomplish God's purposes [Acts 13:1-3; 16:6-10]). In particular the apostle Paul serves as a solid model for prayer; he teaches about God-initiated prayer in the experience of the perplexed believer.

> In the same way, the Spirit also helps our weakness; for we do not know how to pray as we should, but the Spirit Himself intercedes for us with groanings too deep for words; and He who searches the hearts knows what the mind of the Spirit is, because He intercedes for the saints according to the will of God.
>
> And [through this] we know that God causes all things to work together for good to those who love God, to those who are called according to His purpose. (Romans 8:26-28, NASB)

Did you get that?

Through the groaning of the Spirit within, God *prays through us*, and through that praying brings something new to birth, usually in us first, but also in our situations.

God initiates.

We respond.

Stop and take a moment to reflect on the Romans text. Think of a time when you didn't know how or what to pray, and all you could do was groan. Perhaps you are groaning now with the weight of grief or deep despair. Ask the Spirit to pray through you to accomplish some great good.

PEN TO PAPER

1) Think about something that you had to do because you were obligated. It gave you no pleasure. It fact, it filled you with a sense of grim foreboding each time it came to mind. Yet you knew that there was no other choice

except to do what needed to be done. Record that incident here.

2) Now reread John White's words about the nature of prayer as a partnership initiated by God. Stay with the words for a few moments and let them soak into your soul. Now, in your own words, paraphrase what White is saying in the space below:

3) The point of Romans 8:18-30 is that God calls us to a deep sharing, an intimate fellowship, in fact a union with His own activity of prayer. Just as John 17 speaks of us being joined to the Father and the Son, so here in Romans we are joined to the Spirit's praying. Creation is "pregnant" with the promise of some new thing and is groaning with labor pains. God prays *through us* by the movement of His Spirit in the deepest heart of the believer to cause the creation to birth some new good thing, i.e., to "cause all things to work together for good." Reread the text above. What is your place of "groaning that is too deep for words"? Perhaps all that you can record is a name—a place, an event, a time. Record what you can below so that you can offer this to God. Then let Him pray through your soul.

PRAYER CHALLENGE

Sometime today you may sense a stirring in your soul to pray for someone. You may be standing in a checkout line in a grocery store or parked at a gas station and notice someone. Deep within there is an awakening that this one needs prayer. This is God initiating a prayer within you. To respond, simply ask the Lord to pray through you. Ask God to reshape this person's context to bring about some great good. Instead of "praying through" to break into God's presence, let God "pray through" you, by the Spirit of Jesus giving you a prompting inside. Commit to do this each time you are in the presence of other people, just for today.

DAY 5

Jesus' perpetual ministry for us is to pray.

I remember the moment clearly. I was driving down a mountain road in the interior of British Columbia, crying out to God as I was descending. I had gone through three consecutive heart-wrenching experiences, any one of which would have been enough. But three devastating blows in the same window of time clouded my thinking and brought me to a point of despair.

I didn't think I could ever pray again.

In fact, I had resigned my church because (among other reasons) God and I weren't talking to each other very well. It is hard to preach the Bible and proclaim the goodness of God when you are not sure its promises apply to your own life anymore. When we spoke, it wasn't a two-way communication. It was usually just me demanding to know why God had allowed what He did.

Driving along in the car, I cried out, "Why did You do that!"

Sometimes I would shout. Other times I would sob. It seemed that God had abandoned me, though strangely, even in my arguing with Him, I sensed His nearness. There were no clear answers—only His nearness and a great cloud of confusion.

Each prayer initiative that I had offered up to the Lord—that I had lived and hoped to see accomplished—had come crashing down. These were not incidental prayers about minor things. These were the prayers of my life—and they had come to nothing. And yet the unmistakable marks of God's hands had been all over the calling to pray that very way. One divine appointment after another had confirmed that these were not merely things I wanted God to do, but things that God wanted me to pray and live. I was not "praying through" for God to do things my way. I was "being prayed through" for God to do things His way.

But then, why had things gone so terribly wrong?

Was I wrong?

Had He spoken and I messed the whole thing up?

Could I ever hear Him aright?

I needed help.

My conclusion was that I was the problem. Every ounce of my believing had been focused on hearing and obeying God. It was now evident to me that I simply couldn't get it right. And so the best thing to do was to resign my church and retool my life. Careening down that stretch of descending mountain pass felt good. It was solid. I could see the road. I could think. I stopped at a roadside turnoff for a few minutes just to stretch. Then I picked up the book I was reading. It was *The Workbook of Living Prayer* by Maxie Dunnam—a six-week course on what else but learning to pray. On Day 5 of Week 4, Dunnam made an affirmation that was working its way into my soul.

> The Living Christ is praying for you *now*: "Consequently he is able for all time to save those who draw near to God through him, since he always lives to make intercession for them" (Hebrews 7:25, RSV).

> **Ponder this:** *Jesus' prayers are affecting you now.* In addition, *Christ intercedes for you now.* What does this do for you? Immerse yourself in this truth for a few minutes.[6]

It hit me with tremendous force. Jesus was perfect (it was more than abundantly clear that I was not). Jesus was sinless. Jesus was resurrected into glorious, magnificent authority and power. Jesus was seeing reality from the perspective of eternity. There were now no barriers to His perfect knowledge. He could see the start from the finish.

And Jesus was praying—for me.

I found myself weeping like a baby. The tears streamed down my face until it was hard to see. If Jesus prayed, there would be an answer—a perfect one, a sinless one, a glorious one that would unravel all the complexities and produce a wonder. God would see me through.

I asked Him if I could join Him in His perfect praying, and add my imperfect intercessions to His matchless ones. It was then I realized that His Spirit was praying through my groaning, that God was interceding through me, despite me! Somehow, there would be an answer that was waiting to be born.

The story is long, but the answers did come. Over the course of time the confusion turned into clarity. The crisis of faith turned into a process of growth. But it was that crisis moment in the British Columbia interior that began to turn the whole thrust of my life from a negative escapism to a positive outcome. God was still with me. He always had been.

And a primary reason Jesus lives is to pray—for you, for me, for everyone who calls on His name. R. A. Torrey sees this as the motive to pray:

> I know of nothing that has so impressed me with a sense of the importance of praying at all seasons, being much and constantly in prayer, as the thought *that that is the principal occupation at present of my risen Lord.* I want to have fellowship with Him, and to that end I have asked the Father whatever else He may make me, to make me at all events an intercessor, to make me a man who knows how to pray, and who spends much time in prayer.[7]

PEN TO PAPER

1) Dunnam's point to ponder is a good one. Reflect on this: Jesus' prayers are affecting you *now*. Christ intercedes for you now. What does this do for you? Immerse yourself in this truth for a few minutes.

2) Torrey's point is that if Jesus lives to pray, then to know Jesus in any kind of meaningful way is to join Him in that work. What does that mean for you at this point in your life?

3) Could it be that the "groaning of the Spirit in prayer" in Romans 8:26-28 is in fact the praying of our resurrected Lord who intercedes for

us in Romans 8:34? This would mean that His praying *for* us is in fact His praying *through* us. All the more reason to open our hearts to the movement of the Spirit of God in prayer. What are the implications if that is so? What must your role then be?

PRAYER CHALLENGE

Pick three times today (coffee break? waiting at a red light? walking from the bus to your front step?) when you can ponder the fact that Christ's primary role as the Resurrected Lord is to pray for you. Take comfort in His intercessions and know that they will be accomplished.

DAY 6

God "speaks" to us when we pray.

The theme for the day is that God *speaks* when we pray. Italics are used because hearing voices is a rare and unusual occurrence in prayer. Even in the ministry of Jesus Christ, there are only a few recorded instances of a voice being heard (i.e., at His baptism, on the Mount of Transfiguration, and in John 12, just before He went to the cross). Still, it is the uniform testimony of Christians of every age that somehow, some way, the God they love and serve has given them direction. Somehow God has communicated with them. God has "spoken."

Hearing God is linked to having our prayers answered. Jesus did nothing unless His Father told Him (John 5:19-20). Still, He had a jump start on all creation. Like no one else, He was conceived of the Holy Spirit directly. All through His days on earth He was conscious of His Father's initiatives (e.g., Luke 2:41-51), and was able to "learn obedience" by consistently obeying what He heard (Hebrews 5:8-9). This is something that we too have to learn, first of all by "unlearning" doing things merely from common sense. We must acquire sensitivity to the things of God and develop a sense of listening to the voice of the Spirit.

The first step in that process is to immerse ourselves in Scripture, especially in the teaching of Jesus Himself. There are promises connected to that practice. Here is one: "If you abide in Me and My words abide in you, ask what you wish and it will be done for you. My Father is glorified by this, that you bear much fruit and so prove to be My disciples" (John 15:7-8, NASB).

R.A. Torrey speaks to this text in his delightful little book *How to Pray*. He names two conditions for answered prayer. The first is to abide in Christ and the second is for Jesus' words to abide in you. With the first, Torrey looks to the context, which is Jesus' illustration of a vine and branches. Branches have no life of their own, but receive life only as the sap of the vine flows through the branches. The branch can't live independently of the vine. Jesus tells us then not to pursue an independent life, but rather, in Torrey's words, to:

> Give up trying to think our thoughts, or form our resolutions, or cultivate our feelings and simply and constantly look to Christ to think His thoughts in us, to form His purposes in us, to feel His emotions and affections in us. *It is to renounce all life independent of Christ and constantly to look to Him for the inflow of his life and the outworking of His life through us . . . [this way] our desires will not be our desires, but Christ's; and our prayers will not in reality be our own prayers, but* Christ praying in us.[8]

Once again, we are drawn back to the theological principle that God initiates and we respond. Christ is present within through the ministry of His Spirit, bearing witness (pointing, drawing attention) to His Word. We are to ask Jesus to pray *through us* instead of asking God to bless *our* initiatives. We are to connect with Him as the first part of our praying. This involves hearing. Hearing from God is the basis of the second condition for answered prayer.

The second condition is that Jesus' words abide in us.

> If we are to obtain from God all that we ask from Him, Christ's words must abide or continue in us. We must study His words, fairly devour His words, let them sink into our thoughts and into our heart, keep them in our memory, obey them constantly in our life, let them shape and mold our daily life and our every act. . . . It is vain to expect much power in prayer unless we meditate much upon the words of Christ and let them sink deep and find a permanent abode in our hearts. . . . If we thus let the words of Christ abide in us, they will stir us up to prayer. They will be the mold in which our prayers are shaped, and our prayers will be necessarily along the line of God's will and will prevail with Him. *Prevailing prayer is almost an impossibility where there is neglect of the study of the Word of God.*[9]

It is a simple thing, really. God communicates in us, to us, and through us by the Word of Christ. The Spirit moves upon the Word. The Word and the Spirit always work together. One points to the other, and both together shape the life of Christ within the believer. As we are much in the Word, promptings enter our thinking that we should pray a certain way. We realize that it is an idea that conforms to the teaching of Jesus. And so we say, "Let this be so. Bring this to pass, Lord. It is in harmony with Your Word." We ask the Spirit of Christ to deepen that prayer within us, to keep it constantly before us until it is accomplished. We hold it before the presence of God until we receive a prompting in our soul that the prayer has been heard and answered. Then we wait for it to be so.

PEN TO PAPER

1) If you haven't done this before, you may need to just stop and ask the Lord to take up residence in and through you. If you have, but have had no understanding that Christ is to pray through you, pray this prayer:

> *Lord Jesus, I renounce any and all life that is apart from You. You are pictured as the vine. We are pictured as the branches. Connect me to who You are, that Your life may flow into and through me, in my living, in my believing, and most especially in my praying. Make the truth of Your Word alive in me that I might pray Your purposes into existence. Amen.*

Now, as an act of commitment, record the time and date of your commitment to live and pray His way instead of your own. Write down any thoughts or feelings you are having concerning this commitment. Then, to seal it, tell another person what you have done.

2) If you have already made that commitment, perhaps a fresh commitment is needed to immerse yourself in the teachings of our Lord. It is by immersing ourselves in the teachings of Jesus that we come face-to-face with God's initiatives! God initiates through His Word. The Spirit of God moves upon that Word and brings prayer about as we meet our circumstances. Thus, the Word (living in our hearts) made alive by the Spirit of God within us is stirred to pray God's purposes into existence as our lives touch others and our culture. God then prays "through us." If

you have taken the commitment to be joined to Christ the Vine, renew that commitment now by praying this prayer:

Lord Jesus, You are the vine and we are the branches. Reconnect my faith to Your life-giving Word. In Your presence I commit to immersing myself in the Word and works of Jesus Christ, that they may impart the presence of God into my soul. Every day, I shall place myself before Your Word and pray that it take up residence in my heart forever. Amen.

PRAYER CHALLENGE

Write John 15:7 out on a card and carry it with you to read whenever you have an opportunity today. If you are able, commit it to memory and recall it as often as you have a chance to do so. Let the words of that Scripture "abide in you" throughout the day. If it is helpful, write out what that text means to you below (but only after giving it a day of reflection so that it begins to "abide in you").

John 15:7 means

DAY 7

The goal of prayer is to listen to God.
To listen to God is to obey Him.

My sheep hear my voice, and I know them, and they follow Me.
(John 10:27, NASB)

The whole thing sounds mystical.

In fact, many a mystical thought has been penned about this verse. Much attention is paid to forms and methods of giving heed to a voice that is constantly speaking, but that is not the point of this text at all.

Here we have a picture of a shepherd and his sheep. Middle Eastern flocks were small, and the shepherds knew each sheep. The shepherd would earn the trust of his sheep by ensuring their safety and provision. That safety became associated with the shepherd's voice. When the shepherd spoke (and he didn't always speak), the sheep would pay attention and respond. If others spoke, the sheep would not acknowledge them, unless out of fear. The sheep, constantly in the presence of their shepherd, had a lot of time for practice.

Some sheep required more attention than others. The shepherd had, of necessity, to speak more frequently to them than to others in the flock. Hearing the voice, then, was not a mark of more maturity. In this case, it was the sign of needing more attention!

Christians need not be concerned with continually seeking direction, with a hearing of God's voice at all hours of the day or night. God does not "chat." Instead God speaks when something important needs to occur either within or through the believer. (In the account of Elijah, the prophet was sent to a widow in a foreign town for a long time. He acted on the word he had received and waited. First Kings 18:1 (NIV) says, "After a long time, in the third year, the word of the LORD came to Elijah.")

Perhaps a more helpful way to render the text from John 10 would be to indicate that when the shepherd speaks, the sheep pay attention. "My sheep *pay heed to* my voice . . . and they follow me."

When God "speaks," we are to obey.

This understanding removes the pressure of always attempting to make sure we have had yet another specific word of direction. It is sufficient to know that the words of Scripture are working their way through who we are, that we are attempting to practice what we know, and that God's love is fixed on us. Special words from the Shepherd do come, and when they do, we should pay attention. But the point is that words don't need to come every instant of every day. Obedience, however, is a necessity. To obey the promptings of the Lord by both Word and Spirit is one of the conditions of answered prayer: "And whatever we ask we receive from Him, because we keep His commandments and do the things that are pleasing in His sight" (1 John 3:22, NASB).

John in this passage has indicated that God had given him a blank check. He gets whatever he asks. However, this is conditional. It is only because he obeys what God communicates to him by the Word in his life that any answers come at all. If we turn a deaf ear to the commands of God, God is under no obligation to answer. A. W. Tozer, a popular writer and preacher of the last century, makes the point profoundly:

> We must be on what old-fashioned Christians often call "praying ground"; that is, we must be living lives pleasing God. . . . God has not placed Himself under obligation to honor the requests of worldly, carnal, or disobedient Christians. He hears and answers the prayers only of those who walk in His way.[10]

Herein lies an explanation for many of the unanswered prayers of the church. The problem lies on our side. The positive side of "Draw near to God and He will draw near to you" (James 4:8, NASB) is plain and trustworthy. The flip side of that text is that, should we draw away, God is not honor-bound to draw near or answer when we call.

We must make it the study of our lives to discover and do what pleases the Lord. To fail to do this is to remove the promise of answered prayer from our lives.

PEN TO PAPER

1) Can you recall a time when you knew beyond all knowing that God

had given a specific direction for you to pursue? What was it like? What convinced you that it was the voice of God as opposed to just your own thoughts?

2) The promise of answered prayer comes with a requirement to keep His commands. Are there any areas of your life in which you know you are not doing as God would have you? Name them below, and then pray the prayer of renunciation printed here.

> In the name of the Lord Jesus Christ, the only King and Head of the church, I acknowledge that I have turned away from God's leading in this matter: _____. Right now, in the presence of God and the holy angels, I renounce this behavior. I yield it up to God and choose to replace it with obedience to God's Word. As far as I understand the Lord Jesus and His Word, I will obey Him. He is my Lord and Savior. Amen.

PRAYER CHALLENGE

Go through your home today and see if there are any "triggers" (things or circumstances) that set you up to disobey God. As far as possible, remove them from your home and be done with them. Then, as far as possible, replace those triggers with things that would call forth obedience to the commands of Christ.

PRAISE THE FATHER

"Our Father in Heaven, Hallowed Be Your Name."

DAY 1

The Lord's Prayer is more than a guide to prayer.
It is a highway to all of Jesus' teaching.

T ake a moment and pray the words of this well-known prayer, slowly and reverently using the text from the New American Standard 1995 edition. Don't read any further. Get yourself into a comfortable position and follow the directions:

Pray then in this way:
Our Father who is in heaven,
Hallowed be Your name.
Your kingdom come.
Your will be done,
On earth as it is in heaven.
Give us this day our daily bread.
And forgive us our debts, as we also have forgiven our debtors.
And do not lead us into temptation, but deliver us from evil.
[For Yours is the kingdom and the power and the glory forever. Amen.]
(Matthew 6:9-13, NASB)

Was that a meaningful exercise? Do it again, only this time, take a deep breath between each line printed above, and use the time to think on the words you have spoken.

Most of us have prayed the Lord's Prayer. In fact, most have prayed its exact form or used it as a model considerably more than a few times. We have done it in thirty seconds, or for perhaps as long as a minute. If you did the breath exercise with the prayer, you may have been able to pray it a bit longer. We have uttered it in public prayer contexts, or as the final closing at the Sunday evening service. We know this prayer—or at least we think we do. But most of us haven't thought about what this prayer meant in its original context. And most of us certainly haven't prayed this prayer using the concepts and ideas the way that Jesus intended.

Jesus' prayer is a rich vein of pure gold. Sadly, we have buried the vein instead of mining its wealth. I had no idea how much was in this prayer until I had a "conversion" experience related to it in 1994. I met Dr. Carl George, whose prayer life was radically altered by practicing this prayer. He had met a significant prayer leader who used the Lord's Prayer as a model to intercede for three hours a day. The key was to discover just what was in it, using the teaching of Jesus to understand the prayer of Jesus. If Jesus used a word consistently to convey a particular meaning in His teaching and then used that word in the prayer, odds were that this should be the sense Jesus intended and, in turn, how we ought to pray. And so, thinking that this would take a couple of months, I began a study that has continued to the present day! Most of the major themes of Jesus' teaching are found in this one prayer.

For example, the first key word is "Father" as a title for God. The word "Father" with reference to God is used only fourteen times in the entire Old Testament. Almost all of these instances are symbolic or metaphorical allusions to God (e.g., Psalm 103:13 [NASB], "As a father has compassion on his children, so the LORD has compassion on those who fear Him"). There are only two prayers in the entire Old Testament in which the one praying says "Father" with reference to God, and in that material it refers to God's creation of Israel rather than a personal relationship (Isaiah 63:16; 64:8).

In the New Testament, the word "Father" is used for God fifteen times in the Sermon on the Mount alone (Matthew 5-7), and forty times in Matthew's gospel. "Father" is used over 170 times for God's name in the New Testament and *every single prayer of Jesus* begins with this title for God. (The exception is when, from the cross, Christ quotes Psalm 22, saying, "My God, My God. . . .")

Prayer went from utter transcendence in the Old Testament to profound intimacy in the New. For Jesus to teach us to pray using the title "Father" was for Him to profoundly deepen the faith of Israel and to take prayer to an entirely new level.

Each key word in this prayer conveys a new facet of prayer. The key words in order of appearance are:

- Father
- Heaven (two times)
- Hallowed (i.e., consecrated/sanctified)
- Name
- Kingdom (two times)
- Will (of God)
- Daily bread (i.e., provision)
- Forgive (two times)
- Debts (sins/wrongs—"trespasses" in the Common Prayer edition)
- Temptation/trial
- Evil (or the evil one)
- Power
- Glory

These words are keys to the teaching of Jesus. This prayer then is a model to teach us to pray ourselves into the thinking of our Lord Himself. To pray "Your kingdom come" must require that we understand what "the kingdom of God" means. To use the word "Father" with reference to God requires that we understand what it meant to our Lord so that we can appropriate it for ourselves. To do anything less is to shortchange the prayer and do lip service to God instead of entering into prayer from the heart. And so this course is an invitation to live with this prayer for the next seven weeks.

There are six discernable sections to the Lord's Prayer (Matthew 6:9-13, NKJV) that I have shaped into an acrostic using the word "PRAYER." (Others have named seven by separating the "kingdom coming" prayer from the prayer for the "will" to be done. Contextually, though, they seem to belong together. Since the themes of the kingdom and the will are so large, we will dedicate a week to each idea.)

P raise the Father	*Our Father in heaven, hallowed be Your name.*
R equest the kingdom	*Your kingdom come. Your will be done on earth as it is in heaven.*
A sk for provision	*Give us this day our daily bread.*

*Y*ield your sins to God   *And forgive us our debts, as we forgive our*
                                       debtors.

*E*ngage the enemy   *And do not lead us into temptation, but*
                                       deliver us from the evil one.

*R*ejoice in God's victory   *For Yours is the kingdom and the power and*
                                       the glory forever. Amen.

Each week shall take as its principal theme each of the six sections in turn (with two weeks on the kingdom/will material). We will live with each major emphasis until we have done justice to the entire prayer.

PEN TO PAPER

To get started on this adventure, attempt to put into your own words what Jesus meant by the phrases that are part of this prayer. Make each of the sections your own. Attempt to render ancient concepts into modern language. Let me give you my attempt to do justice to the first line, just to get you started:

> God in radiant, uncreated light, You are utterly beyond our grasp, yet You reveal Yourself in the humblest form—as the strong provider for a very human family—"Father." Better yet, "Dad." Your reputation, Your good name has been treated so poorly in our society. Some treat You as irrelevant and do not deign to speak of You at all. To disregard Your name is to treat it with contempt. Some mutter the name of Your Son when they cut their hands or stub their toes, not thinking or knowing that You would want that name reserved for the highest regard and worship. This must change. Grant that I may be a change agent to show that You are worthy of only the highest love and sacrifice. Grant that I might live a life of praise, and make looking up the first part of all my praying. Grant that in my life and through my presence, others will speak well of Your reputation. Hallowed be Your name.

The point of praying is to speak your heart to God's. Take your time here. These are Jesus' deepest words. Ask Him to pray through you as you attempt to understand and pray His thoughts after Him.

1) Our Father in heaven, hallowed be Your name.

2) Your kingdom come. Your will be done on earth as in heaven.

3) Give us this day our daily bread.

4) And forgive us our debts, as we forgive our debtors.

5) And do not lead us into temptation, but deliver us from the evil one.

6) For Yours is the kingdom and the power and the glory forever. Amen.

PRAYER CHALLENGE

Decide that you will pray the Lord's Prayer today whenever you have a free moment. It can be done is as little as twenty seconds. Perhaps at lunch or after work, you could slow this prayer down. Pray each phrase using the method you started with at the beginning of this exercise—take a deep breath, thinking all the while about what the line means. Then proceed to the next line, letting the truths of Jesus' prayer soak in and out of your soul with each breath.

DAY 2

We need to start where Jesus did— with God, first and last.

L uke 11:1-4 tells us that the disciples saw Jesus at prayer and asked to learn how He did it. They realized that they wanted what He had—a profound relationship with God that permeated every thought and every decision, and bore fruit in a God-focused life. After all, this is what disciples did—they learned from their teachers. John's disciples learned prayer from John; Jesus' disciples, then, should learn prayer from Jesus.

Some of Christ's disciples had been disciples of John. They noticed that there was something more to Jesus' prayer life. And it was true. Jesus' very conception of God was profound—deeper than anything that had appeared on the world stage before. He called God "Father," not occasionally, but regularly (even always). As stated in the first day of this week, virtually every prayer of Jesus began with this designation (Psalm 22 being the exception).

This was extremely unusual for a Jew. No one dared to utter the Hebrew name of God at all for fear that it would be mispronounced and thus His name taken in vain. Every time the name of God (transliterated YHWH) was recorded in Scripture and was to be read, another name would be substituted out of reverence and respect for the holiness of God—Adonai. (The correct pronunciation of the name YHWH has been forever lost because of this attitude of reverence.) He was so holy that even His very name should not be polluted by its utterance on tainted human lips (see Isaiah 6:1-8, esp. 5)!

In all of Hebrew Scripture, a designation such as "Father" was almost nonexistent. It can only be found directly in the following Old Testament texts: Deuteronomy 32:6; 2 Samuel 7:14; 1 Chronicles 22:10; 28:6; Psalm 68:5; 89:26; 103:13; Isaiah 63:16; 64:8; Jeremiah 3:4, 19; 31:9; and Malachi 1:6; 2:10. There were a few other allusions to a Father-son relationship between Israel's king and God (e.g., Psalm 2:7-9) or the people of God and

God Himself (Exodus 4:22-23; Deuteronomy 14:1, implied in Deuteronomy 32:18-19 from 32:6, etc.). Yet the paucity of references makes the following point clear: *No one else had prayed it as Jesus did.*

No one in Hebrew history ever prayed to God as "Father" with the specific intention of making clear that God was personally involved in his human existence, and that the relationship was "Father-son"! The Isaiah passages do name God as the Father of Israel directly, though here, God's Fatherhood is a corporate reality; these texts speak of Israel's creation as God's people, rather than of an individual who had God as his Father. These two references (Isaiah 63:11, 64:8) are far more formal—more removed than the intimacy that Jesus had with God His Father. It was prophesied in 2 Samuel 7, 1 Chronicles 28, and Psalm 89:26 that one born through David's line would call God "my Father." This was a promise that became Messianic prophecy (and shows up without the word "Father" in Psalm 2:6-9, 12). The marks of the Messiah appearing on earth would include a "Father-son" relationship with God, through someone directly descended from the line of King David.

Jesus began His prayer with that.

This prayer, steeped as it was in the promise of the Jewish Messiah, was filled with our Lord's self-awareness that He was the Chosen One.

Now while it was one thing for the Messiah to pray it, it is quite another for the followers of the Messiah to parrot the same words. After all, unless we are thinking delusionally, we know that we are not the Messiah. Jesus' prayer, however, starts with a promise—that God can be our Father by adoption through Jesus Christ. We get joined to Jesus' body; then His Father becomes "our Father . . ."

To get there, we must be born a second time. And the mark of that rebirth is the ability to call God "Father" and relate to Him as a child does to a caring parent, only better. Our human fathers (and mothers) are bent with sin. God's Fatherhood toward us is sinless, deathless, and profoundly life-giving. It is linked to receiving God's Spirit, and with that Spirit touching ours, we receive confirmation of the reality that God has become our Father. The Lord's Prayer is rooted in *our sharing in* Jesus' experience of having God as *His* Father. This is supernatural in origin and it becomes ours through the experience of the Spirit of God entering our lives through faith in Christ.

This experience is described in Paul's letter to the Romans:

For the Spirit that God has given you does not make you slaves and cause you to be afraid; instead, the Spirit makes you God's children, and by the Spirit's power we cry out to God, "Father! my Father!" God's Spirit joins himself to our spirits to declare that we are God's children.

Since we are his children, we will possess the blessings he keeps for his people, and we will also possess with Christ what God has kept for him; for if we share Christ's suffering, we will also share his glory. (Romans 8:15-17, GNT)

Jesus' prayer begins with His personal awareness that God was His Father, and that He was the Messiah, sent from the Father to save the world. That was the heritage of His Hebrew faith. Though we are not the Messiah, by being joined to Him, His *inner* life is extended to us, in that we participate in His Spirit. His *outer* life, His mission, is also extended to us inasmuch as we are joined to His life by the Spirit of God.

This prayer, then, begins with a declaration of partnership; Jesus merges us with Himself, and through that union we receive *His Father as our Father.* He is the Father of Jesus Christ, and, through Jesus' Spirit who resides within, *our* Father as well.

Jesus began His prayer with God first.

He didn't begin to meditate on the things that needed to be done (though they were legion). He didn't focus on the needs that had to be met (though they were too numerous to count). He didn't begin with the trials He faced or the people He offended or blessed. He began with God first, known to Him as an intimate. So should we.

PEN TO PAPER

1) To try and capture the shift from the Old Testament to the New, pray through the two texts below. The first is one of only two texts from the Old that addresses God as "Father," and the second, the Romans passage that speaks about receiving God as our "Father" through an encounter with the Holy Spirit. The way to do this is to read and reread them several times, until you discover that these words are in fact yours. Do that now, taking several minutes for each text. Give yourself some silence between

each reading to let yourself enter the thinking and believing of the prayer. Then record your impressions:

> There is no one who calls on Your name,
> Who arouses himself to take hold of You;
> For You have hidden Your face from us
> And have delivered us into the power of our iniquities.
> But now, O LORD, You are our Father,
> We are the clay, and You our potter;
> All of us are the work of Your hand.
> Do not be angry beyond measure, O LORD.
> (Isaiah 64:7-9, NASB)

> For the Spirit that God has given you does not make you slaves and cause you to be afraid; instead, the Spirit makes you God's children, and by the Spirit's power we cry out to God, "Father! my Father!" God's Spirit joins himself to our spirits to declare that we are God's children.
>   Since we are his children, we will possess the blessings he keeps for his people, and we will also possess with Christ what God has kept for him; for if we share Christ's suffering, we will also share his glory. (Romans 8:15-17, GNT).

What was the point of calling God "Father" in the Isaiah passage? Is it a warm image or a distant one? Why is Isaiah praying and what is the desired outcome? (Note that this is the most intimate "Father" prayer in Old Testament Hebrew Scripture.)

What is the point of Paul calling God "Father" in Romans? Is it a warm image or a distant one? What is the point of the text? What does this mean to you right now?

2) Now go back and pray through the Lord's Prayer again. Think about what Jesus' disciples would have felt on hearing this for the first time. Then offer up to God your own paraphrase from yesterday in your praying.

PRAYER CHALLENGE

As you go through this day, do so knowing that you have been invited into Jesus' relationship with the Godhead. Through Jesus' Sonship, and via the Spirit's work in your inner being, you have been given the privilege to call God "Father" through being joined to Him. Ponder that through the day and return blessings to God using your own words.

DAY 3

Heaven is not only the Father's home, but also ours.
We are to live there in our hearts.

Jesus started to pray by looking up, an act of praise. He immediately thought of God as His Father. Here was something utterly new. The God in glory was now the God resident within the believer. Yet the world in which Christ was living and working was not as heaven should be. There was dissonance between what He knew of God and what He knew the world to be. So He prayed for heaven's presence and power to become real, rich, and tangible on earth—but we are getting ahead of the prayer itself.

In this first line of the prayer, Jesus began by focusing His thinking and His praying on God in heaven. Nothing would distract Him from this. Prayer begins with God and prayer ends with God. Jesus didn't merely think of God. He thought of God in sinless, radiant, perfect, uncreated glory. Unlike any of us, Jesus thought of heaven as the dwelling place of God because He knew *exactly* what heaven was like. He came from there and was going to return there. He was reflecting on the glories of heaven from personal experience. Therefore, the center of His existence was there. This reality—of heaven's power and glory—was the reality that would need to "come to earth."

Some years ago, I had a Nigerian roommate who had come to Canada to study theology. His goal was to return to his native country and teach those who could not afford to travel abroad.

He made a conscious decision *not* to assimilate.

He had seen it happen before: Friends would go to Canada, England, Australia, or the United States to study with the thought of returning home to teach. Most would discover the wealth of those societies and decide to remain in the new culture. They would become "Westernized."

He had decided. He would live for Nigeria.

His clothing didn't fit the norm among Canadians (and he didn't care). He ate food that didn't agree with our tastes. He made regular long-distance calls to his friends and relatives (and only truly laughed with them—not us). He had Nigerian friends over at all times. He always pointed out the subtle and the not-so-subtle cultural assumptions of Canadians (and Americans as well), making clear what was Canadian, what was Nigerian, and what was neither! And he kept our room temperature *hot!*

My roommate achieved his goal. He lived for Nigeria and returned there to teach. His home was not the country in which he studied, but the place from which he came.

Jesus made a conscious decision *not* to assimilate.

Only He went one step further.

He made a conscious decision to export all of heaven's power and glory here.

Keeping His mind and His life focused on this one goal, Jesus began His praying with this beginning: *Our Father in heaven . . .*

Heaven or "the kingdom of heaven" is mentioned in sixty-one different verses in the twenty-eight chapters of the Gospel of Matthew alone. It is hard *not* to notice that Jesus was oriented to His home country, the realm from which He came. He was utterly conscious of heaven's realities, despite being surrounded by all that was and is part and parcel of the material realm.

Jesus was "heavenly minded"—and much earthly good. He is our model. We are to think of God's abode in heaven—to reflect on His marvelous presence in that perfect place—even as we praise Him first. To hallow the name of the Father is to recognize that He lives in hallowed space! Let's think on heaven.

Paul saw heaven: "I know a man in Christ, who fourteen years ago . . . was caught up to the third heaven. And I know how such a man . . . was caught up into Paradise and heard inexpressible words, which a man is not permitted to speak" (2 Corinthians 12:2-4, NASB).

The writer of Hebrews contrasts the revelation of heaven with the giving of the Law on Mt. Sinai, and describes heaven:

> But you have come to Mt. Zion, and to the city of the living God, the heavenly Jerusalem, and to myriads of angels, to the general assembly and church of the firstborn who are enrolled in heaven, and to God, the Judge of all, and to the spirits of the righteous made perfect, and to Jesus, the mediator of a new covenant, and

to the sprinkled blood which speaks better than the blood of Abel.
(Hebrews 12:22-24, NASB)

Our Lord Himself returned to His former glory, the glory of heaven, for a
passing moment on the Mount of Transfiguration.

Six days later Jesus took with Him Peter and James and John his
brother, and led them up on a high mountain by themselves. And
He was transfigured before them; and His face shone like the sun,
and His garments became as white as light. . . . A bright cloud
overshadowed them, and behold, a voice out of the cloud said,
"This is My beloved Son, with whom I am well-pleased; listen to
Him!" (Matthew 17:1-2, 5, NASB)

These texts give us a passing glimpse of heaven, the place in which God
dwells. To begin to pray biblically, we are to locate our thoughts, our praises,
our prayers not on earthly reality, but on the God who dwells in unapproachable
light, whose sinless perfection is so holy that we experience utter inadequacy
to stand, let alone speak before His reality. We are to recognize that God lives
there (even as we do not), and that our highest aspirations and hopes are far
below the lowest thought of that magnificent place of existence—and that
God would raise us to that place.

Spend some time thinking of heaven.

Decide not to assimilate.

Decide to export heaven's glorious power to earth by first entering into its
reality in your praises.

PEN TO PAPER

1) When was the last time you thought about heaven? Spend some time
thinking about what it might be like. Perhaps you or someone you
know has had a vision of heaven, or been resuscitated from a near-death
experience. Jot down words or word-pictures that have to do with that
place and record them here.

2) Now go back and reread today's three texts. Try and put into words what those texts are saying about heaven. What is it like? Who lives there? What is heavenly existence like compared to earthly existence?

3) Now return praise to God once again. If it is helpful to you, turn to a psalm that focuses on the praise of God and recite it verbatim, then say it again, paraphrasing the words using your own thoughts (e.g., Psalm 145 is pure praise rooted in theology and prayer). Focus your thoughts on God's praise and, this time, picture God in heaven above. If you know a hymn about heaven, sing it now. Then sit silently, reflecting on the God of heaven, the Father who dwells in unapproachable light.

PRAYER CHALLENGE

Reginald Heber was the Bishop of Calcutta. He had a vision of heaven based on Revelation 4:8-11 and wrote this very famous hymn (published after his death). It is a hymn to the holiness of God and to the mysteries of heaven. Perhaps today you can sing it or recite it. Let it come to mind today whenever you have a passing moment and let its truths call you to think of God in heaven:

Holy, holy, holy, Lord God Almighty!
Early in the morning our song shall rise to Thee!
Holy, holy, holy, merciful and mighty,
God in three persons, Blessed Trinity.

Holy, holy, holy, all the saints adore Thee!
Casting down their golden crowns around the glassy sea.
Cherubim and seraphim, falling down before Thee,
Which wert and art and evermore shall be.

Holy, holy, holy, though the darkness hide Thee!

Though the eye of sinful man Thy glory may not see.
Only Thou art holy. There is none beside Thee—
Perfect in power, in love and purity.

Holy, holy, holy, Lord God Almighty.
All Thy works shall praise Thy name in earth and sky and sea;
Holy, holy, holy, merciful and mighty!
God in three persons, Blessed Trinity!

DAY 4

The first movement in Jesus' thinking was to hallow
God's name—an act of praise.

Praise is something we do either to acknowledge a person's character or
to positively highlight something he or she has done well. All through
the pages of Scripture we find the people of God engaged in praise of
God. In fact there are scores of texts in both Old and New Testaments that
command us to praise the name of God. The following text from Hebrews
tells us what praise is: "Through Jesus, therefore, let us continually offer to
God a sacrifice of praise—the fruit of lips that confess his name. And do not
forget to do good and to share with others, for with such sacrifices God is
pleased" (Hebrews 13:15-16, NIV).

Praise is a sacrifice. It is something that we do to please God. It must cost us
something to do it. Time. Effort. Money. In Hebrew worship, it was unthinkable
to come to the temple of God without a material offering for sacrifice (see
Deuteronomy 16:16-17). To worship was to sacrifice. Even the very poor would
bring a grain offering; the marginal (those we would call the "working poor")
would bring a pair of turtledoves; and those who were doing well would bring
a sheep or goat as an offering for sin (see Leviticus 5:5-13). The sacrifice of
worship must include at least the giving up of the other things that we could
and would do if we didn't have a life of prayer. Much more is implied!

Praise is reshaping our lips (and our living) around the glory of God. We
use our words for everything else. We practice speaking for work, for school,
for interacting socially. We must also practice (and that sacrificially) to honor
God with our words. The text speaks of the "fruit of lips that confess his
name." Fruit begins in a blossom; then it takes time to become full grown and
ready for harvest. Fruit doesn't develop quickly, but over time, given the right
conditions—the right soil, the right moisture, the right amount of sunshine,
the right amount of care, pruning as needed, just enough fertilizer—all this
and more.

The fruit of praise must be nurtured and cultivated in the garden of obedience.

There are many who can help us learn. Our Lord praised His Father. In Matthew 11, after the apostles (unschooled and working class) had returned from cities that didn't repent, Jesus used that occasion to praise God: "At that time, Jesus said, 'I praise You, Father, Lord of heaven and earth, that You have hidden these things from the wise and intelligent and have revealed them to infants'" (Matthew 11:25, NASB).

There is more thanksgiving in the apostle Paul than in any other ancient writer (both inside the New Testament and outside of it). Praise is riddled throughout his letters. Listen to Paul praise the Lord:

Oh the depth of the riches both of the wisdom and knowledge of God! How unsearchable are His judgments and unfathomable His ways! For who has known the mind of the Lord, or who became His counselor? Or who has first given to Him that it might be paid back to him again? For from Him and through Him and to Him are all things. To Him be the glory forever. Amen. (Romans 11:33-36, NASB)

The Psalms are rich sources of praise affirmations. Here are two of my favorites:

Bless the LORD, O my soul,
And all that is within me, bless His holy name.
Bless the LORD, O my soul,
And forget none of His benefits;
Who pardons all your iniquities,
Who heals all your diseases;
Who redeems your life from the pit,
Who crowns you with loving-kindness and compassion;
Who satisfies your years with good things,
So that your youth is renewed like the eagle.
(Psalm 103:1-5, NASB)

I will praise you, O Lord, with all my heart;
I will tell of all your wonders.
I will be glad and rejoice in you;
I will sing praise to your name, O Most High.
My enemies turn back;
they stumble and perish before you.
For you have upheld my right and my cause;
you have sat on your throne, judging righteously. . . .

The Lord is a refuge for the oppressed,
a stronghold in times of trouble.
Those who know your name will trust in you,
for you, Lord, have never forsaken those who seek you.
(Psalm 9:1-4, 9-10, NIV)

PEN TO PAPER

1) Praise must be learned. Get yourself in a private place—one where no one will see or hear you. Put yourself in a posture in which you know you will worship God (sitting, kneeling, or relaxed in a recliner if that helps you). Now, slowly and deliberately read out loud Paul's words of praise from Romans 11. Read them several times until you find you are able to speak them as your own words. Then simply be still. Record what the practice of praise did within you here below.

2) Repeat these steps for Psalm 103:1-5 above. First read it aloud. Then read it again, until it is your own praise. Continue this until you know you are done. Come to a place of quiet and record your impressions about your inner being in response to praising God.

3) Finally, repeat these steps for Psalm 9 printed above. Record your impressions below.

4) What was the effect of praising God first? Were you lifted? Do you need to practice this more?

PRAYER CHALLENGE

Don't ask God for anything today. Instead, praise Him for who He is and turn the requests you want to make into praises instead.

DAY 5

The name of our God is to be revered.

What does it mean to revere or "hallow" the name of God? Isn't His name already holy? Why then does Jesus instruct us to begin our praying by setting that name apart? There are two issues here for our praying that we need to understand. The first is the nature of the name, and the second is what it means to set that name apart as holy.

So what is the "name" we are called to hallow? The name cannot be the simple utterance of the syllables that make a particular sound. There is more than enough profanity around to make clear that those who speak the name "God" or "Father" aloud are not necessarily invoking God at all! Besides, the sound of God's name is different in each language group (*Dios* in Spanish, *Bok* in Russian/Ukrainian, *Theos* in ancient Greek, *Adonai* and *Elohim* in Hebrew, etc.). Beyond that, there are many in history who thought they acted in the name of God when, in fact, they were doing just the opposite, doing evil instead of good, representing their own ideas instead of God Himself.

So what is "the name"?

The prayer found in John 17 provides some clues to help us discover what the "name" is. The "name" shows up four times there (17:6, 11, 12, 26). It is inextricably intertwined around several themes: the nature of eternal life, the utter and complete unity of the Father and the Son, and the possibility and promise that Christian believers can be joined as intimately with the Father as Christ Himself was. This unity is not something that was incidental to the life of Christ. Rather it was the heartbeat of His devotion. If we are to join Christ in praying about the name we must understand the nature of that name. Let's look at this material:

> I am no longer in the world; and yet they themselves are in the world, and I come to You. Holy Father, keep them in Your name, the name which You have given Me, that they may be one, even as

We are. While I was with them, I was keeping them in Your name which You have given Me. (John 17:11-12, NASB)

This text makes clear that the Father has a "name." The Father bestowed that same name on the Son, and the Son Himself, through His presence (and from the context, through the Word of truth He spoke and lived) brought the disciples into that name as well.

It can be pictured as a funnel in which God's name, I AM, is poured into who Jesus is. The I AM in who Jesus is, is then expanded out to the disciples:

I AM THAT I AM

Into Christ Jesus

Into disciples (us) who receive the name

Let's look at these verses later in the chapter:

O righteous Father, although the world has not known You, yet I have known You; and these have known that You sent Me; and I have made Your name known to them, and will make it known, so that the love with which You have loved Me may be in them, and I in them. (John 17:25-26, NASB)

Here, the intimate caring of the Father and the Son toward each other is extended to the disciples through the name. It is through that name that the love of the Father is revealed within the believer, and it is through that name that Christ Himself will dwell in them.

The name, in Scripture then, is the very character and nature of God Himself. The name contains the *power* of God as well as the *presence* of God. The two are inextricably woven together, and cannot be separated. The name has been described as the "power-sphere" of God's very essence and being. Perhaps a more accurate phrase would be the "power sphere of His presence."

The name is:

- God's reputation
- God's presence
- God's power
- God's action
- God's love
- God's being
- God's holiness
- God's grace
- God's judgment
- God's calling, and
- everything else that pertains to God

While "hallowing the name" includes reverent speaking, that is merely the beginning. To "hallow the name" is to enter into the very heart and life of who God is, and to dwell there. It is to find our identity as loved of God there, and it is to flow with God's very authority and power as we obey His promptings. How do we do this? It is by the Spirit of God Himself.

> I will ask the Father, and He will give you another Helper, that He may be with you forever; that is the Spirit of truth . . . you know Him because He abides with you and will be in you. . . . But the Helper, the Holy Spirit, whom the Father will send in My name, He will teach you all things, and bring to your remembrance all that I said to you. (John 14:16-17, 26, NASB)

We know that Jesus acted in the name of His Father. Here the Father answers the prayer of Christ by sending the Spirit to us in Jesus' name (though we know that this "name" was given to Him by God and that it was the same name as the Father's). Putting all of this together, it is clear that the presence of the Father, the Son, and the Holy Spirit all come to us through the name. God the Father reveals His presence in Christ and makes that real to us through the Holy Spirit. We are to set apart this name in our thinking through our experience of God Himself.

What does it mean to "hallow" or "sanctify" or "make holy" that name? Simply put, we don't make it holy (i.e., show that God is holy by living a godly life). Rather, we *enter into* the action of God, who is showing forth His name as holy (i.e., God sends His Spirit into us and gives us the power to live for Him). This prayer to God is that God Himself will accomplish the hallowing of His name, through us, as we enter the "power-sphere" of His character and nature together. Despite the sin and evil that resides in the created realm, God will act through us to accomplish His purposes. This is a partnership prayer. We are asking God to flow through us to make clear to the world that He lives and that He is holy.

PEN TO PAPER

1) When we say, "Bill went and made a name for himself," to what does this refer? "I need to clear my good name" carries a similar connotation. How do we use the word "name" in our conversations?

2) The concept of the "name" also carries a meaning of both personality and power in our culture. If we use a checkbook, we sign our name. When the check is cashed, it carries the weight of our resources as well as our personality. If there were no money in the bank, then our name would be ruined. If someone else signed our name, our name would be falsely used. What then, does the "name" mean?

3) Reread the Scripture passages above. What does God want accomplished through the name?

4) Make a list of ways that you can hallow the name. Share that with your group.

PRAYER CHALLENGE

As you go through the day today, ask the Father to grant you His Spirit through the name of Christ. Ask God to remind you of what you need to remember to hallow that blessed name. Return to this resource tonight and list the ways you discovered that God could and would hallow His name through you.

1. _____

2. _____

3. _____

4. _____

DAY 6

The name of God is the character of God within the believer.

"You shall not take the name of the LORD Your God in vain."
(The Third Commandment, Exodus 20:7, NASB)

From the time of our first lessons in Sunday school, the Ten Commandments have been before us. We have taken the third commandment as a word of warning, an admonition never to use God's name for anything other than worship, teaching, Christian service, or genuine prayer. There is certainly truth in that. But there is a deeper level related to the concept of the name. There are those who attempt to claim the name of Christ who simply do not have His presence or power within them. They use Christian language, belong to Christian associations, but have no dynamic connection with Christ Himself. This is to profane that name, empty it of all meaning, and render it useless.

The risen Lord made this clear when He spoke to the church of Sardis: "I know your deeds, that you have a name that you are alive, but you are dead" (Revelation 3:1, NASB).

Beyond this, there are those who attempt to do things in the name of God when God has not commanded them to do anything at all. This is also to misuse the name of God and to claim to represent His presence and character when neither is involved. It can have awful results. Notice the unclean use of the name of Jesus in this passage:

> Some of the Jewish exorcists, who went from place to place, attempted to name over those who had the evil spirits the name of the Lord Jesus, saying, "I adjure you by Jesus whom Paul preaches." Seven sons of one Sceva, a Jewish chief priest, were doing this. And the evil spirit answered and said to them, "I recognize Jesus, and I know about Paul, but who are you?" And the man, in whom

was the evil spirit, leaped on them and subdued all of them and overpowered them, so that they fled out of that house naked and wounded. This became known to all, both Jews and Greeks, who lived in Ephesus; and fear fell upon them all and the name of the Lord was being magnified. (Acts 19:13-17, NASB)

This text makes clear that the name "Jesus" or "Father-God" is not some sort of a magical incantation that can be uttered to invoke the power of God. Those in whom the Spirit of God did *not* reside could not claim the power of the name.

Without the *presence* of God, there is no *power* of God.

It is not enough to simply speak the name "Jesus." In fact, according to the Acts text above, it is not enough to hold that name in high regard (something those exorcists did) and attempt to use it based on their awareness of and respect for the incredible power in the name. While that kind of respect for the name goes a lot farther than the misuse of the name through profanity, it does nothing to access the power of God against evil. All that this kind of respect got for the seven sons of Sceva was a beating. According to Revelation 3:1, neither is it acceptable to have a reputation for walking in the name when in fact there is no dynamic sense of God's presence in one's life. (Jesus calls that church "dead.")

To honor and hallow the name of God is to live in the very nature of who God is. It is to encounter Him, invite Him to dwell within by His Spirit, and it is to dwell in His presence. The only way the name of God has power is if one lives the name, joins one's own reputation and destiny to the name, trusts the name, believes the name, and stakes one's own good name on God's name. It is to utterly and totally identify with the name in the inner being as well as on our lips. The twelve apostles were arrested and whipped for the name (Acts 5:40-41). Paul was called to suffer for the name of Jesus (Acts 9:16) and was ready to die for His name (Acts 21:13). Barnabas joined Paul in this when both risked their lives for the name of the Lord (Acts 15:26).

Perhaps the closest parallel in John to this first section of the Lord's Prayer was the moment in which Jesus knew that He was going to go to the cross and die so that we might live. He saw the hour of His death approaching, acknowledged as much, and said, "Father, glorify your name" (John 12:28,

NASB). In John that meant, "Take me to the cross. I will offer myself to You utterly and totally for the accomplishment of Your purposes." There could be no more total identification with the purposes of God than for Jesus to offer Himself up to death.

Jesus, the apostles, and prophets of the early church all understood that to hallow the name of the Father was to line their lives up completely and totally with the purposes, the presence, and the plans of God. Anything less was to take the name of the Lord their God in vain. It was to share God's goals and have God's Spirit within directing them toward these goals.

PEN TO PAPER

1) The desert fathers of the early church used a prayer that brought them into the dynamic presence of God. It was a simple prayer that they could pray when they went about their work or when they wanted to meditate on the character of Christ. It is called "the Jesus Prayer." Some would pray this prayer all day. Others would pray it on those occasions in which words seemed to fail them. This simple little four-line prayer, an adaptation of the prayers of blind Bartimaeus (Mark 10:47) and the Syro-Phoenician woman (Matthew 15:22) has been a fountain of blessing for generations of believers.

> *Lord Jesus Christ,*
> *Son of God,*
> *Have mercy on me,*
> *A sinner.*

Take ten minutes and get yourself into a comfortable position. Deliberately tell the Lord that you want to hallow His name, to line yourself up with His purposes, and that to do so you need not only the words of any prayer you might pray, but, above all, His very presence within. To settle yourself, take several deep breaths and repeat the Jesus Prayer.

Picture the cross of Christ, place yourself under His care, and receive His salvation.

Spend ten minutes now sitting in one place, repeating this prayer. Attach each line to every breath that you breathe. Be still.

2) What was it like to pray that prayer? Journal your experience in the space provided below:

3) Now return to praising God in whatever way you know. Use the Psalms or Paul's expression of praise from Day 4 of this week's adventure. Close out your prayer time by saying the Lord's Prayer slowly and reverently. Record what comes to mind as you do this.

PRAYER CHALLENGE

During those times today when you are frazzled or hassled, pray the Jesus Prayer. It can be used when you are driving, walking, waiting in a line, buying a soft drink, or interrupted at a task. Let it draw you to Christ and to knowing the power of His presence within.

DAY 7

To glorify the name of the Father is to enter into spiritual warfare.

There is much to understanding the doctrine of the name of God, both as it relates to the Father and to the Son. This study won't begin to cover all that is found in that teaching. However, there is one aspect to the hallowing or consecrating of the "name" that needs to be explored to fully understand its significance for the Lord's Prayer. We have already learned that the name is a "power-sphere" linked to the character of both Jesus and the Father. What we have not explored up to this point is how that power-sphere relates to the rest of the world—and the other powers at work here. That power-sphere is in direct opposition to another power-sphere—that of the forces of evil and darkness. This is most clear in the use of the name in John's gospel.

As Jesus contemplated His impending death on the cross, He uttered these profound words that give us insight into what it means to hallow or glorify the name of the Father. This is John's functional equivalent to the first line of the Lord's Prayer.

> And Jesus answered them, saying, "The hour has come for the Son of Man to be glorified. Truly, truly, I say to you, unless a grain of wheat falls into the earth and dies, it remains alone; but if it dies, it bears much fruit. . . . Now My soul has become troubled; and what shall I say, 'Father, save Me from this hour'?
>
> But for this purpose I came to this hour."
>
> "Father, glorify Your name."
>
> Then a voice came out of heaven: "I have both glorified it, and will glorify it again." . . .
>
> Jesus answered and said, "This voice has not come for My sake, but for your sakes. Now judgment is upon this world; now the ruler

of this world will be cast out. And I, if I am lifted up from the earth, will draw all men to Myself." (John 12:23, 27-28, 30-31, NASB)

Here the purpose of the life of Jesus on earth comes to the forefront. He was sent to glorify the name of the Father. The voice that responded signaled God's complete approval of all that Christ had done and would yet do through His death on Calvary. The task had been accomplished. God had been glorified in the life, signs, teaching, and solemn witness of the Lord. Taking the message of the Gospel of John as a whole, the Father had been glorified through the impartation of "the name," first in and through Jesus, and through Him to the apostles (and later us).

In fact, so complete was the identification of Jesus of Nazareth with the name of God that when the soldiers came to arrest Him, they met something other than what they expected. When they asked if He was in fact Jesus of Nazareth, Christ used the Hebrew name for God, "I AM," to identify Himself. The use of that name was so very powerful that it knocked the disciples, the soldiers, and the betrayer off their feet. Attempting to arrest what they thought was a troublemaker, they discovered that they were arresting God Himself—something they could not do without God's tacit consent (John 18:4-6). They were so overcome at the revelation of God's name "I AM" in Jesus that they could not even stand up. Jesus, in complete control of His destiny, offered Himself up for death. With the power to stop it, He took up the cross voluntarily. This was God, the only begotten God, making the Father understood! The unity of the name of the Father and the Son was so complete that Jesus could say, "I and the Father are one" (John 10:30, NASB) and "before Abraham was born, I AM" (John 8:58, NASB).

To return to this specific text, at John 12 the emphasis shifts from God receiving glory through Jesus' signs and teaching, to God receiving glory through Jesus' death on the cross. Jesus prays for the Father to glorify His name—ostensibly through His life.

The answer comes and Christ "explains" it to us. Here the power-sphere of the name of God in Jesus was to be completely revealed. It would include:

- The casting out of dark powers; the ruler of this world, Satan, would be expelled through

- The death of Jesus on the cross, so that
- The preaching of the cross of Christ would
- Draw all people everywhere into who Christ Himself is (i.e., the power-sphere of His name)—God revealed in human flesh

When we pray for the Father in heaven to be hallowed, we are in fact lining up with God's purposes to destroy the influence of another power-sphere. We are declaring that God's name will expel the rule of evil from earth itself. We are lining our lives up with God's purposes to destroy all the works of the devil, to cast out all hatred, all animosity, all despair, all disease, all meaningless suffering, to remove all things that subvert or oppose God's true rule and destroy people. In the end, to pray this prayer is to cast out Satan himself through the proclamation that Jesus died for us and rose again to become the risen Lord.

To pray "Glorify Your name" is to assert that all of our lives be put on the line to destroy evil everywhere, up to and including following Christ in the offering of ourselves in martyrdom.

The Lord's Prayer is no prayer to pray if you don't mean business about God's purposes to destroy evil. It is no prayer to pray if you wish to have a carefree existence. To pray this prayer is to enter into the sphere of God's transcendent goodness and to declare war on all evil everywhere. God has determined to destroy all principalities and powers that subvert His rule, and He is asking us to partner with Him in the retaking of earth from the forces of darkness.

Be careful what you pray! God will answer you. Now that you know this from the teaching of Jesus, the Lord's Prayer will take on a whole new significance. Before you go to the next section of this material, determine that you will not pray flippantly or lightly. To pray the first line of the Lord's Prayer is to declare open warfare on Satan and his evil hordes. They will counterattack.

PEN TO PAPER

1) We have spent the last seven days examining what Jesus meant by the words and phrases of the Lord's Prayer. I suspect that what they imply and what we have traditionally thought about the prayer are two very different things. Go back and review your paraphrase of the Lord's Prayer

from Day 1 of this week. Then rewrite the first line, based on what you have learned from the last seven days.

2) On Day 5 of this last week we examined the truth that the Spirit of God would be sent by the Father through the name of the Son to teach us of Christ. Return to that day and reread John 14:26. After you have done this, ponder these truths from that text:

- *We need the name* to receive all the blessings of Christ.
- *God gives us the name* to be able to send the Spirit of Christ to us.
- *Christ bestows the name* upon us so that we can have the same unity with the Father that He has with the Son.
- *The Spirit flows through the name* between the Father and the church (us), bringing teaching and reminders of what Christ has already given to us.

Spend a few minutes thinking on these truths, and then return thanks to God for the power-sphere of the name, sent from the Father to the Son, and given to us by His Spirit. Record your thanksgivings below.

PRAYER CHALLENGE

As you go through this day, ask God to reveal to you what it means to pray, "Father, glorify Your name." Ask Him to give you concrete ways that you can live out your prayer. In essence you will be asking God to be so very present in and through you that every action will be impacted by His presence. How would God's name be glorified in your water-cooler conversation? How would God be glorified as you are visiting with your neighbor? How would God's name be glorified at your workplace or your school? Ask Him to reveal that, and pray the first line of the Lord's prayer at each place.

Week Three

REQUEST THE KINGDOM

"Your Kingdom Come."

Part 1

DAY 1

The Kingdom of God will change the one who prays!

Now we turn to the second movement of the Lord's Prayer. So far we have seen that Jesus began His life of prayer with a focus on the glorious nature of God and the hallowing of His name (and at the close of the prayer we shall see that He will end the same way as He began). The second movement is very nearly the same. Though the focus of the second movement is not *directly* upon the worship or praise of God, it is still centered in God's agenda—not ours! It is a prayer about the rule of God and the accomplishment of God's express purposes. Since this material is so very rich, it will take us two weeks to even begin to sound out the implications of the second line. So though the two thoughts are intrinsically intertwined, the first week will focus primarily on the phrase "your kingdom come," and the second will examine "your will be done."

To put all of this in perspective, let's pray the Lord's Prayer again, this time from a different perspective. Listen to a modern rendering in the translation/paraphrase of Rev. Eugene Peterson.

> Our Father in heaven,
> Reveal who you are.
> Set the world right;
> Do what's best—as above, so below.
> Keep us alive with three square meals.
> Keep us forgiven with you and forgiving others.
> Keep us safe from ourselves and the Devil.
> You're in charge!
> You can do anything you want!
> You're ablaze in beauty!
> Yes. Yes. Yes.
> (Matthew 6:9-13, *The Message*)

Take a few minutes now to read and reread Peterson's rendering. Get it into your thinking. Position yourself in a comfortable place and pray it. Slow it down by taking a deep breath between each line. Then simply be still for five minutes. Do that now.

Was that exercise meaningful? What did you notice about this prayer that was different or new compared to your usual praying of the Lord's Prayer? Reduce that to writing here:

While Peterson's rendering doesn't capture the exact nuances of every part of the prayer (no translation does), he has captured the thrust of the second movement well: "Set the world right; Do what's best—as above, so below."

Take a moment right now to pray the second line of the prayer with this paraphrase in mind. Think for a moment about the parts of the world that aren't right, from the injustices on the world stage to the quarrels in the workplace to the petty squabbles of children in the nursery! Then ask God to reorder our fallen world—to do what's best on earth, just as in heaven. Be bold in your asking. God wants the world set right, far more profoundly than we do. He commanded us to pray this way for that very reason! Take five more minutes and commit your prayer to writing below.

What's wrong with the world

1) _____
2) _____
3) _____
4) _____

Set the world right

1) _____
2) _____
3) _____
4) _____

The theme that emerges from this kingdom prayer is that there are things on earth that are not as they should be. Heaven's way is the better way. That includes how *I* live. Listen to these parables of the kingdom of God from the teaching of Christ.

> The kingdom of heaven is like a treasure hidden in the field, which
> a man found and hid again; and from joy over it he goes and sells
> all that he has and buys that field.

> Again, the kingdom of heaven is like a merchant seeking fine
> pearls, and upon finding one pearl of great value, he went and sold
> all that he had and bought it. (Matthew 13:44-46, NASB)

In these two parables, Jesus compares the discovery of God's kingdom to the finding of tremendous treasure. We all know what we would do if we found treasure—we would do whatever we could to obtain it, including selling off everything else to get it. There are two ways of reading these parables. The classic approach is to understand that this refers to *our* doing everything we can to obtain entrance into God's kingdom, sacrificing, giving up other things, saying good-bye to all hindrances that prevent us from keeping God's purposes central to our lives, etc. There is merit in this interpretation.

There is a second way to take these parables however, and it is based on how other kingdom parables work. In every other kingdom parable with an explanation, *God* is the one taking the action and *we* are the recipients of whatever He gives and brings. Applying the same interpretive grid to these two parables, it would mean that we people are the hidden treasure or the pearl of great price, and that God gave up everything, including His own Son, to obtain us.

The jury is out on which way we should take the parables. Perhaps they are left without explanation for a purpose! Putting the two views together, it means that God highly esteemed us and gave us His Son. We in turn are to do everything we can to esteem God in our lives. Since He gave up everything for us, we in turn should give up everything for Him.

This means that to pray this prayer is for us to decide to change. To pray for the kingdom to come and for the will to be done is for God's rule to begin right in our hearts and lives. This is no prayer to pray if we wish to remain the same!

PEN TO PAPER

1) Have you ever discovered something precious and realized that you needed to act quickly in order that it might become yours? What did you do to make sure that you could move ahead quickly?

2) We know God sacrificed everything for us. We also know that this is reciprocal from other parts of Jesus' teaching. Christ has told us to "take up our cross and follow" Him as well. Taking up the cross means dying by degrees until we are completely dead! Is there anything in your life that you know you need to give up for the kingdom of God to take deeper root in your life?

3) If the kingdom of God means the rule of Christ over our lives and over our society, what changes are needed? Where is your time being spent? On what do you spend your money? What is your principle worry this week? Are your relationships with your co-workers authentic or false? After reflecting on this for a few minutes, write down what needs to occur for God the Father to become your true King in each area:

   a. My use of time _____

   b. My use of finances _____

   c. My main worry _____

   d. My relationship with co-workers _____

   _____

   e. The thing I need to change but haven't acted _____

   _____

   f. My neighborhood _____

   g. My city government _____

   h. My family life _____

   i. Other _____

PRAYER CHALLENGE

Perhaps the list above seems daunting—too many changes too quickly. You know what the Lord wants, but find that too many priorities prevent you from working on one. Pick one area today and ask God to cause His kingdom to come and His will to be done in that one area. Every time the issue arises (perhaps by seeing the person who you would rather avoid), pray the kingdom prayer until you come to a sense of what you should be doing. Then do it.

DAY 2

Kingdoms need a king!

A story from the Arthurian legend will make today's point clear:

"What are we supposed to do?" The knight muttered shaking his head so that the bedraggled plume on his helmet flopped pitifully back and forth. "The merciless heathen roams the land at will; our people are starved, murdered or enslaved. And we are powerless to stop it. What kingdom is this? We have no kingdom!"

"True," Merlin agreed. "We have no kingdom because as yet we have no king. But the sword is still there in the stone, and someday the one for whom it is reserved will come and pull it out. Then when the king comes, the kingdom will come. Where the king is, there the kingdom will be. As strong as the king is, so strong will the kingdom be. They will sing songs about us, my friend, for when *that* king comes, we shall have a kingdom indeed—and then we shall have peace."

"Whoever you are," the knight said fervently, "I've got one thing to say: thy kingdom come!"[11]

What is a kingdom without a king? Merlin and the knight above would indicate, quite truthfully, "Nothing, for where the king is, there will the kingdom be." What was true of the legendary kingdom of Camelot is far more profoundly true of the kingdom of God. Without the God of heaven as King, there is no kingdom of heaven! There are forty-nine references to "the kingdom of heaven" in the twenty-eight chapters of Matthew's gospel alone (Mark refers to it sixteen times, while Luke uses the term thirty-eight times). The theme fairly screams off every page in the teaching of Jesus.

What is the common thread that binds all these pieces together? Simply put, the kingdom of God refers to the kingly rule of God over every aspect of life. Each "kingdom" section begins with the presupposition that kings of any sort are absolute rulers. Their word is law and cannot be questioned. Kingdoms require kings, and kings in the Middle East of Jesus' day had the power of life and death (e.g., John the Baptist was killed on the word of a king, even though that king had been manipulated into that action [Mark 6:14-29]).

For God the Father to be King is for God the Father to hold absolute sway over our lives. To pray "Your kingdom come. Your will be done on earth as it is in heaven" is to make a commitment of allegiance to a ruler that brooks no compromise. Since God "lives" in heaven (the domain totally given over to His rule) and we live on earth (a domain in rebellion to His rule), it is to commit to a King who is returning with an invasion force to reclaim what is rightfully His own. It is to pray for God to rule as effectively and directly on earth as He does in heaven and to partner with God in causing that reality to be accomplished.

It is clear that this is no prayer to pray if we wish to remain the same. To pray this prayer is to invite God to radically redirect our existence forever. It is to invite heaven's power to overlap earth through the medium of your life! It is to export heaven's influence to earth, despite the screaming protests of the usurper demons that want nothing of the sort, and will be cast out only by force. It is to be part of a task force that will retake the ground that was lost in the original battle for earth by our first parents.

One thing is clear: there is a contrast between God's will being done perfectly and instantly above and God's will being done only partially or imperfectly on earth. The center of this line from the prayer is that the Father's purposes be carried out as wonderfully below as they are above. In heaven where God is the undisputed King, when the Father speaks, reality is altered, and "the will" is done immediately. On earth where God gives us the choice to make Him King, when the Father speaks, some choose to obey, some to ignore, some to resist, some to reject, some take years to come to a place of obedience, and the occasional believer listens again, unsure if it was really God speaking.

Heaven and earth are not identical! But the thrust of this prayer is that the earth respond to God just like heaven does! That is quite a faith-filled prayer, given Jesus' knowledge of the human condition! This isn't mere optimism however, partly clothed in the language of believing. It is realism, with the sordid facts and events of human life and reality faced and considered. It is a receiving of a gift of faith to believe that God can and will accomplish even that through the blood of Christ and using His sanctifying Spirit upon a miserable lot of humans caught in their sins.

To return to our main theme, to speak of a kingdom implies a king. Kings in Bible times were to be obeyed on pain of death. To be a king was to have one's will done. This phrase implies that God was, and is, King in heaven. There His will is done, and there are no other pretenders to the throne.

God's desire was that He be the King of His chosen people by raising up leaders by His Spirit when need arose. Yet historic Israel chose to have an ordinary king, just like the kings of the nations around them—something that grieved God's Spirit. In speaking to the prophet Samuel about the nation's desire for a monarchy with an installed king, the Lord said this to him: "Listen to the voice of the people in regard to all that they say to you, for they have not rejected you, but they have rejected Me from being king over them" (1 Samuel 8:7, NASB).

So painful was this decision to have a human ruler rather than the direct rule of God by His Spirit that the grief is named as a rejection of God's rule altogether. Samuel said this when Saul was set apart as the first king of Israel:

> Thus says the LORD, the God of Israel, "I brought Israel up from Egypt, and I delivered you from the hand of the Egyptians and from the power of all the kingdoms that were oppressing you." But you have today rejected your God, who delivers you . . . ; yet you have said, "No, but set a king over us!" (1 Samuel 10:18-19, NASB)

The sordid history of the kings of both Israel and Judah shows us why. Saul failed in his leadership and had to be replaced by David. David ruled well until he committed adultery and abused his legitimate power to commit murder in the first degree. God rebuked and punished him. David repented, but his family life and his kingly rule were wounded forever thereafter.

His son Solomon began well, but turned to the worship of idols at the end of his life. After Solomon, the kingdom divided into north and south. The north then had nineteen rulers in just over two hundred years—and all of them were wicked. The southern kingdom had seventeen rulers for over three hundred years—eight followed the Lord to greater or lesser degrees, but nine were utterly wicked, including a king named Manasseh, who through fifty-two years of awful rule "filled Jerusalem with innocent blood" (2 Kings 24:4).

Kingdoms need a king, but more than this, the kingdom of God needs a *godly* king! So God reestablished His kingly rule by using the very thing that was "thrown in His face" at the time of Samuel. God became a human, born of the family line of King David. He entered our stream of existence by becoming one with us. We celebrate that every Christmas.

Yet what we often fail to ponder is that He came among us by using the very means that had been the utter and complete rejection of God's effective rule in Israel's history—kingship! Jesus our Lord was born into the family of Mary and Joseph (descended from David's line) to take up the role of being the true King who would rule us through His Spirit's presence being given to us all. He would show us what His kingship was really to be like.

God through Jesus began His kingship by entering the very means of His rejection to take up our embrace! What a King this is!

Yet David knew that God's rule was better than his! Listen to how he describes God's kingly rule:

> The LORD is gracious and merciful;
>> Slow to anger and great in lovingkindness.
> The LORD is good to all,
>> And His mercies are over all His works.
> All Your works shall give thanks to You, O LORD,
>> And Your godly ones shall bless You.
> They shall speak of the glory of Your kingdom
>> And talk of Your power;
> To make known to the sons of men Your mighty acts
>> And the glory of the majesty of Your kingdom.
> Your kingdom is an everlasting kingdom,
>> And Your dominion endures throughout all generations.
> (Psalm 145:8-13, NASB)

PEN TO PAPER

1) Reread the story from the Arthurian legend above. Spend some time thinking about the strength of King Jesus. What makes Him "strong"? Then pray
   for those strengths to become a part of your following of His Kingship.

2) For God to be king, God must be obeyed. What do you currently know
   that God wants you to do? (Don't struggle with this one. Start with the
   obvious, such as "love your neighbor as yourself" [Leviticus 19:18, NIV]!)
   Commit three of these to writing and make a plan to do them.

3) Reread the Psalm above. Notice the characteristics of God's kingly rule.
   What makes this a king who is easy to serve? Take one characteristic of
   how God rules and reflect on what that means for you personally. Then
   thank the Lord for the kind of a King that He is.

PRAYER CHALLENGE

The Psalm today indicates that people shall "speak of the glory of Your kingdom" (Psalm 145:11, NASB). Think of one of the benefits of following "King
Jesus" and ask God for someone that you can tell about this. Then speak. Pray
and then obey.

DAY 3

God began to take up his kingly rule again when
Jesus became our Second (and Last) Adam.

Kingship as it was understood in the Bible is an alien concept to the Western mind (though it is still alive in the Middle East and parts of Africa). This became crystal clear when visiting family in Minneapolis-St. Paul in Minnesota. Our son, Ben, was all of four years of age when we took him to the children's museum there. That museum teaches children by using all the sensory inputs—sight, touch, hearing, fragrance, taste, and beyond all this, participation in the displays. As it turned out, there was a medieval court area among the displays that had live actors and actresses to play out their respective roles. Ben took great delight in putting on regal garments—the crown, the scepter, and a magnificent cloak of rich cloth. He began to parade about in his royal robes when he was escorted to the throne to be seated as king before the adoring court. As he sat down, a young woman dressed for the ancient English court threw herself down before him, utterly prostrate, loudly pleading for mercy. By her performance it was plain that she was willing to do anything and everything to obtain it—her act was extremely convincing. It was clear to everyone that our four-year-old, in putting on that clothing, had been given "the power of life and death."

The effect on the child was profound. He immediately tore off the crown, tossed the scepter aside and ran right out of the room. It was one thing to put on the clothing and to sit on a pretend throne. It is quite another to take up the absolute power of life and death—and to use it.

He didn't want that kind of power!

But another did . . .

The enemy of our souls usurped that power from our first parents—and has used that right to introduce death into our fallen world. In fact, Satan's rule is that of an overlord rather than a kindly benevolent. When we pray our Lord's Prayer, we are praying for the dethroning of a horrid king, and the reestablishment of the kind and gentle rule that was intended in the first place.

On earth we are in a cosmic battle: will the earth itself be subject to God, or to a false spirit who presides over death, destruction, disease, despair, misery, gloom, and pain? The account of the fall of humanity lies behind the kingdom teaching of Jesus' ministry. It was there that God the Creator-King shaped the human race to be Servant-Rulers under His dominion. It was also there that we learn that a false spirit usurped the kingship of creation from God by deceiving our first parents in order for him to become the de facto ruler. Notice the two key concepts of "dust" and "spirit" and how they intertwine. In a nutshell, from Genesis 2-3 we know that:

1) God, a being of pure *Spirit*, created the earth and formed the creatures from its *dust*.

2) To oversee the planet, God formed humans out of the elements (*dust*) and breathed His very breath (*Spirit*) into them. God made us as creatures of two realms—earth and heaven, "dust" and "spirit." In this way we were in perfect harmony with both God (*Spirit*) and the creation (*dust*) at the same time. We were "intermediaries" in fellowship with creation and Creator like no other creatures on the planet. We were granted the unique purpose of the stewardship, care, and oversight of earth in submission to God. Under God the Ruler-King, we were made coregents of the creation, "underrulers" uniquely designed for perfect fellowship with both our Ruler and the ruled under our care.

3) Satan, a false spirit, using the voice of a serpent, usurped the kingship of the planet. He deceived Eve and Adam. Through that deception, humans found themselves obeying the serpent's will instead of God's. If our King commands us at the same time as another, and we choose the other, we are guilty of high treason, rejecting the true King and ceding obedience to a usurper. This puts us in a mutiny against God the true King. Our first parents' choice of the serpent's voice in direct opposition to the Lord's command ceded the kingship from God to Satan (for kings are to be obeyed on pain of death). Thus, Satan became the lord of the ones who had been given oversight of earth. With him as the new overlord, three painful new realities entered the creation—sorrow, sin, and death.

4) God acted immediately to win creation back. In an ancient messianic

prophesy, God promised that a descendant of the human line would crush the Serpent's head, even though the Serpent would bruise His heel (Genesis 3:15).

This takes us to the fulfillment of that promise made to our first parents. God (*pure Spirit*) entered the human line (becoming *dust* with us) through Jesus Christ (*born of dust and Spirit*). This Messiah, born as our first parents were, a human of both heaven and earth, receives heaven's power to accomplish His ministry. As soon as the *Spirit* of God came upon Him at His baptism, He (like the first Adam) immediately faced the powers of darkness. (This is why Jesus is referred to by Paul as the second and last Adam.)

As soon as Jesus was baptized, he went up out of the water. At that moment heaven was opened, and he saw the Spirit of God descending like a dove and lighting on him. And a voice from heaven said, "This is my Son, whom I love; with him I am well pleased."

Then Jesus was led by the Spirit into the desert to be tempted by the devil. After fasting forty days and forty nights he was hungry. The tempter came to him and said, "If you are the Son of God, tell these stones to become bread."

Jesus answered, "It is written: 'Man does not live on bread alone, but on every word that comes from the mouth of God.'"

Then the devil took him to the holy city and had him stand on the highest point of the temple. "If you are the Son of God," he said, "throw yourself down. 'For it is written:

"'He will command his angels concerning you,

and they will lift you up in their hands,

so that you will not strike your foot against a stone.'"

Jesus answered him, "It is also written: 'Do not put the Lord your God to the test.'"

Again, the devil took him to a very high mountain and showed him all the kingdoms of the world and their splendor. "All this I will give you," he said, "if you will bow down and worship me."

Jesus said to him, "Away from me, Satan! For it is written:

'Worship the Lord your God, and serve him only.'"

Then the devil left him, and angels came and attended him. (Matthew 3:16-4:11, NIV)

In the text above, Jesus took on human existence. He entered the creation and became, like us, one "born of dust." Like the first Adam, Jesus also received the "breath of life"—the Spirit was upon His mother Mary in His conception (see Matthew 1:20; Luke 1:35). This means that He was born of dust and Spirit, like no one else. Beyond this, the Spirit descended upon Him at the beginning of His ministry.

As both "dust and Spirit" (and without sin) He was in exactly the same condition as our first parents prior to the original temptation. He is in perfect union with both creation and Creator. Just as the enemy appeared to our first parents, so the enemy appeared to tempt Jesus away from the leadership of the true Spirit; the devil wanted to obtain Jesus' allegiance. Why?

Satan's rule of earth was only through the fallen nature of humanity.

The appearance of a human made (just as Adam was) of dust and Spirit and without sin, in perfect fellowship with the True Ruler-King was a very real threat to his rule of "all the kingdoms of the world and their splendor" (Matthew 4:8). Jesus could take creation back from the usurper.

- The first revelation granted Christ by the heavenly voice was that He was the Son of God and loved.
- The first attack to drive a wedge between God and Christ was to act on His own to prove it.

The enemy demanded that He prove it twice by acting *apart* from God's initiative instead of acting *in concert with* the Spirit of God, acting merely from the dust!

Though the terms were different than that of our first parents, Jesus was being tempted exactly as they had been—to act out of harmony with the Spirit. Unlike our first parents, Jesus refused. In the third temptation, Satan showed his hand. He offered Him (note the language) all *the kingdoms* of the world in exchange for what he really wanted, the rule of earth demonstrated by the adoration of all his subjects. He said, "All this I will give you . . . if you will bow down and worship me" (Matthew 4:9).

Two kingdoms came face-to-face in that encounter: the kingdom of God in Christ and the kingdom of darkness under Satan. Unlike the first Adam, the second Adam, Jesus, didn't yield to deception or to the lie, nor did He embark on a path of disobedience. He gave the false ruler no quarter and insisted that God was His Ruler, His true King. Since only a human could give the rule of the creation away to Satan, only a human in fellowship with the true Spirit could take it back. This was the beginning of the kingdom of God reclaiming this fallen world from the usurper. All through Jesus' ministry, He proclaimed the rightful rule, the kingdom of God. To paraphrase the dialogue between the knight and Merlin, "when the King came, so also did the kingdom!" His rule was regularly characterized by undoing the works of the devil. He healed the sick, raised the dead, taught unearthly truth, confounded world systems, and, especially, demonstrated that He would retake earth from evil by casting out demons!

The ultimate promise made to all humanity, to all fallen "creatures of dust," is that He would rejoin us to the true rule of God in our lives through the rule of the Spirit. John the Baptizer indicated He would baptize in the Holy Spirit (Matthew 3:11; Mark 1:8; Luke 3:16; John 1:32-34). The Risen Lord reaffirmed that teaching (Acts 1:5, 8) and it was carried out in the ministry of the early church (Acts 2:4, 17, 33, 38-39; 4:31; 10:44; 1 Corinthians 12:13; see Paul's rebuke in Galatians 3:2-5).

Simply put, to pray "Your kingdom come, Your will be done" is to pray a spiritual warfare prayer. This prayer is to say to God that you, with Jesus' Spirit, are partnering together against all the forces of wickedness in making God's rule effective to usurp the evil rule of the devil. Don't be afraid, though. Jesus told us that "the gates of hell shall not prevail" against the church (Matthew 16:18, KJV). It means that we storm those gates rather than let the enemy set up citadels for evil. That is what this prayer is about.

PEN TO PAPER

1) Jesus' ministry rested on doing things through the leading of the Holy Spirit, rather than "just doing nice things." God wants us to follow the leading of His Holy Spirit as well. Think of a time when you knew that God was giving you a direction, whether it seemed a small thing or a heavy burden. Record it below.

2) Just as the name of God was the power-sphere of God's character as opposed to that of other names, so also the kingdom of God pertains to God's rule as opposed to any other kind of rule. To get at what this means, take the word "evil" and brainstorm what that word means. Then write down the exact opposite on the other side of the page.

Evil means   The opposite is

_____   _____
_____   _____
_____   _____
_____   _____

3) To pray "Your kingdom come. Your will be done" is to partner with God to replace evil with good, death with life, sickness with healing, etc. Turn this into a personal prayer. Name the areas in which evil, sin, or despair are active in your life. Then pray for the kingdom of God to come by renouncing the evil and replacing it with good. Record that below:

PRAYER CHALLENGE

The kingdom of heaven is the rule of God, a situation in which everything works God's way. Think about what life would be like in heaven anytime you have a moment today. When you see things that are not at all like heaven, pray quietly for the kingdom of heaven to come to earth, right there. Spiritual warfare can be as simple as an act of kindness when animosity or sarcasm or a reprimand is expected. Pray for the things that make Jesus strong to become strong in each situation.

DAY 4

The kingdoms are at war! To pray the Lord's Prayer is
to commit to battle in a war zone.

Some time ago, while teaching on the kingdom of God, I would ask
people to brainstorm two words: "heaven" and "war." What invariably
came out is that the two were diametrical opposites.

For "heaven," people would say things like "bliss," "rest," "reunion," "joy,"
"light," "freedom," "resurrection," etc.

For "war," people would say things like "violence," "death," "despair,"
"famine," "hatred," "murder," "loss," etc.

With this being the case, it was a terrific surprise to discover that the two
words show up side by side in a picture of heaven from the book of Revelation:

> And there was *war in heaven*, Michael and his angels waging war
> with the dragon. The dragon and his angels waged war, and they
> were not strong enough, and there was no longer a place found for
> them in heaven.
>
> And the great dragon was thrown down, the serpent of old
> who is called the devil and Satan, who deceives the whole world;
> he was thrown down to the earth, and his angels were thrown
> down with him.
>
> Then I heard a loud voice in heaven, saying, "Now the salvation,
> and the power, and *the kingdom of our God and* the authority *of His
> Christ* have come, for the accuser of our brethren has been thrown
> down, who accuses them before our God day and night.
>
> "And they overcame him because of the blood of the Lamb and
> because of the word of their testimony and they did not love their
> life even when faced with death. . . .
>
> Woe to the earth . . . because the devil has come down to
> you. . . ."

So the dragon was enraged with the woman, and went off *to make war with the rest of her children*, who keep the commandments of God and hold to the testimony of Jesus. (Revelation 12:7-11-12, 17-18, NASB, emphasis mine)

Revelation gives us a "two- (and sometimes three-) tiered view" of reality. We see heaven and earth at the same time (and sometimes also hell and judgment). With this two-tiered perspective, events of heaven and earth are telescoped or collapsed into condensed sections containing vivid metaphorical imagery. Revelation 12 is an example of this.

Revelation 12:1-6, the verses that precede the above passage, contains a condensed picture of the story of redemption. A woman (the Virgin Mary, representing the people of God—Israel and the church) gives birth to the future ruler (Messiah Jesus). A dragon (Satan/the devil) tries to destroy the child, but fails to do so. The child ascends to heaven and takes up His rightful throne, despite the threats of the usurper. As soon as the child becomes the heavenly king, war occurs in heaven between the forces of God under Michael the archangel and the forces of evil under the dragon.

As soon as the true king, Jesus, comes to heaven, God's kingdom is inaugurated, war is declared on the false king Satan. Then the false one, after a season of battle, is thrown out. The kingdom of God is declared as a present reality only after all evil is thrown out and removed from heaven's realm. While evil and evil influences remained, it was clear that the kingdom had not yet come!

There is more. This dragon is thrown down to earth to make war on all those who follow Jesus. The kingdom is coming, but the kingdom of our God has not yet come to planet earth. That remains for the time after the evil one (and all evil influence) is thrown out and destroyed forever. It will occur completely when the King returns!

Until the return of the King and His influence is exported to earth (i.e., until His "kingdom comes" and His "will is done on earth as it is in heaven"), the church of Jesus Christ is at war with evil in all its forms. Our job is to do exactly what the angels in heaven did—to cast out evil as we wage war against the author of evil, leading to his expulsion from earth forever.

The legend of Robin Hood is a similar kind of story. Wicked King John had usurped the rightful throne from Good King Richard the Lionhearted.

Robin Hood, a servant of Richard, was at continual war with the usurper king until the return of the rightful one. When the true king returned, so also did justice and truth, and the wicked king was expelled.

And so we wait. We know our God and we know our enemy. To pray "Your kingdom come, Your will be done on earth as it is in heaven" is to declare open war on evil in all its forms. It is to partner with God in destroying sickness with health, in casting out evil with good, in upholding the name of our true King whenever the false one attempts to control us or destroy us. It is to identify completely with His name, His rule, and His love.

PEN TO PAPER

1) Think about what is needed in time of war. What did our forebears do when the Allied forces and the resistance movements in conquered nations (and Germany itself) fought against the evil of Hitler? What then is required for us as Christian believers at war with evil? How then should we pray?

2) Satan immediately declared war on the people of God. Why? He hated the Child Messiah and has transferred his hatred to those who follow Him. What does this mean for those of us who follow the Lord?

3) Go back and reread the passage from Revelation. There are three weapons that were used to defeat the dragon and usher in the return of the king. What were they?

    a) _____

    b) _____

    c) _____

    Make a plan to use all three weapons. It is not enough to commit to one or two of them. Enemies probe for weakness until it is found, and then they attack. All three are necessary to defeat evil. If we use one, and make no commitment to the other two, attack will occur in the other two areas.

4) Get into a prayerful posture in a private place. This one will take time. Give God a minimum of half an hour to start this prayer (you may not finish that quickly). It is time to take up the kingdom-promoting weapons of Revelation 12. Without these instruments, the kingdom of God will not move forward in your life, and it most certainly will not grow in your circles of influence.

a) The "blood of the Lamb" is the means by which we are forgiven. Ask God the Father to cover you with the sacrificial blood of Christ. Stay with this until you are sure that it is accomplished. This is the means by which God identifies with us completely.

b) The "word of your testimony" is your solemn word ("testimony" is your word about what you have seen or heard, etc.) about your experience of God's grace in your life, pointing to the reality of Jesus Christ. Commit yourself to speak to, of, and about Jesus whenever opportunity arises. Plan not to shirk the open invitation to identify with Him, especially when people ask about your walk with God. This is a first step, a means by which we identify with God's identification with us.

c) Commit to *complete* identification with Jesus' cross. We are to "love not our lives even unto the death." This means that we commit to loving the Lord so profoundly that we identify with Him whether it is easy or risky. We are to speak for Him when all speak against Him. We are to name Him as our Lord, even when under threat of death and loss. We are to be so one with Him that we are willing to die for Him. This one should not be done lightly or quickly. Can you "take up your cross and follow Him"?

PRAYER CHALLENGE

Carry the thought through the day that we are at war with evil and especially with the evil one. Count the cost, place yourself under Jesus' death, plan to speak what you believe, and understand that you need to be fearless in sharing your Christ-life. Make preparations for attack and counterattack.

DAY 5

The kingdom of heaven and the Holy Spirit's presence and power are connected.

It is very clear from the teaching of Jesus that our Lord was intimately concerned about the coming kingdom of His Father. That is the plain sense of this second line from the Lord's Prayer. In fact, it is striking that Jesus told us to ask for that kingdom to come—as if our prayers in this matter would make a difference.

In fact, they do.

There is a sense in which the kingdom of heaven is coming—there will be an end to time when all evil will be destroyed and truth will prevail. But there is another sense in which the kingdom of God is already here—by the presence and power of the Holy Spirit. Many texts point to this, but we will examine a couple in the next two days to determine exactly what the relationship between the kingdom of God and the Holy Spirit's presence and power is.

In my former book, Theophilus, I wrote about all that Jesus began to do and to teach until the day he was taken up to heaven, after giving instructions through the Holy Spirit to the apostles he had chosen. After his suffering, he showed himself to these men and gave many convincing proofs that he was alive. He appeared to them over a period of forty days and spoke about the kingdom of God. On one occasion, while he was eating with them, he gave them this command: "Do not leave Jerusalem, but wait for the gift my Father promised, which you have heard me speak about. For John baptized with water, but in a few days you will be baptized with the Holy Spirit."

So when they met together, they asked him, "Lord, are you at this time going to restore the kingdom to Israel?"

He said to them, "It is not for you to know the times or dates the Father has set by his own authority. But you will receive power when the Holy Spirit comes on you; and you will be my witnesses in Jerusalem, and in all Judea and Samaria, and to the ends of the earth."

After he said this, he was taken up before their very eyes, and a cloud hid him from their sight.

They were looking up intently into the sky as he was going, when suddenly two men dressed in white stood beside them. "Men of Galilee," they said, "why do you stand here looking into the sky? This same Jesus, who has been taken from you into heaven, will come back in the same way you have seen him go into heaven." (Acts 1:1-11, NIV)

Now take a pen and underline every reference to 1) the Holy Spirit and 2) the kingdom. Do that right now.

Did you notice the relationship between the Holy Spirit and the kingdom of God in the mind of both Christ and the apostles?

- Jesus gave *instructions* ("injunctions" or "commands") *through the Holy Spirit* to the apostles in the forty days between His resurrection and His rising to heaven.
- In those forty days He spoke about one topic only—*the kingdom of God.*
- To explain this further, and to indicate the content of the kingdom teaching, Acts 1 indicates that Jesus spoke of how they would be *baptized in the Holy Spirit.*
- The apostles immediately asked about whether *the kingdom* would be restored to Israel.
- The Lord indicated that their timing was off (and off-limits!) but that they would receive power when *the Holy Spirit* would come upon them.
- Then the Lord, the Messiah-King, was taken up with a promise that He would return at the end of time (ostensibly to bring in *the kingdom*).
  Spirit.
  Kingdom.

Spirit.
Kingdom.
Spirit.
Kingdom.
To think of one was to name the other.

It is plain from this text that the kingdom of God has a future fulfillment. The kingdom of God is on the way, and it involves Israel and the rule of the Jewish Messiah, Jesus Himself. It is also plain that the teaching of the kingdom of God is directly related to the presence and power of the Holy Spirit in the lives of believers in the "now." Jesus indicated that the *timing* was not their concern, but the *experience* of the Spirit was to be the thing for which they must wait. The kingdom of God is "already here/not yet arrived."

What is clear in the teaching of Jesus is also found in the epistles of Paul. There are fourteen references to "the kingdom" in the epistles. In most, the kingdom refers to the practice of right living rooted in the experience of the Holy Spirit ("The kingdom of God is . . . righteousness, peace and joy in the Holy Spirit" [Romans 14:17, NIV]). In the remaining places, the kingdom refers to the last day when all things will be handed over to God the Father that God might be all in all (1 Corinthians 15:20-28). In both types of contexts, the underlying teaching is that God is exercising His rule. In this age, God does this in those who love Him by shaping them, empowering them, and making them holy through the presence of His Spirit. In the next age God will exercise His rule by dismantling evil and by casting away everything that exalts itself against the knowledge of God. This is summed up beautifully in 1 John 3:2-3. Even though the phrase "the kingdom" isn't in this text, the two realities of how we live now and what we can expect at the end of time are placed in parallel here.

> Beloved, we are God's children *now,* and what we will be has *not yet* appeared; but we know that when he appears we shall be like him, because we shall see him as he is. And everyone who thus hopes in him purifies himself as he is pure.
> (1 John 3:2-3, ESV, emphasis added)

We are "now/not yet" people. We are *already* children of God. We are *not yet* sinless perfection. We are saved from our sins (though we sin from time to time). We are filled with the Holy Spirit, but we leak! God needs to fill us again, until we come to the time when we become just like Jesus at the end of time. This is motivation to keep purifying our hearts and minds as we await the return of Christ at the end of time.

PEN TO PAPER

1) When the disciples wanted the kingdom to come, Jesus redirected them and told them to focus on waiting for the gift of the Holy Spirit. Reread the Acts passage above. What did Jesus tell them would be the effect of their being "baptized with the Holy Spirit"?

2) How would the disciples know that they had received the power promised in that gift? What then should we be asking from the Lord for "the kingdom to come on earth as in heaven"?

3) First John indicates that "now" we are God's children and that we are "not yet" as we shall be when we see the return of Christ at the end of time. He then indicates that this is a motivation to become more like Christ now. List the things that motivate you to become more like Christ. Then pray for the Spirit to give you power, to make you able to share your faith, and to live a life that pleases God.

PRAYER CHALLENGE

Commit 1 John 3:2-3 to memory. Each time you remember it, ask God to increase the presence of His Spirit in your heart and mind, for power to be granted to live a God-honoring life, and for power to share your faith in Jesus.

DAY 6

Jesus' kingdom rescues us from the devil's rule of sin and evil.
Kingdom versus kingdom means "Spirit versus spirit."

T o take us forward in our understanding of the Lord's Prayer, we are
going to revisit an old friend! It is likely that you know this Old
English folk carol. Regardless of the season, sing out this familiar
tune (or read it aloud if vocally challenged!).

> God rest ye merry, gentlemen, let nothing you dismay!
> Remember Christ our Savior was born on Christmas Day—
> *To save us all from Satan's power when we were gone astray.*
> O tidings of comfort and joy, comfort and joy!
> O tidings of comfort and joy!

Doubtless you have heard this song before, every year at Christmas—but
did you notice the words? The ancient songwriter had his finger on the point
of the second line of Jesus' prayer—when we pray for the kingdom to come
and for God's will to be done, we are inviting Jesus to save us from our sins,
which is the power of Satan. All who go astray from God's grace are under
that false, unclean power. Jesus came to destroy that unclean power! John says
it succinctly:

> Little children, make sure no one deceives you; the one who
> practices righteousness is righteous, just as He is righteous; the one
> who practices sin is of the devil; for the devil has sinned from the
> beginning. The Son of God appeared for this purpose, *to destroy the
> works of the devil.* (1 John 3:7-8, NASB, emphasis added)

God rules His people by love, truth, and right living.
The devil rules his people by sin, the lie, and the practice of evil.

God's rule is selfless and empowering.

The devil's rule is selfish and power-mongering.

The contrast between the two is quite striking.

Once when asked how to tell the difference between the voice of the Holy Spirit and the voice of the unclean spirit, I replied that it was really quite simple:

1) When the Holy Spirit tells us about our sin, it is to free us from its power. God speaks to bring deliverance.
2) When the devil tells us about our sin, it is to lock us into more sin. The devil speaks to ensnare the unsuspecting and bring despair.

Now here is the good news: Jesus came to destroy the power of that second voice. That is the thrust of Jesus' teaching about the kingdom of God. Let's examine another "kingdom" text from Jesus' teaching:

> Then they brought him a demon-possessed man who was blind and mute, and Jesus healed him, so that he could both talk and see. . . . But when the Pharisees heard this, they said, "It is only by Beelzebub, the prince of demons that this fellow drives out demons."
>
> Jesus knew their thoughts and said to them, "Every kingdom divided against itself will be ruined, and every city or household divided against itself will not stand. If Satan drives out Satan, he is divided against himself. How then can his kingdom stand? And if I drive out demons by Beelzebub, by whom do your people drive them out? So then, they will be your judges. But if I drive out demons by the Spirit of God, then the kingdom of God has come upon you." (Matthew 12:22, 24-28, NIV)

Notice that Jesus has been accused of partnering with the devil, of using unclean spirit-power to cast out unclean spirit-beings as a con job to win people over to darkness, all the while using His "false light" as a mask. This section is loaded with kingdom language for both clean and unclean uses of kingdom power. But for our purposes, notice that to speak of a kingdom implies a king who must not work against himself. There are two kings here, God and Satan. Both of them rule by the power of their spirit. Here we have two kingdoms at war, and the kingdom of God expands as demons are cast out, just as in the passage from Revelation 12 that we read on Day 4 this week. The key for our purposes today is the last line: "If I drive out demons by the Spirit of God, then the kingdom of God has come upon you."

Once again, to speak of the presence and power of the Spirit is to imply the presence of God's kingdom, coming to earth as it did in heaven. To pray the Lord's Prayer then is to ask for the power of the kingdom, that is the power of the Holy Spirit. It is for us to immerse ourselves in every part of our beings with His presence so that God might use us to drive out evil wherever and whenever we meet it.

PEN TO PAPER

1) In 1 John 3:7-8, it is clear that Jesus and the devil are at war. They both are spiritual powers, though the effect of their spirits is very different. What is the mark of those who belong to the devil? What is the mark of those who belong to Christ?

2) The difference between the two voices—of the Holy Spirit and the devil—is contrasted in today's lesson. How do you tell the difference between the voice of God, the voice of the devil, and your own thoughts?

3) Reread the Matthew passage. What did the presence of the Holy Spirit in Jesus accomplish? What does this mean for us as we pray for the kingdom to come?

4) Spend some time praising God. Then ask God for a list of things you know need to happen for the kingdom of God to come. Don't be afraid to "ask big." God's answering will always be superabundantly beyond all that we could even ask or imagine! So ask and imagine.

PRAYER CHALLENGE

Ask God to grant you the Holy Spirit's power today. If you do not sense the Spirit's presence and power experientially, then commit to wait on the Lord until this becomes tangible and real in you. Then pray for God to "save you from your sins," to let the Spirit of God release you from the things which the enemy uses to destroy us. Jesus came to destroy that voice! Celebrate this. Whether in season or not, sing the first verse of "God Rest Ye Merry, Gentlemen" from time to time today. Thank God for its truths!

DAY 7

The "will" in God's kingdom will always include knowing God better.

I n *The Lord's Prayer* William Barclay makes clear that the two thoughts of Jesus' prayer, "Your kingdom come, Your will be done," are in fact one single thought:

> If . . . [the Lord's Prayer] is an instance of . . . Hebrew parallelism, and the second arm of the parallel explains and defines the first, then we can arrive at the definition:
>
> The Kingdom of God is a society on earth in which God's will is as perfectly done as it is in heaven. That is to say, to do the will of God and to be in the Kingdom are one and the same thing. To be a citizen of any kingdom, and to be a subject of any king, necessarily involves obedience to the laws of that kingdom and to the commands of that king. To be a member of the Kingdom of God necessarily involves acceptance of the will of God.[12]

The Lord's Prayer makes abundantly clear that the will of God is linked to the kingly rule of God. It also makes clear that our prayers cause earth to be opened up to the influence and power of heaven itself. We now know that this prayer is a "two-spirit" prayer, in which we resist evil in heaven's name, until God expels all evil forever.

But what is the will of God for us today? Most of us think of the will of God as some task that God is calling us to accomplish. We strain in prayer as we choose between two jobs, or we struggle to determine which is best—extra work to pay for our children's education or more time at home to nurture them. We find ourselves torn between continuing in current tasks and making a potential career change, and we want to know that God is in these decisions.

Jesus' message is that the *tasks* take second place to the *relationship*. He speaks to this in the Sermon on the Mount:

> Not everyone who says to Me, "Lord, Lord," will enter the kingdom of heaven, but he who does the will of My Father who is in heaven will enter. Many will say to Me on that day, "Lord, Lord, did we not prophesy in Your name, and in Your name cast out demons, and in Your name perform many miracles?" And then I will declare to them, "I never knew you; depart from Me, you who practice lawlessness." (Matthew 7:21-23, NASB)

Here many elements of Jesus' prayer intersect: (a) the kingdom, (b) heaven, (c) the will, (d) the Father, and e) the name. There is a future kingdom with a Judgment Day. Here we find some truths about the kingdom and the will of God:

1) the kingdom of God is to be entered (entrance is *not* automatic)
2) entering that kingdom is linked to doing the will of the Father
3) the Father *wants* His will done on earth
4) without obedience to the will, no one gets into the kingdom
5) some will attempt to enter the kingdom based on the power of the name, but will not be allowed in
6) some attempting to enter will claim that they succeeded in casting out demons/evil, based on the power of the name
7) Jesus will declare He never knew them.

This is a sobering text for everyone. It at least implies that it is *possible* to tap into God's power (or to suffer from the illusion that we did), and to miss God altogether, to think we are "in the kingdom and doing the will" but to fail altogether. Here were those who understood the two-spirit battle, and had sided with good over evil. Yet they were missing an important element—knowing and loving God through Jesus Christ. This makes a most decisive point in our understanding of the will of God: *The will of God can never be reduced to some task or event that we have done, ostensibly in the name of our Lord.*

God's will is first and foremost a *relationship*!

To do the will of God is to focus on knowing God at all costs. Any task that we do *for* God must draw us into a deeper relationship *with* God or the task was simply not within the *will* of God, however noble the task or pure the motive.

The rejected servants had a false understanding of the will as mere tasks, even tasks for which they received power. Their understanding focused on *power alone* and not on the person and character of Jesus and God. Power in and of itself is a vain use of the name of God. It is profane to "use God and lose God." Some would call it blasphemy. Why? The answer is simple: *Doing the "will" of God always creates a magnificent unity between God and us.*

To "hallow the name" is to know God in all His holiness and love. To live in and for "the will" is to recognize this and live for this, and then to use the power of the name when need arises. This text implies that some can cast out demons and use the power of the name *and not do the will of God.*

The will of God is larger than dealing with what some call "power-encounters." Living in the will certainly means to participate in the name, which *includes* power, but only power as *a secondary reality.* The point of doing the will is to know Jesus, His character, His nature, His person, His very life. It is to be in intimate communication with Him, and through this, it is to know *exactly* what God wants done.

God's will then can never be reduced to some task—even if it is a "power-encounter." God's will is first and foremost *friendship with God.* Listen to what Jesus said about this matter: "No longer do I call you slaves, for the slave does not know what his master is doing; but I have called you friends, for all things that I have heard from My Father I have made known to you" (John 15:15, NASB).

It is to know the Son, and through Him, to enter into the will of the Father. To fail to know Jesus and His true name is to practice lawlessness, regardless of whether the so-called "good things" we do look powerful or not. All tasks that we are required to do must arise from knowing and loving God in a relationship in which we are alive to God.

There is no clearer exposition of this than "the other Lord's Prayer" found in John 17. As we heard in Week 1, Day 3, this "high priestly prayer" indicates that there is a true center in taking God as King and doing His will. Here it is: "This is eternal life, that they may know You, the only true God, and Jesus

Christ whom You have sent" (John 17:3, NASB).

In other words, all of Jesus' life was focused not on some great deed or task (though His life was filled with many tasks, including His death and resurrection), but on a magnificent reunion of lost children to a loving Father. To be in the kingdom of God is to leave our alienation from God behind forever and to become rejoined to the God who made us to fellowship with Him forever.

Once this is settled, then the tasks God wants done are assigned to us—but each task, whether simple or difficult, will only serve to draw us closer to knowing the Lord we love, who calls us "friends" by showing us what is for us.

PEN TO PAPER

1) Think for a moment about "servants" and "friends." What is the difference between the two?

A servant: _____

A friend: _____

It is clear that the relationship is very different. Go and reread John 15:15 and record here what the text means for you today.

2) Now ask for the kingdom to come in your life—for a richer, closer friendship with God, even while you sort through what tasks need to be done today to help you earn a living.

PRAYER CHALLENGE

Take some time today to just "be" before God. Praise Him. Specifically remember the good things that He has done for us—in biblical history through His birth, His life and teaching, His death and resurrection, and in your life through how He has worked with you. Thank God that you are friends with Him, and that the whole point of His coming was to make us His friends. Thank Him that any tasks that God assigns will only make us closer to Him. End by remembering that eternal life is to know Him.

Week Four

REQUEST THE KINGDOM

"Your Will Be Done . . ."

Part II

DAY 1

The King's Presence—His Spirit—shows us what
God desires for us to do.

I t is time to reexamine our understanding of the Lord's Prayer again.
Teaching about God's kingdom and God's will are deep waters—and
most of us have not sounded out how deep it really is. We need a second
week to attempt to grasp these realities!

Very likely, we are in a similar position as the novice dealer who sold what
he thought was a pretty rock to a man named Roy Whetstine. In February of
1986 Whetstine went to a gem show in Tucson, Arizona. His two sons each
gave him $5 and asked their dad to find some souvenir for their collections.
The hope was that he might stumble onto a bargain or two.

Whetstine went about his business; then on a whim he walked through
an area in which amateur dealers were displaying their wares. He walked up
to one dealer and saw a box of stones and rocks marked $15. Inside the box
was an egg-shaped, brown-black stone the size of a small potato. Whetstine
picked up the stone, examined it, and said, "You want $15 for this?"

Immediately the dealer cut the price to $10.

Whetstine took the rock home and had it appraised. It turned out that the
brown-black rock was a 1,905-carat star sapphire worth $2.28 million USD.
At the time, it was thought to be among the world's largest.[13]

Though subsequent appraisals have disputed the value of Whetstine's find
(one appraiser put the value as low as $10,000), the point is still valid: we need
to value what we have in our own backyard. The dealer had no idea what was
in the stone he was selling.

Most of us are in the same position when it comes to praying the Lord's
Prayer. We have an incredible treasure in our hands, but haven't the vaguest
idea of just what we have! In fact, we value it less than we should. Since this is
Week 4, and our stereotypes of what is in this prayer have been lessened, let's
return to "tradition" with a twist! Most of us learned either the King James

Version, the Douay translation from the Latin Vulgate, or the version found in the Book of Common Prayer. The treasure has been there all along. Listen now to the traditional rendering from the KJV. Compare it to the Peterson translation right beside it, and pray the prayer with an open heart:

Our Father which art in heaven,	Our Father in heaven,
Hallowed be thy name.	Reveal who you are.
Thy kingdom come,	Set the world right;
Thy will be done in earth,	Do what's best—
As it is in heaven.	as above, so below.
Give us this day our	Keep us alive with three
daily bread.	square meals.
And forgive us our debts,	Keep us forgiven with you
As we forgive our debtors;	and forgiving others.
And lead us not into temptation,	Keep us safe from ourselves
but deliver us from evil:	and the Devil.
For thine is the kingdom,	You're in charge!
and the power,	You can do anything you want!
and the glory,	You're ablaze in beauty!
for ever. Amen.	Yes. Yes. Yes.
(Matthew 6:9-13, KJV)	(Matthew 6:9-13, *The Message*)

Sometimes we can find treasure more easily when we see what someone else has mined! Compare these two renderings and record anything new that comes to you below, and then pray out that new meaning.

Was that helpful to you? What was the most important thing you prayed as a result of this discovery?

Let us refocus on what it means to pray the second line of the prayer. If it wasn't clear before, it is now apparent that we will always be learning what it means to pray for the kingdom to come and the will to be done. What is obvious is that we are entering the very heart of everything Jesus lived and died and rose again for! Yet the question we raised at the close of last week is still with us. How do we know the specific tasks that God wants us to do? What must we be and do for the "will to be done"?

We know the will of God *generally* (i.e., keep the Ten Commandments) but we are not sure what the will is *specifically* for our lives at this particular time. How can we get there?

God longs for us not only to know Him, but for us to be in intimate "two-way" conversation with Him so that we can know what pleases Him. He will communicate and we will be able to follow God.

So how then do we "hear" when God speaks and obey when we are pressed to understand which of two equally godly alternatives is the one God wants us to follow? The answer is to pay attention to the Presence!

From time to time, God resorts to speaking human language—as He did when He spoke to Moses on Mount Sinai, to Mary about the birth of Christ, or to Peter when He called him to preach to the Gentiles. Most of the time though, God "speaks" through the increase of (or the withholding of) His presence. It was the presence of God that guided Israel in their wilderness journeys and set Israel apart from all other nations (Exodus 33:14-16). We can see this in the closing words of Exodus—the book depicting Israel's departure from Egypt, and in Numbers—a book describing the journey to the Promised Land:

> In all the travels of Israelites, whenever the cloud lifted from above the tabernacle, they would set out; but if the cloud did not lift, they did not set out—until the day it lifted. So the cloud of the LORD was over the tabernacle by day, and fire was in the cloud by night, in the sight of all the house of Israel during all their travels. (Exodus 40:36-38, NIV)

> Whenever the cloud lifted from above the Tent, the Israelites set out; wherever the cloud settled, the Israelites encamped. At the

LORD's command the Israelites set out, and at his command they encamped. (Numbers 9:17-18, NIV)

Israel learned to go nowhere unless the presence of the Lord went there first. Here the command was not an audible word spoken. Rather it was God's *presence* that moved and beckoned them to follow.

We need to learn this lesson as well—and we have a better heritage. Now the Holy Spirit has been given to all believers everywhere. It is the presence of the Holy Spirit in our hearts that sets Christians apart from the rest of the world (see Ephesians 2:22; Romans 5:5, etc.). It is this presence that can show us which assignments He has for us. Listen to this word from the apostle Paul:

> Let the peace of Christ rule in your hearts, to which indeed you were called in one body; and be thankful. Let the Word of Christ richly dwell within you, with all wisdom teaching and admonishing one another with psalms and hymns and spiritual songs, singing with thankfulness in your hearts to God. Whatever you do in word or deed, do all in the name of the Lord Jesus, giving thanks through Him to God the Father. (Colossians 3:15-17, NASB)

Over years of seeking to know what God wanted done (with many false trails along the way) five steps have regularly provided helpful guidance. They are as follows:

- The Word of God
- The Witness of the Holy Spirit
- The Workers in God's kingdom
- The Worship of God
- The Will of the believer

1) The Word of God: Colossians indicates that the Word should dwell in us richly. What better way to discover what God wants than to saturate our souls with His specific teaching! If the Word within us is rich, so also will be the guidance that God sends through that Word. There are biblical principles that we should know. Read the gospels until their teaching is second nature. Study the epistles and the Revelation. Immerse yourself in the prophets. Commit Scriptures to memory and feed your soul with them. There will be no *specific* guidance if we are disobeying the *general principles* of godliness that are ours for the learning. If this step is not taken, then we will not be guided well. Obey what you know. Refuse to disobey what you know, and then God can give specific steps to take.

2) *The Witness of the Holy Spirit:* The peace is to "rule" in our hearts. The word rendered "rule" here is used in ancient Greek for "umpire" or "referee." The peace of Christ then is to mediate between two (or more) directions or judge whether one is in or out of the game. The peace "calls the decision." There should be a general sense of peace in a Christian's life. This comes from the presence of the Holy Spirit. Should this peace become diminished, jarred, or out of kilter, "Peace," the referee, is saying "Wait. Test this one out." If the peace is consistently absent, God is saying "no." If the peace grows deeper as one considers a direction, test this further. If it continues and grows more profound, then this is a signal that God *could* be leading in this direction. It is best to keep this tentative; since this area is subjective, there needs to be a further testing out of this sense of leading.

3) *The Workers in God's Kingdom:* Find someone who is a person saturated in the Word of God. Ensure that this is a person who is open to the leading of the Spirit and sensitive to God's flow of peace. Place the situations before him and pray together. Let this be a person with no vested interest in the decisions (i.e., if you are thinking about taking on a new job, don't pray with the old boss!). Let him ask you probing questions until he and you together come to a place in which the peace of God in his soul and yours is ruling, and indicating that this decision is "in the game" and "fair play." This is what it means to be "called in one body." The result should be a sense in which the Word of God is in harmony with this decision. The sense of leading in the soul of the seeker is peaceful and clear. There should be a consensus within unbiased third parties that the Word and Spirit together are pointing in this direction. With these three in place, the last two steps can be taken.

4) *The Worship of God:* At this point, a decision to proceed with a direction is taken. The outflow of this process should be "psalms and hymns

and spiritual songs"—praise, worship, mutual teaching, and a release of intimacy with God in the souls of all concerned. Sometimes a heavy decision doesn't lead to this kind of release. Ordinarily, however, there should be a sense of rightness that facilitates being able to worship God in openness and joy.

5) *The Will of the Believer:* Once the decision is taken, believers set their will to live with the consequences of whatever decision is taken. There will be ups and downs with each major decision taken. Regardless of how one feels, there is a specific calling on each believer who has sounded out the mind of the Lord. *Thankfulness* will be the calling in the times when the decision is tough. "Whatever you do in word or deed, do all in the name of the Lord Jesus, giving thanks through Him to God the Father" (Colossians 3:17).

To pray "Your Kingdom come. Your will be done on earth as it is in heaven" is sounded out through discovering God speaking this way. Here, God speaks through relationship, through abiding in the Word and keeping it, through openness to a leading mediated through peace and through mutual submission of the believer to other godly Christians.

PEN TO PAPER

1) Is there a decision that you need in which you are not sure of the will of God? Commit the options to writing below. Now ask the question, "Does this conform to the Bible's clear teaching?" "Do I have a consistent sense of peace as I pray this through?" "Do other godly Christians agree with me?" "Do I have a release of intimacy with God as I commit to this decision?" "Can I commit to this direction, knowing that it will have ups and downs, confident that God was with me as the decision was taken?"

The Issue: _____

The Bible: _____

The Peace: _____

Other Christians: _____

The Worship: _____

The Will: _____

2) Perhaps you are not yet sure. Wise counsel ensures that all options are examined. It is best to wait, trusting that God will make all things known in time. Place this before God and ask for His leadership. Put the "on hold" things before Him below and commit them to Him.

3) Close out your prayer time by praying through the Lord's Prayer as far as you understand it (and are able to pray it) now. If it is helpful to you, use another translation to help you see some other aspect of the prayer.

PRAYER CHALLENGE

To know and do the will of God (and to pray for it to be done) is more than simply mouthing words. It is a relationship. Be conscious today of the peace in your soul. Let the peace guide you. When your peace leaves, ask if you have stepped out of something you are supposed to be doing. When the peace grows strong or deeper, ask if you are entering into something that you are supposed to be doing. Look for opportunities to speak of your faith, to do an act of kindness, to pray a blessing, to learn a new principle, etc.

DAY 2

Do the general will of God until the specific will of God is given.

There are many people who spend huge amounts of time in what can be called "priority paralysis." They don't know what "the will of God" is, and therefore they cannot pray the will into existence, nor can they do what they aren't sure of. Some are looking for a mystical experience. Others are looking for a clear biblical principle, but find that two or three principles can lead in different directions.

"Go ye into all the world and preach the gospel" (Mark 16:15, KJV) is clear. So is "Honor your father and your mother" (Exodus 20:12, NIV). What is not clear is which command predominates when we have to choose between the two! How are we to obey God's calling to do both when our aging parents need our presence, and we are doing godly service in another country with positive results? Change the scenarios, but many a believer has been confused about which godly option is the right one—which job to choose, which area of service to take up, which course to follow, which fellowship of believers to join, etc.

The best counsel I ever received on this matter was to do the general until God gives the specific. This means that we are to find out what is biblically commanded for the will; then we are to simply do and pray what we know from the Bible that pleases the Lord. Then in the midst of doing the things that we know please God generally, we give room for the Lord to direct us into the personal calling on our lives, whether a short-term assignment or a long-term career choice.

There are texts that indicate what we *can* do, regardless of which decision we take for a specific life task. Here are some texts that make that clear:

> See that no one repays another with evil for evil, but always seek after that which is good for one another and for all people.

Rejoice always; pray without ceasing; in everything give thanks; for this is God's will concerning you in Christ Jesus.

Do not quench the Spirit; do not despise prophetic utterances. But examine everything carefully; hold fast to that which is good; abstain from every form of evil. (1 Thessalonians 5:15-23, NASB)

The way the material is shaped, all of the above commands are modified by the phrase "for this is God's will concerning you in Christ Jesus" (1 Thessalonians 5:18). This gives us clear direction for praying "Your will be done." It is always God's will to pray for these kingdom initiatives to succeed in your life, in the lives of others, and in your local church. To pray for the kingdom to come and the will to be done then includes at least the following:

- It is always God's will to pray for a gracious nature that doesn't return evil for evil.
- It is always God's will to seek after good for another and for everyone (especially when you have been slighted or done an injustice).
- It is always God's will to pray for and to practice joy.
- It is always God's will to deepen your prayer life.
- It is always God's will to give thanks.
- It is always God's will to test out when someone claims to speak for God (you do not have to immediately accept every word spoken, but you do need to listen and to test this by Word, Witness, Workers, Worship, and the Will of the believer).
- It is always God's will to cling to the things that Scripture makes clear are right and true.
- It is always God's will to avoid or turn away from evil (and in this text to reject false prophecy/spirituality).

With these things in mind, we can now pray for some specific things that are the will of God in our own life and in the lives of others. Perhaps there is someone who has done some injustice to you. Likely, the first instinct was to react and to return the same to her. This, according to the passage above, is *not* the will of God. Take a moment and pray good (and not evil) toward her. Make a plan as to how you will seek good for her. Do that right now.

The person who has injured me: _____

My plan to do good to her: _____

My timeline to make it happen: _____

_____

A person to hold me accountable to do it: _____

_____

If you managed to do the above, you are beginning to pray for the will to be done on earth as it is in heaven, simply based on a Scripture text about the will. Jesus' prayer is now beginning to shape your praying. All that you have done is take one of the clear words about "the will" and incorporate that into your relating to another. To pray longer in this vein, simply take the next clear word (rejoice always) and pray that for yourself and for the one who wounded you.

Then do it!

Sing praises to God. Read the Psalms aloud. Record the specific answers that you know you have received to prayer. Ask others about their answers to prayer and commit them to writing. Bring this out and thank God for each answer. Anytime you are tempted to despair, plan to celebrate the presence of God, even in times of darkness. This is the will of God in Christ Jesus concerning you.

Take five minutes and do this very thing. Rejoice.

Did you succeed in rejoicing for five minutes? Then you are praying and partnering with God in the will of God. Though you may not know whether you should take on the new job, move to a new town, stay close to your parents, or propose to your girlfriend, you have had success in doing a part of what you do now know to be "the will." It is best to regard the will of God as a *journey* of faith. We know many things about the will that we *must* do (i.e., keep the Ten Commandments). In time we will know *some* things that are specific to us as God leads us through the five steps we named yesterday (e.g., perhaps you will be called to become a computer programmer instead of a journalist, etc.). We also know that, for some reason beyond our understanding, some things must wait in a trusting relationship with God. God will reveal what we need to know for the future when the time is right.

Other texts make some things clear:

It is always the will of God to pray for sexual purity and to ask God for that to be true within family, friends, and society. This means celibacy in singleness and faithfulness in the "one man/one woman" marriage bond. "For this is the will of God, your sanctification; that is, that you abstain from sexual immorality" (1 Thessalonians 4:3, NASB).

It is always the will of God to pray that others hear about Jesus Christ and His salvation. "For this is the will of My Father, that everyone who beholds the Son and believes in Him will have eternal life, and I Myself will raise him up on the last day"(John 6:40, NASB).

It is always the will that we baptize and coach those who take that step: "Go therefore and make disciples of all nations, baptizing them in the name of the Father and the Son and the Holy Spirit, teaching them to observe all that I commanded you" (Matthew 28:19-20).

It is always the will of God that we become a people of God with other believers together as the power of the Holy Spirit flows through us, and that everything in heaven and on earth be "summed up," joined together under the Lordship of Christ. "He made known to us the mystery of His will . . . the summing up of all things in Christ, things in the heavens and things on the earth" (Ephesians 1:9-10, NASB).

The list is enormous. One way to deepen our understanding of the will of God would be to pick up a concordance and look up every reference to "the will" in the teaching of Jesus and in the epistles. You will discover that simply praying according to what is clearly outlined as "the will of God" will inform all of your praying. There is more than enough to keep our hearts filled with what needs to be done on earth as it is in heaven.

PEN TO PAPER

1) Take a moment and write down the things you know that are the will of God below:

Now pray that each one become true in your life and in the lives of those that these truths impact.

2)   Now take a moment and write down the things that you are not sure of when it comes to the will of God below:

Ask God to clarify each one according to what you know. If you are still unsure, simply entrust these items to Him.

3)   Return to the act of praise. Name God's goodness and grandeur and thank Him for who He is. Complete your time by thanking Him for His deep desire to reveal His will to you!

Prayer Challenge

Each time you are not sure of what God's will is today, return to doing exactly what you know God wants done. Trust God to intervene and tell you what you need to know as the need arises.

DAY 3

"We don't pray about things. We bring things
about by prayer."

*—Armin Gesswein (a leader in the Norwegian Revival and a primary prayer
partner of Billy Graham)*

It is more than abundantly clear that the Lord Jesus did not regularly pray any "if it be Your will" kinds of prayers. His relationship with His Father was such that He simply knew *exactly* what to pray into existence (for that is the role of prayer in a life yielded to God). He did what the Gospel of John calls "abiding" or "remaining" in His God. Their fellowship was so very rich and so intimate that nothing Jesus did was His action alone, but His action as an expression of the Father's. Numerous passages make this one clear. Perhaps the clearest testimony to this reality is when Jesus said, "I and the Father are one" (John 10:30, NIV). Some texts, especially in John's gospel, point this reality out clearly for our purposes of prayer (we will look more closely at this in Week 8, Day 3):

> Most assuredly, I say to you, the Son can do nothing of Himself,
> but what He sees the Father do; for whatever He does, the Son also
> does in like manner. For the Father loves the Son and shows Him
> all things that He Himself does . . .
>
> I can of Myself do nothing. As I hear, I judge; and My judgment
> is righteous, because I do not seek My own will, but the will of the
> Father who sent Me. (John 5:19-20, 30, NKJV)

Once again, this indicates that the will is based both on knowing the clear teaching of Scripture, and more importantly, on cultivating a relationship with God that is intimate and ongoing.

Knowing the Bible, important as it is, is not enough.

Atheists know the Bible. Some know it well and learn it to mock it.

In fact, knowing the Bible and believing it to be true isn't enough either. James says this very well indeed: "Do you believe that there is only one God? Good! The demons also believe—and tremble with fear" (James 2:19, GNT).

Rather we need to know it, believe it to be true, *and* cultivate a growing positive relationship with the God who inspired it so that we might discern what God is saying through it! Then we need to pray the things God wants done into existence.

Armin Gesswein, a man who served regularly as one of the first prayer-anchors for Billy Graham, used to say it this way: "We don't pray about things—we bring things about by prayer."

Perhaps there is no better illustration of this principle than Elijah the prophet—one who had a nature just like ours. In Week 1, Day 4 we learned an important prayer principle: God initiates, and we respond. Elijah's life was based on that principle. He had been told by God to show himself to wicked King Ahab so that God could send rain on the earth (1 Kings 18:1).

It sounded so very simple.

Show up, speak to the king and it will rain.

In fact, it was far more complex than that. Elijah had to "pray into existence" what God was telling him was to come to pass.

After rebuking (and in fact embarrassing) the false faith of the king and the false prophets through proclaiming a three-year drought and calling down fire from the sky, Elijah declared to the king that the rain was about to fall. He did that based on the fact that God had told him to say this. But it is the *method* used by Elijah that helps us today.

> Then Elijah said to King Ahab, "Now, go and eat. I hear the roar of rain approaching." While Ahab went to eat, Elijah climbed to the top of Mount Carmel, where he bowed down to the ground, with his head between his knees. He said to his servant, "Go and look toward the sea."
>
> The servant went and returned, saying, "I didn't see a thing." Seven times Elijah told him to go and look. The seventh time he returned and said, "I saw a little cloud no bigger than a man's hand, coming up from the sea."

Elijah ordered his servant, "Go to King Ahab and tell him to get in his chariot and go back home before the rain stops him." In a little while the sky was covered with dark clouds, the wind began to blow, and a heavy rain began to fall. (1 Kings 18:41-45, GNT)

Elijah had a life based on prayer and obedience. From his knowledge of the Law of Moses, he knew it was the will of God that Israel turn from worshiping other gods. When they did, God's blessing of rain could be restored.

Notice what occurred. Elijah had some kind of an auditory experience in the Spirit realm. He "heard" the rain coming. In fact, so strong was his conviction that he declared the sound of the rain and the approach of the storm to the king, long in advance of it happening. Remember, the land was parched from three years of drought.

Then, instead of simply waiting for the rain to fall based on the Word of the Lord to him, *Elijah prayed for the very thing he knew God wanted to send.*

The evidence was nonexistent for the first six attempts at praying in the rain. But he knew three things:

1)   God had spoken.
2)   He had to speak of his faith conviction aloud.
3)   He had to pray for the thing God wanted done to be done!

There were six attempts without any evidence of success. On the seventh attempt to pray in the rain, Elijah's servant indicated that there was meager evidence of rain—a cloud the size of a hand, not enough for two drops—and what is that to a land parched by a three-year drought?

Seeing the tiny evidence, he proclaimed that God's rain would happen. And it did. Here is the order of events:

Elijah:
• Perceived/heard in his spirit what God wanted done.
• Spoke what God wanted done.
• Prayed for what God wanted done.
• Kept praying repeatedly until he
• Saw the barest of beginnings of evidence of what God wanted done.

- Declared that it was done.

Then God sent the answer.

God initiated.

Elijah responded—by *praying.*

God brought the first evidence to pass through the prayers of the intercessor. Then Elijah spoke that it was done. Then God brought the rain.

To quote Gesswein again: "Prayer is not everything, but everything is by prayer."[14]

Elijah knew what God wanted done before he prayed for it to be so.

So did Jesus.

So also must we.

Read the stories of George Mueller of Bristol, and you will find the same story occurring over and over again. Mueller took in and raised thousands of orphans, even though he didn't have the means to feed them. He determined simply to pray and watch God supply without telling anyone of his needs. There are verified accounts of Mueller setting the breakfast table though there was not a crust of bread in the house. Nevertheless, he had prayed, he had the assurance in his spirit that God had heard his prayer. So he would emerge from his prayer time and would say, "Let's thank the Lord for His provision." At the close of the prayer, someone would bring in food and the children would receive everything needful for the day.

Mueller built buildings, fed thousands, and blessed many other faith endeavors based on the principle that God would supply in direct answer to prayer. He would bring about by prayer what God wanted done. He would perceive what needed to be done, pray until the assurance was granted, and then would confess that it was done until the food landed on the table.

We have already examined John 17 and the nature of that material for our participation in the Godhead. The point there is that eternal life is to know God and to know Jesus in the same way as Jesus and God know each other (John 17:3). It is to participate in that same kind of knowing and abiding that Jesus had with God His Father and the will of God (John 17:11, 20-23).

Search the Scriptures and you will search in vain for any prayer in which Jesus *didn't* know what His Father wanted done. There were a few times when He was surprised (e.g., the faith of the Roman centurion compared to the faithlessness of His own people). However, even in those instances, He would wait to understand what God wanted done, and then He would pray in perfect, sinless harmony with God's purposes. Through that praying, the will would be done on earth, just as in heaven. His role, as the Second Adam (of both earth and heaven, dust and Spirit), was to bridge the two realms, invoking heaven's presence and power through the mediation of His earthly nature.

- Heaven and earth *intersected* in the man Jesus and opened earth to heaven's influence.
- Through being joined to Christ Himself (by virtue of His atoning death and His Spirit residing within) heaven and earth *intersect in us too*.

Our praying also opens earth to heaven's influence as well. Through our intercessions, we act as a conduit through which the power of the Lord can flow through us to reshape the fallen creation back into something that suits God's purposes. That is the thrust of Romans 8:18-30, as we learned in Week 1, Day 4. We are to discern what God would have us pray, rather than simply to pray, "God do this, if it be Your will."

Know God.

Know God's heart. Then:

Pray God's heart into the creation.

Creation is waiting for that reality to be so—for the people of the Spirit to retake the rightful oversight of the creation under God the True Spirit. "For the earnest expectation of the creation eagerly waits for the revealing of the sons of God" (Romans 8:19, NKJV).

This is the paradigm for prayer ministry—to know the will from the clear teaching of the Bible and by the experience of the Spirit, and then to pray it into existence. Ponder this thought and record your impressions of what this means for your prayer life now in the space below.

Pen to Paper

1) Reread the passages from John 5 above. Note that the Lord Jesus Christ Himself could do absolutely nothing on His own merits! We know He is

the sinless, perfect, holy Son of God, so this catches us by surprise. What does this text tell us about how Jesus accomplished His ministry tasks?

2) Now reread the account of Elijah praying for rain. What does this text tell us we need to do in praying effectively?

3) Those who have prayed for years can testify to this truth. Sometimes they know that God gives them a prayer assignment. They are to pray for _____ to be done, and they have no peace until it is done! Can you remember a time when God called you to a specific prayer for something to be done? What was the burden like? What was the desired outcome of the prayer? Did you see an answer? If you did, then you have experienced something of what happened to Elijah and what regularly happened to our Lord in His ministry. God initiated. You responded. Record the incident here.

PRAYER CHALLENGE

Praying Christians have known about this principle all their days of prayer. A burden to pray enters their heart. They know the person, and they are given some sense of how they are to pray. Then they pray until the intercession is accomplished.

Today ask God for Him "to initiate" in your praying. When you find yourself thinking of someone and offering a prayer, take this as God at work, reshaping your inner prayer life.

DAY 4

Knowing God's will and liking it are not the same!

There are times when to know the will does not mean to relish what it will cost us. We know this from Jesus' teaching: it is no easy thing to love our enemies—yet that is God's will! Jesus had a thorough knowledge of the will of God based on His relationship with the Father. Though Jesus always *embraced* God's will and did it, even our Lord didn't always *want to do* what God wanted in the realm of His physical and emotional existence.

Now we come to holy ground. This, of all texts, is the clearest case of the will of our Lord and the will of the Father coming into some kind of agonizing tension (and here it is clear that embracing God's will is not automatic or easy all the time).

> Then Jesus went with his disciples to a place called Gethsemane, and he said to them, "Sit here while I go over there and pray." He took Peter and the two sons of Zebedee along with him, and he began to be sorrowful and troubled. Then he said to them, "My soul is overwhelmed with sorrow to the point of death. Stay here and keep watch with me."
>
> Going a little farther, he fell with his face to the ground and prayed, "My Father, if it is possible, may this cup be taken from me. Yet not as I will, but as you will."
>
> Then he returned to his disciples and found them sleeping. "Could you men not keep watch with me for one hour?" he asked Peter. "Watch and pray so that you will not fall into temptation. The spirit is willing, but the body is weak."
>
> He went away a second time and prayed, "My Father, if it is not possible for this cup to be taken away unless I drink it, may your will be done."

When he came back, he again found them sleeping, because their eyes were heavy. So he left them and went away once more and prayed the third time, saying the same thing.

Then he returned to the disciples and said to them, "Are you still sleeping and resting? Look, the hour is near, and the Son of Man is betrayed into the hands of sinners. Rise, let us go! Here comes my betrayer!" (Matthew 26:36-45, NIV)

This is the only place in the New Testament where the will of God was clearly revealed to our Lord, and *Jesus clearly didn't want to do what it implied.* It was very rare for a Jewish believer to pray with His face to the ground. Here Christ did just that. There was tremendous tension in His soul. He had loved the will of God and lived the will of God. Yet here, the outcome was so disturbing that He asked for the will to be altered. Why? Many indicate that this was the fear of death that is part of what it means to be human. But there was more.

Up to this point it was clear that Satan had wanted Him dead.

Here it became plain to Christ that God wanted Him dead too!

For a passing moment, God's will and Satan's will looked (and in fact were) the same. So He entered a time of searching, yearning prayer. He knew that God was not a demon. He knew that the outcomes of His Father's dealing would be very different from that of the lord of darkness. Satan just wanted Him dead. God wanted Him to pass through death that He might destroy the false kingship of the devil, destroy death's hold from the inside and rise again.

Satan's *ultimate* purpose was Jesus' death.

God's *ultimate* purpose was the restoring of all things lost.

In harmony with the ancient promises found in Ezekiel 37, there would be death and then life again from death, a true king from the line of David, and God filling up His people with the Spirit of the living God. There would be deliverance, freedom, healing, and a return of the rightful kingship of creation to God Himself (1 Corinthians 15:20-28). This was the beginning of life from the dead.

But the *means* to accomplish their purposes—Satan's short-sighted one inspired by hatred, anger, and fear, and God's long-term plan inspired by redeeming love—were both identical. The will of God for the sinless Lamb of God was a horrible, agonizing death—and this was enough to make God the

Son lie down prostrate on the ground in death-anguish and grief.

Here it is plain that Jesus had His own human will. He did not automatically choose to do what the Father asked of Him. Rather, God asked Him to offer His life. Jesus asked if there were any other way.

Jesus sensed God say a wordless "no."

Then Jesus asked again!

Jesus heard the same "no" to His request for release three times before He stopped asking the question.

It is no sin to ask God for a way out, to get a "no," and to ask again. It is simply a part of the process of getting down to the divine decision, and embracing the painful part of the call of God on our lives.

Jesus had to choose, to "learn obedience" (see Hebrews 5:8) by choosing to align His human inclinations with the divine decision—not an easy thing to do. The will of the Father had to be chosen and embraced by the will of the Son.

This is the model for believers who are born of the Spirit. We must, through our relationship with the Father, "sense" or "discern" the will. Then, whether it is joyful (marry the one you love), or whether it involves sacrifice at great cost (go to another culture and serve the poor), we must choose it. Sometimes it will seem that the enemy of our souls is winning a horrible battle, but the point of this passage is that our Father can be trusted and that, however horrible this path looks, God's ultimate purpose is for our deliverance and for the blessing of the many.

There are three possible answers to any prayer we pray. God can say:

1) "Wait. There are things that you cannot know. Be still and trust Me."
2) "Of course. I have heard your prayer and the answer is already on the way." Or
3) "No. My purposes are larger than what you are currently seeing."

To pray, "Your will be done on earth as it is in heaven" is to accept all three possible answers in our lives of faith.

There is a word of relationship that comes through this account. Jesus *knew* the will. He asked for another way. When we know the will, it is not wrong to ask for a different path or outcome. History is filled with examples of the people of God crying out for hope in the midst of judgment. Jeremiah was told to proclaim a word of repentance in the hope that his people would hear God's voice so that the Lord would not be forced to destroy them (Jeremiah 18:5-12). Hezekiah was told he would die, and he cried out to God to spare him and he was granted fifteen more years of life (Isaiah 38:1-6). There is a *provisional* will and there is an *ultimate* will. The provisional will can be altered and the means is prayer. The ultimate will can never be changed, regardless of all the prayer in creation. God would have us commit to the ultimate will and to pray through the provisional will. We will look at these two concepts more closely tomorrow.

PEN TO PAPER

1) Go back and reread the account of Gethsemane. Jesus was looking for a provisional will and learned that He was facing God's ultimate will. Do you have any "Gethsemane" decisions—in which you know exactly what God wants done, but you would search for another way? Some things can be changed by prayer. Some must remain exactly as they are. Place these before the Father and ask as you feel led.

2) If you knew that your King was right before you, and that you could ask Him anything to make His kingdom move ahead, what would that request be?

3) What would it take for God to be King of your home, your city, your country, the world God loves? Commit that to writing below:

Home: _____

City: _____

Country: _____

World: _____

Now ask for that, knowing that you are asking for God's kingdom to come and His will to be done. Don't be afraid to ask boldly. God is much bigger than your largest thought!

PRAYER CHALLENGE

Rather than praying "If it be Your will" when you are not sure how to intercede, pray very specifically about anyone and anything that crosses your path. Be clear about what kind of blessing you sense would be appropriate for the lady at the checkout line, for the gas station attendant, for the worker in the next booth from yours, for the retiree in the library browsing books, the mother and babe in the playground, or the coal miner underground. Pray specifically, pray by name, and ask in faith. Decide to pray "this is Your will—bring it to pass" any time you sense a call to pray.

DAY 5

God's *ultimate* will cannot be changed. The *provisional* will
can be altered by prayer based on God's character.

W e cannot escape the plain truth that Jesus prayed for the will of
God to be changed, and that He did so without sinning. Neither
can we escape the fact that God said "no" three times, and that
our Lord submitted to the painful realities of the will of God in His redemptive
life. His march toward the cross from Gethsemane was the remainder of this
prayer. Through mocking, beating, the lash, the cross bearing, and slow suffo-
cation He lifted His torn back on splintered wood. The death He died, shorn of
dignity, was the ultimate expression of praying "Your will be done."

Once again we are face-to-face with the reality that the Lord's Prayer is no
prayer for the faint of heart. To utter "Your will be done" may mean praying
away your life!

But the fact that Jesus dared to pray for God to find another way at all
raises a startling question: Are there elastic boundaries around the will of
God? Can the will of God be changed?

Jesus' prayer was based on a long tradition of relationship-based praying. Christ was involved in dynamic engagement with His Father all the way
through this prayer process. He didn't evade the will, nor did He hide from
God. Rather, He wrestled in anguished prayer and sweat blood; through that
process He embraced the will that He abhorred because He knew that it was
the ultimate will of God.

This is the stuff of intercession. Here we see Jesus' embrace of "the will"
through deep prayer to discern the mind of God. This is what the apostle
meant by the Spirit praying "with groanings too deep for words" (Romans
8:26, NASB). Jesus did this in His ministry. In fact, others in biblical history
had prayed for God to change His mind as well.

Brother Andrew, known as "God's Smuggler," the Dutch believer who
smuggled Bibles behind the Iron Curtain to build up the suffering church,

authored a book with a startling title: *And God Changed His Mind.*[15] The book is entirely about praying to that end.

The title comes from the intercession of Moses against the anger of the Lord (Exodus 32:14). It seems strange to imagine that God would *want* to do one thing and that He would call us *to pray against* the thing that He is about to do—yet that is the case when it comes to this example.

Moses had been called to Mt. Sinai to receive the Ten Commandments in the fiery cloud of God's Presence. Exodus tells us that he was in the manifest presence of God for forty days and nights (Exodus 24:18). While there, the people began to worship a golden calf—violating the first and second commands of God's holy covenant. They did this immediately after God had accomplished incredible acts of power to take them out of slavery to freedom.

God's anger burned—and God was on the verge of destroying the people who so quickly forgot about His goodness and power. God would complete His *ultimate* purpose—that Israel's descendants would inherit the Promised Land. But He was so grieved by the rejection of the Israelites, that He made another *provisional* plan to carry it out—use Moses' family to start again.

It is important for us to notice this prayer principle: the only thing that stood between God's destruction of the people was Moses himself—a person of their own line. This same Moses *prayed against* the burning wrath of God, reminding the Lord of His promises to bring the children of Israel out of Egypt:

> Then the LORD spoke to Moses, "Go down at once, for your people, whom you brought up from the land of Egypt, have corrupted themselves. They have quickly turned aside from the way which I commanded them. . . . Now then *let Me alone*, that My anger may burn against them and that I may destroy them; and I will make of you a great nation."
>
> Then Moses entreated the LORD his God, and said . . . "Turn from Your burning anger and *change Your mind* about doing harm to Your people. Remember Abraham, Isaac, and Israel, Your servants to whom You swore by Yourself, and said to them, 'I will multiply your descendants as the stars of the heavens, and all this land of which I have spoken I will give to your descendants, and they shall inherit it forever.'"

So *the LORD changed His mind* about the harm which He said He would do to His people. (Exodus 32:7-8, 10,-14, NASB, emphasis added)

Moses' praying in this matter was complex. God told Moses to leave Him alone—to get out of the way. Moses refused! He stayed right in the middle, placing himself between God and the people and as an intercessor. He was positioned between God's anger and God's people. And so began the intercession.

This was not a single request that he prayed once, but a series of prayers that went deeper with each request. Later the prayer of Moses against God's anger became all the more bold—he prayed to be damned that Israel might be saved. "Alas, this people has committed a great sin, and they have made a god of gold for themselves. But now, if You will, forgive their sin—and if not, please blot me out from Your book which You have written!" (Exodus 32:31-32, NASB).

God's reply to Moses was "no." He would punish whom He would punish.

But then it appeared that there would be a divorce. God would keep His word of sending them to the Promised Land—but His Presence would not go with them.

They would get the goods, but they would not get their God! The holy marriage between God and His chosen people would be destroyed forever. The Word would be upheld. The Spirit would be withdrawn. Seaparating Word and Spirit is disastrous!

Moses knew that to lose the presence of God would make Israel like every other nation, so he prayed for God to change His mind again! He prayed like this: "Do not divorce Your Presence from Your people. Above all else, give us Yourself."

"If Your Presence does not go with us, do not lead us up from here. For how then can it be known that I have found favor in Your sight, I and Your people? Is it not by Your going with us, so that we, I and Your people, may be distinguished from all the other people who are upon the face of the earth?"

The LORD said to Moses, "I will also do this thing of which you have spoken." (Exodus 33:15-17, NASB)

The principle behind this praying is that God has an ultimate purpose—that there be a people set apart for His glory, marked off by His presence forever. It began when God chose Abraham, Isaac, and Jacob in the history of Israel; it is fulfilled in those who embrace Jesus (in whom all the promises to Israel are collapsed and find their fulfillment) as their personal Lord.

Some will embrace this and the ultimate will of God will be done.

Others who should accept this will not, and God will either work to redeem those who have rejected Him through the praying of His people, or He will choose others to get the job done.

Here we have an ultimate will and a provisional will.

God told Moses that the promise would be fulfilled—a multitude born of Abraham's line would receive the land and be in the presence of God. Moses himself could have that prerogative and the "letter of the law" would be done—he was from Abraham's line, after all! Moses on the other hand, simply returned to the same promise and pleaded that God keep His Word to *all* those descended from that line.

God listened to His own Word carried to Him by one set apart to pray. Moses stood between the anger and the mercy of God, inspired by the word of God's promise.

Standing on the promises given brings joy to the heart of God.

It is always permissible to pray that God complete His purposes. It is also permissible to ask God not to destroy those who fail in their walk with God. There were times in biblical history in which "God changed His mind."

When Jonah preached to Nineveh that they were about to be destroyed because of their great sins, they repented and God "changed His mind." He didn't destroy them (see the book of Jonah). The reality was that God didn't want to destroy them in the first place. He wanted them to live lives acceptable to Him—and the coming judgment led to their changing their ways—and God had no choice *except* to change His mind based on His very own nature—they became what pleased God in the first place.

The *ultimate will* was done—lives that pleased Him.

The *provisional will* (take them out because they were so awful) was averted by repentance—they changed the way they lived.

Scripture is filled with other examples of the ultimate will being done, and the provisional means that God used changing because of sin or repentance.

God raised up Saul to be the first king of Israel—and after he consistently refused to listen to the Lord, he was removed. It began with the withdrawal of God's presence from his life. Then David, the son of Jesse took his place! The ultimate will—a godly king—took place. The provisional will, David replacing Saul due to sin, happened.

Moses was supposed to take the first wilderness generation into the Promised Land. Moses, at one point (when absolutely fed up with rage at the utter unbelief of God's people) treated God's command with contempt. He was to *speak* to a rock to make water flow out of it by a word spoken. Instead of speaking to the rock, he pounded it twice, indicating that he and Aaron were producing the water; in the process Moses made it appear that his blow brought the water instead of God (see Numbers 20:2-13). His calling to take the people in then was given to Joshua. The *ultimate* will—that Israel's descendants enter the Promised Land was fulfilled. The *provisional* will—that Moses be the one to take the first generation in—was laid aside based on the principle of God's holiness.

We can pray for the will to be changed based on God's character—and He will enable us to pray that way. The ultimate will is that we be a people set apart for God's glory—people who are marked off by repentance, kindness, gentle love, with God's presence shining through everything we do as we take back our fallen world from all the things that are called "evil." The provisional will depends entirely on our response to God's calling. Should we fail to follow the Lord when He calls, God will raise up another.

Based on this biblical history, and the awareness that His God was so large that another way could be possible, Jesus prayed: "My Father, if it is possible, may this cup be taken from me. Yet not as I will, but as you will" (Matthew 26:39, NIV). Then Jesus submitted to what He knew was the highest best in His life.

PEN TO PAPER

1) Have you ever asked God to "change His mind"? If so, describe the experience here.

2) Reread the account of Moses praying for Israel. What "speaks" to you from that story? Is it possible to pray that way now?

3) Mothers and fathers plead for lost sons and daughters like this. Their children sin terribly, wounding others and themselves, but the heart of the parent is moved with compassion, pleading with God that his or her child must not be lost. Through praying this way, many sons and daughters are brought back to God. Yet some will not turn from their destructive path. So, when the day is done, even as Moses and our Lord Jesus submitted to what God told them to be and to do, we must submit to God's purposes. They embraced the ultimate will. This must be our final prayer when the prayer process reaches an end. The only reason God "changes His mind" is because God's people choose what pleases Him in the first place. What impossible circumstances bring you to plead for God to change His mind? Place them before the Lord here, and pray "Your will be done on earth as it is in heaven."

Prayer Challenge

Perhaps you know someone who has turned away from God's best, and it disturbs you. Pray that God move in his life again. Bring this to God continually unless God leads otherwise. The best result is that "God change His mind" because the lost one becomes found again.

DAY 6

Pray for the wandering ones to return, and make sure to welcome them!

It had never happened before.

In fact, it never happened again.

I served that congregation for five years and this kind of thing only happened once.

We had a guest preacher that day—a famous author whose life and writings had inspired hundreds of thousands, if not millions. It was astonishing to us that he came to our little church in Lac La Biche, Alberta, a congregation of only about eighty to ninety souls at the time.

His first message to get us started was a simple declaration of God's desire for the church to be so utterly loving and accepting that the most undeserving, sin-sated, callous soul would not be able to resist the good news of Christ. He warned us against judging anyone, even those that everyone else just "wrote off." Using Luke 15, three parables of the lost and found (the lost sheep, the lost coin, and the lost sons), he told us that Jesus told the three parables with a single message in mind—God is in the business of seeking and saving the utterly lost (not just the "almost nice" who need a bit of moral improvement) and finding them a welcoming home in our families of faith. So don't judge them when they return. Instead, throw a party!

In the middle of the message, he said something that startled the church. "I don't care if the town drunk shows up and sits at the back of the church by the exit so you can't avoid tripping over him. When he arrives, you need to love him and care for him, and help him get started with God again. Even if it seems a hopeless case—make sure that you love him to the uttermost—or else the church is just a pack of 'elder brothers' with their noses stuck up in the air."

When the sermon was done I closed out the service and walked to the back door to greet the church.

There he was.

Sitting at the back of the church in a chair right by the exit was an utterly intoxicated man. He was barely able to form a sentence due to how drunk he was. He was impossible not to notice: everyone who wanted to leave the worship service had to walk around and by the fellow.

But we had heard the message.

Our eyes got very large. It took us a few minutes to figure it out, but in the end, we knew what we had to do: An elder took him home, gave him a place to sleep, sobered him up with coffee and a meal. Afterwards the elder told him of the love of God.

I met the man on the street a couple of days later. He was embarrassed that he had gone to church drunk. In fact he had never been to church before at all! He sure hadn't planned on showing up like that. We spoke warmly to each other and I asked him to come back.

He didn't. But we did at least attempt to pass the test.

Perhaps you know someone who is what might be called a "hopeless case." Long ago they did the right things, but they are caught up in a lifestyle that is so contrary to the right that most think they can never return. Listen to this parable about the kingdom of God and doing God's will. Bear in mind that Jesus was speaking to people who were meticulous about doing good things in exactly the proscribed way, whose rules and regulations were so strict that those who had wandered away couldn't possibly return. He was speaking to them of their need to celebrate the success that John the Baptizer had had, calling people back to walking with God. This text is a calling for our praying. A warning shot across the bow for us all:

> "But what do you think? A man had two sons, and he came to the first and said, 'Son, go work today in the vineyard.'
>
> And he answered 'I will not'; but afterward he regretted it and went.
>
> The man came to the second and said the same thing; and he answered, 'I will, sir'; but he did not go. Which of the two did the will of his father?" They said, "The first." Jesus said to them, "Truly I say to you that the tax collectors and prostitutes will get into the kingdom of God before you.

"For John came to you in the way of righteousness and you did not believe him; but the tax collectors and prostitutes did believe him; and you, seeing this, did not even feel remorse afterward so as to believe him." (Matthew 21:28-32, NASB)

Here we have a parable of the kingdom of God. It includes a father and speaks of the accomplishment of the father's will. It includes two "half-ish" responses to the call of the Father. Neither model was exemplary, though in the first case, the work that had been assigned did in fact get done. In the second case, saying that something would be done, and then not doing it, was worse than saying nothing at all. In the case of the second, the Father's will was abandoned completely, despite the loud affirmations that it would be accomplished.

So which are you, the first or the second? How so? Take a moment and record your thoughts on this matter.

It is clear that the Lord was rebuking an attitude of rejection and judgment. In fact, Jesus was cultivating an attitude of complete acceptance of people from any and all walks of life, an attitude that would call people back to loving God and living their lives that way regardless of how awful their sin had been.

The lowest on the social rung of his day were contrasted with the highest. In that culture, praise was heaped on the meticulous law keeper with a rule for every occasion. Scorn was poured down like burning coals on the heads of those tax collectors who would collaborate with a conquering power that took away the right of self-determination and imperiled the temple worship. The collectors could charge whatever they wanted and keep the extra for themselves. Very often, the helpless suffered.

Lower than this group were the harlots. Prostitutes would sell sex to any and all with cash for services rendered, including godless pagan conquerors and worse, to the tax collectors who worked with them, and got their money through robbing the weak!

We would have as much respect for a child molester.

Yet God would have us pray for the kingdom to come and the will to be done on earth as in heaven—and this means that they can be one of us! All that it takes is the decision to start again with Jesus Christ as their Savior. We are to be pleading with God to be given opportunity to meet and love people like that, to "be" with them and live our lives before them so winsomely that they want to follow the God we serve. We are to be seeking for their lives to be saved. We are to be asking that God use us to call people like that to be reconciled to God and to learn of him from us! Then God would have us welcome them into our midst as soon as it is clear that they truly mean business about living for the Lord. If fact we need to be welcoming them into our midst before they choose to walk with God at all, just to get to know us.

Will we accept them?

If yes, then we are on "kingdom-ground."

If no, then we are just playing church.

How then will you pray?

Pen to Paper

1) What is the highest level in the society in which you live? The professor? The politician? The doctor? The entrepreneur? The CEO? Name the best, the highest role that people try to attain as the pinnacle of society.

2) Now name the worst that society scorns with contempt and ridicule. Who lives at the lowest rung. Name the very worst.

3) Think for a passing moment. Which group does your congregation welcome? In fact which group would you welcome into your home? Do you know of a church that seeks God for and welcomes both groups?

4) Name the ones that you know are "hopeless." Pray for the kingdom to come and the will to be done in their lives. Ask God for opportunity to be among them to win them to God's grace.

5) Which "brother" are you? Pray that God lead you to become like the first instead of the second.

PRAYER CHALLENGE

Ask the Lord for this part of His will to be done today. Ask to notice anyone that is "written off," the hopeless ones that no one seems to care about. Pray for them. In fact, make a plan to remember them before the Lord as often as they come to mind. Each time you think of someone that seems an impossible case, ask the God of the impossible to "bring them home" to God.

DAY 7

The kingdom and the will "on earth as in heaven" is a people filled with God's empowering presence.

There is a theme that pervades the entire teaching of the Bible from cover to cover. God has always sought to establish a people who would bear the glory of His name. So He set apart our first parents to do this very thing. When they failed, He called Abraham and His descendants, passing them through prosperity and despair. When their success in Egypt became their slavery, God promised them a new hope by returning them to the land of Canaan. He would give them (1) a law to shape a just, God-honoring society and (2) a land to live in that would be their very own.

And when it came time for them to receive both of these blessings, God brought them out of bondage and despair. He led them by miracle, and brought them to the place in which His Law would be revealed to them (and to us) forever. Just before that Law was given, God told them His purpose in calling them to Himself.

They would be a "kingdom people," a nation set apart to show how good God is!

> You yourselves have seen what I did to the Egyptians, and how I bore you on eagles' wings, and brought you to Myself. Now then, if you will indeed obey My voice and keep My covenant, then you shall be My own possession among all the peoples, for all the earth is Mine; and *you shall be to Me a kingdom of priests and a holy nation.* (Exodus 19:4-6, NASB, emphasis added)

When the Covenant with Moses did not produce this kind of a God-honoring kingdom, a promise was made that there would be a new and better covenant . . .

"Behold, days are coming," declares the LORD, "when I will make a new covenant with house of Israel and with the house of Judah. . . . I will put My law within them and on their heart I will write it; and *I will be their God, and they shall be My people.* (Jeremiah 31:31, 33, NASB, emphasis added)

The prophet Ezekiel spoke of this hope and took it a step further. Not only would the law be written within by His Spirit's presence, but when the people of God were truly in love with God Himself, the Lord would restore the Promised Land:

Moreover, I will give you a new heart and put a new spirit within you; and I will remove the heart of stone from your flesh and give you a heart of flesh. I will put My Spirit within you and cause you to walk in My statutes, and you will be careful to observe My ordinances. You will live in the land that I gave to your forefathers, *so you will be My people, and I will be your God.* (Ezekiel 36:26-28, NASB, emphasis added)

The promises made to Israel were completed in Jesus Christ.

He received the Spirit of God, in order to grant us the gift of the Spirit. God entered the human race in Jesus, so that God could enter the human race in us through His Spirit dwelling within us. That is why He is the "baptizer in the Holy Spirit."

But it was never intended that this be an individual gift alone. God does not merely give any one person His Spirit. Rather God's desire is that we receive His Spirit as individuals with a specific end in mind: God's desire is to finish the task—to make us "a kingdom of priests and a holy nation." When we receive the Spirit, we become forged together in utter unity with all those who have also received the same gift. We receive God's very being in us so that we become a "people of God" together.

When we pray "Your Kingdom come, Your will be done on earth as it is in heaven," we are praying that God's desire from the beginning of time be completely fulfilled. His desire was that a people (created by the sacrifice of Christ and joined by their common experience of the Spirit of God) who are utterly different than anything the world has ever seen before, be set apart just for Him.

In fact, the last two chapters of the last book of the Bible say this very thing. When God brings about the new heavens and new earth, it will be said beyond all of this, that there is *a new people*, described as both a bride to Christ and a city, the New Jerusalem. And God and the city will be so very one, that it will be well nigh impossible to tell them apart. God will be seen by looking through the transparent walls of the city. The city will shine with the glory of God. There will be no need for the sun, because the glory of God will be its light.

This will be the people of God, forever "at home" in who God is, and God Himself, forever "at home" in the people of God, who will shine with His glory forever: "And I heard a loud voice from the throne saying, 'Behold, the tabernacle of God is among men, and He will dwell among them, and *they shall be His people*, and God Himself will be among them.'" (Revelation 21:3, NASB, emphasis added).

This is "big praying." Ponder this thought for a few minutes. Put the book down and reflect on this. Then record what this means to you:

And yet while we are on earth, the prayer for the kingdom to come includes us becoming a "kingdom of priests."

What do priests do?

Priests stand between God and the people. When facing God, they represent the people's needs to the God who can answer. In return, when they turn to face the people they speak of the glory of God and His calling on their lives to the people. The only thing that makes it possible for priests to do either is that they stand in the middle because a sacrifice has been offered on their behalf so that there is no sin barrier between them and God.

Priests, in that intermediary place, based on the sacrifice, make it possible for each to connect to the other. When Moses refused to get out of the middle between God's anger and the people's sin, and prayed against that anger, he was acting as a priest. His brother, Aaron the priest, was set apart to offer sacrifices and to pray against God's anger, preventing God from destroying God's people because of their sins.

Priests pray to God for the blessings of God to be given.

Priests also speak to people to call them to God, and to invite them to the sacrifice, so that they might be reconciled to God.

Jesus is our High Priest. When we receive His Spirit through accepting His sacrifice, we receive His ministry—we join him in praying that all the world be reconciled to God.

God wants a kingdom of people who do just that! His will is that the whole world be brought to him, by a whole kingdom of people who shine with His grace in every corner of the world.

PEN TO PAPER

1) Think for a moment about what priests do. Write down a few thoughts about their role.

2) What would a "kingdom of priests" look like? How many priests would that entail?

3) Based on this, what then does it mean to pray "Your kingdom come, your will be done on earth as it is in heaven"?

4) We have been living with the second line of the Lord's Prayer now for two weeks. It is clear that the kingdom of God is enormous. So is the will of God. Perhaps it is time to rethink what it means to pray that line. Write a fresh paraphrase of that prayer below.

PRAYER CHALLENGE

You have now successfully journeyed through two lines of the Lord's Prayer. Look for opportunities to pray for the kingdom to come and for the will to be done. As you read the paper or listen to the news on the radio, pray for God's rule to be reestablished. As you watch the grocery store attendant care for customers, pray for her. As you work through a ticklish situation at work, pray for God's intervention. Finally, return by giving thanks to God that He is involved in all your labors.

ASK FOR PROVISION

"Give Us This Day Our Daily Bread."

DAY 1

God provides for kingdom purposes (and not merely for our own purposes).

Almost every resource on the Lord's Prayer sees the petition "Give us this day our daily bread" as a break point in the prayer. According to the common view, going back as far as the early church fathers Tertullian, Cyprian, and Augustine, it is here that we shift from purely divine initiatives to human ones. Rather than the advance of God's kingdom, common interpretation holds that this now concerns *us*: We need "bread," "forgiveness," and "safety."

There is much truth in this approach: it is more than true that the human dimension of existence is dealt with in this part of the prayer. However, it is also more than clear that a neat division of the prayer into two parts is not quite so neat. In the first two lines we were dealing with a prayer for heaven's influence to invade earth, to retake the ground lost by our first parents. We have seen that the concept of the name and hallowing the name involves a "power-sphere" in which God's rule and reputation are at war with any other rule or reputation. We have also seen that to know and do the will of God is first and foremost a *relationship* between God and us—something utterly and warmly human—something that our first parents had as the foundation of all that God intended to be *fundamentally* human.

The first half, then, includes not only the divine, but also the human. The second includes not only the human, but also the divine.

In particular, the two-spirit war motif continues throughout the remainder of the prayer. The second half includes a petition to be kept from severe trial as we face the evil one. The prayer ends with a declaration that God's kingdom, power, and glory be ascribed to God forever. The battle for earth includes the battle for personal and corporate holiness (as opposed to personal and corporate sin). It means forgiveness and dealing with temptation and the tempter. The tempter's power is real and must be prayed against in order for victory to become ours, and for the kingly rule of God to result in personal and/or corporate righteousness and justice.

What becomes clear here is that the Lord's Prayer is a unity with a single theme—the retaking of all that was lost, to the glory of the Father. This next section is really a continuation of the same theme—the war between the powers of good and evil. The first section has to do with declaring war on the powers of darkness and entering their territory. This next line has to do entirely with maintaining the supply lines to ensure that the battle for the hearts and souls of our race can continue without interruption. God does not merely supply "daily bread" to any and all who ask (though in His grace He usually does!). Rather He supplies daily bread for those who are involved in the grand scheme of hallowing His name, in praying the kingdom rule into existence, and accomplishing the divine will on earth as it is in heaven.

The first two lines constitute the commitment to the battle. This third line is a request for K rations to maintain the troops on the front lines.

In the ministry of Jesus, the first reference to "bread" was in fact a two-spirit scene, a text we examined on Day 3 of Week 3. In Matthew 3:16-4:11, the Holy Spirit had been given Him to carry out His ministry, after His baptism. The Holy Spirit "drove" Him to meet the unclean spirit in the battle that we have come to call "the temptation." Let's revisit some of that material here.

> Then Jesus was led up by the Spirit into the wilderness to be tempted by the devil. After he had fasted forty days and nights he then became hungry. And the tempter came and said to Him, "If you are the Son of God, command these stones to become bread." But He answered and said, "It is written, 'Man shall not live by bread alone, but on every word that proceeds out of the mouth of God.'" (Matthew 4:1-4, NASB)

Note that Jesus had abstained from all food for an extended period *specifically in order to have His calling tested.* The test was divine in origin—God sent Him *by the Spirit* to have His calling sounded out. The first test involved His allegiance to God around the issue of "bread"—necessary food for the body. This should not surprise us. The very first temptation in the

Bible involved allegiance to God around food for the body. Our first parents chose to obey the serpent around the issues of provision instead of God (see Genesis 3:1-6). In this narrative, Jesus was called to a fast by God. He chose to forgo provision to obey God *over against* the devil.

Bread, in this material, is a true need (and not ordinarily forbidden).

Bread was, at the same time, the lure to a hungry man to disobey the lesson just learned from the Holy Spirit. Instead of accepting that He really was the Son of God demonstrated by the voice of God, the enemy was asking Him to prove it at Satan's command.

Jesus understood.

Power could be used to meet legitimate need, but it could never be used to do that alone. Power from God should always be put to God's use at God's command, and never because of a dare to prove a fact already established by God through a holy experience.

God must be the overlord of our bread. Need, even legitimate need (and what could be more legitimate than food for a hungry believer completing a fast?), must never be the center of our existence. God must always be at the center. He must be the Lord, even of our need. God must supercede our need, even when the need is profoundly legitimate.

We serve the kingdom. God's power is at the service of the kingdom. Needs must always come a distant second behind the kingdom goal. No appeal to the senses, to an innate sense of worth or loss, nor to a calling to the satisfaction of even a clean desire, can ever take first place. God supplies bread to reestablish His kingly rule, for kingdom purposes, not for the personal gratification or the achievement of any individual for whatever reason, however noble or legitimate. God must be God, even when the need screams to us that it *must* be satisfied (urging us to use God's power if necessary).

To this temptation, Jesus said a profound "no," quoting a passage from another time in Hebrew history when bread was a test of allegiance to God. In another wilderness, at another time, Moses reminded the people of the exodus that their receiving of God's bread was to humble them and test them to see if they would obey God.

> You shall remember all the way the LORD your God has led you in
> the wilderness these forty years, that He might humble you, testing

you, to know what was in your heart, whether you would keep His commandments or not. He humbled you and let you be hungry and fed you with manna which you did not know, nor did your fathers know, that He might make you understand that man does not live by bread alone, but man lives by everything that proceeds out of the mouth of the LORD. (Deuteronomy 8:2-3, NASB)

Hunger was God's humbling of His people. Hunger was the test in terrible adversity. If God remained their center during trial, God would provide. However, if the *need* became the center, then the need would be the god—and that was to replace the true God with a false one, a violation of the first commandment.

In the Lord's Prayer, we begin with God. We move to invite God's power and kingly rule to take first place in our lives and through us on earth. Then and only then, we bring our needs to Him, to ensure that we can get the work done that needs to be accomplished. Needs, even something as basic as bread, take second place to God's rule.

PEN TO PAPER

1) What needs take center stage in your praying? What are the things you find are basic to your very survival? In survival cultures (i.e., regions devastated by war), literal bread is the center of the praying. In first-world contexts, people have the luxury of being concerned about things like career or location of home. In both extremes, these issues are "daily bread." When you ask "Give us this day our daily bread," what comes to mind for your heartfelt concern?

2) The temptation is to make our needs the center of our praying rather than God's kingdom. You have just generated a list of "bread and butter" issues above. How would these issues cause God's kingdom to move

ahead? Are they focused on you (or even your family/friends), or are they focused on getting God's agenda done? Take each one in turn and ask the Lord if this is something you need to do His work, or if this is merely something you believe you want.

3) What are the kingdom issues about which you are concerned? Name the things you know need to happen in your home, your church fellowship, your school, your business, your friend network, etc., for the kingdom to come. Then name before God what is needed for the kingdom to come in each case. Ask then in confidence.

Kingdom issues at   Kingdom needs
a) Home _____   a) _____
b) Church _____   b) _____
c) Work _____   c) _____
d) School _____   d) _____
e) Friends _____   e) _____
f) _____   f) _____

PRAYER CHALLENGE

Ask yourself, "What does God's kingdom need for it to move ahead in my life?" Simply pray that your needs would be subservient to God's kingdom. Pray that you would avoid the sin of asking God's kingdom to *focus* on your needs (i.e., putting our "kingdom" ahead of God's) instead of placing your needs under the care of God's kingdom.

DAY 2

With God's rule as the center of our existence, God provides in a faith-building way.

Judaism and Christendom have their favorite texts. You can find them in promise boxes and collections of texts in theme books and reprinted on plaques to place above the doorway. One of those texts pursued me in a way that forever marked my devotional life. You likely know this one from your own promise box: "And my God will supply all your needs according to His riches in glory in Christ Jesus" (Philippians 4:19, NASB).

The following account indicates how I learned the truth of this text!

At university, I belonged to a small campus ministry for students. I also belonged to a Thursday evening Bible study. Though the two were not at all connected (except that I was involved in both), the lessons learned in one had an uncanny way of finding a regular overlap in the other! Perhaps the most extraordinary lesson learned this way had to do with "daily bread"—trusting God to supply, even while practicing generosity. I was learning to give the tithe (giving the first 10 percent of one's income to God's work), though there was great resistance to this one within me! I would show up at Bible study and ask, "Why does God need my money?" and invariably end with the familiar but utterly nonbiblical "God helps those who help themselves!"

Gradually, however, as we began to study about giving and receiving, it became plain that I must practice the tithe. And so, I began by putting the first 10 percent in an envelope and praying about where to put it to good use.

In the campus ministry, I had met a couple (let's call them Bill and Sue) who were praying about overseas ministry work. Every now and then we would bump into each other, and they would speak about their desire to go to Southeast Asia. They had student loans to repay, however, and wanted to be debt free before beginning their service.

The university year ended. I started to earn some money from a summer job. Soon the tithe fund was up to $120. I sensed that it was time to give it away. I knelt beside my bed to ask God where it should go.

The time was 4:00 p.m. on a Friday afternoon.

As soon as I started to ask, Bill and Sue came to mind and wouldn't leave my thoughts. So, with that settled, all that remained was to decide how much to give. I started a conversation with God that forever changed my understanding of "daily bread."

"Should I give them $110?" I asked.

The only way I can describe what happened is that I experienced a physical jolt, right in the center of my being. I took that to be God's "no"! Then came a sense that I should try again with a little less for them.

"Should I give them $109?" I asked again.

This time, the sense of being "jarred" lessened considerably, though I didn't have a complete peace.

"How about $108?" I prayed.

Suddenly I found myself on my feet with a profound sense of strong peace and even urgency. Fire and joy permeated my inner being and I knew beyond all knowing that Bill and Sue were to have $108 as soon as I could arrange to get it to them.

That night, after work was done, I took a plain opaque envelope, put their names on the front, inserted a card with Philippians 4:19 printed on it and added the cash inside. I went to their home and discovered that their porch light was burnt out. In the dark, I went up to their mailbox, dropped the sealed envelope inside, and left without their knowing of my presence. Two weeks later, I learned the "daily bread" lesson that forever altered my pattern of living and giving.

I was walking down the street where they lived (not far from my home) and Bill saw me. Waving to me he said, "Dave! Have I got things to tell you! God is supplying our needs according to his riches in glory! Come on in!"

Feeling rather smug, I walked over and said, "What's up?" Then I got the story.

"Two weeks ago," said Bill, "Sue and I were trying to figure out what to do. It was a Friday afternoon about 4:00 p.m. We were wanting to go to Asia, but I needed to finish my degree. We sensed that God would have us complete this before taking the new step. Now I had to take an evening course and enroll by Monday. Trouble was that we were strapped for cash. We were both going to get paid by Wednesday, but we had to pay up front to take the course. We needed $158 by Monday morning, and all that we had was $50. So about 4:00 p.m. we started praying that God would send us $108 by Monday morning. We kept praying all through the weekend. Finally on Sunday afternoon, I received an assurance that our prayer was heard and that God would send the money to us in time for us to enroll for the course. I checked the mail on Monday and there was an envelope with the cash inside and a card that said God would supply our needs! Isn't that incredible?"

My jaw dropped, the hair stood up on the back of my neck, and we prayed large prayers of thanksgiving together. I didn't tell them I was the giver at that time. Years later I did, when it was clear that they needed to remember what God had done. But at that moment they didn't need to know, as they were still in awe at the power of God to meet their needs when they put the kingdom first.

Friday at 4:00 they needed and asked for God to send them $108.

Friday at 4:00 I was in prayer and God commanded me to send Bill and Sue $108 as quickly as I could get it to them.

It was the *exactness* of the incident that astounded me. It was also the truth that God could and truly did communicate with me and I actually managed to "hear" exactly what He said needed to be done!

Suddenly I knew that if God did that for Bill and Sue, who were putting the kingdom of God first, God would do that for anyone who was putting the kingdom of God first. A gift of faith was born within to trust the Lord for daily bread from that time forward.

The money was a test to see if I would put the kingdom of God first! The obedience yielded a rich reward. It taught all three of us to believe God, to trust when trusting made no sense, and to submit to God's leading even when doing so was difficult to do. I remain friends with Bill and Sue to this very day!

To return to the wilderness theme from Deuteronomy from yesterday, we are to live on every word that proceeds from the mouth of God. Peter Craigie in his commentary on Deuteronomy states this well:

> When the people were hungry, God fed them manna; the provision of manna was not simply a miracle, but it was designed to teach the Israelites a fundamental principle of their existence as the

covenant people of God. The basic source of life was God and the words of God to his people; *every utterance of the mouth of the Lord . . . was more basic to Israelite existence than was food.* This principle did not mean that the Israelites were to expect the miraculous provision of food, as in the instance when God provided manna. Normal circumstances would involve the normal acquisition of food supplies. But if the command of God directed the people to do something or go somewhere, the command should be obeyed; shortage of food or water, lack of strength, or any other excuse would be insufficient *for the command of God contained within it the provision of God.* (emphasis mine)[16]

Jesus knew that with obedience would come provision. That was why He put the kingdom of God first, and our legitimate needs second. It is important to recognize that Paul wrote Philippians 4:19 while imprisoned for his faith. His *needs* were supplied (he ate, slept, and had a roof over his head and a mission to accomplish). His *wants* (including his freedom!) didn't happen according to his own desire or timetable. His *wishes* had to be submitted to God as well (knowing he could either live or die, he had a longing to join Christ, but chose to endure prison and suffering for the church [Philippians 1:22-26]).

There are differences among the three. The sorting out will occur over years and a fervent searching out of the mind of God. But the attitude must be clear and forthright. Put God first. Then trust Him for the things that are necessary to get the work done.

PEN TO PAPER

1) All of us have needs, wants, and wishes. It is right and proper to speak to God about everything, including the things that may or may not be granted. The issue is not the *needs*. The issue is the *relationship* with Him. Take a moment and reduce to writing what you know are your needs to get God's work done. Follow that with your wants, and then your wishes:
    Needs:

    _____

    _____

Wants:

_____

_____

Wishes:

_____

_____

2) Is there an area in which it seems that the legitimate needs are not getting met? Reread Philippians 4:19 above. Paraphrase that text below to "get at" the main point it is trying to teach us. With that done, review your needs, wants, and wishes above and commit them to God in prayer, trusting that He has heard your prayer.

3) Is there someone you know who is in need of "daily bread"? Perhaps you are the one holding the resources to answer that need. Ask God about your need to practice generosity, and commit to use your resources to advance His work. If you know of someone whose need you can meet, make a plan to do it anonymously. Commit to this below, make a timeline to get it done, and then do it (without being known). This way, God gets the glory, and not you.

The people/situation:

The plan to send them the "bread" they need:

The timeline to complete it:

Prayer Challenge

Daily bread is not just physical provision. It can include affirmation or encouragement. Practice this today as your prayer to supply hope and joy to another. Encourage someone as soon as you see him doing something well. Make that your prayer for that person today.

DAY 3

God's provision for our needs is a daily relationship.

Begin today by praying rather than by going right to the learning. Here is the Lord's Prayer in the CEV translation. Read it slowly, and then pray it by pausing between each line:

> Our Father in heaven,
> Help us to honor your name.
> Come and set up your kingdom,
> So that everyone on earth will obey you
> As you are obeyed in heaven.
> Give us our food for today.
> Forgive us for doing wrong, as we forgive others.
> Keep us from being tempted
> And protect us from evil/[the evil one].
> [The kingdom, the power and the glory are yours forever.]
> Amen. (Matthew 6:9-15, CEV)

This edition of the prayer underscores different emphases than those we have prayed before. What was fresh and new in this translation for you today? Record that here:

Did you notice? The bread is daily!
It can't be stored up for future use.
The assumption behind this prayer is that the disciple has a daily walk with God, and that in the midst of doing regular tasks to reestablish God's rule, provision is given as the needs arise. The wilderness generation learned this lesson as they traveled through the desert en route to the Promised Land.

God sent them daily provision as a test to see whether He would be obeyed.

> Then the LORD said to Moses, "I will rain down bread from heaven for you. The people are to go out each day and gather enough for that day. *In this way I will test them and see whether they will follow my instructions.* . . .
>
> That evening quail came and covered the camp, and in the morning there was a layer of dew around the camp. When the dew was gone, thin flakes like frost on the ground appeared on the desert floor. When the Israelites saw it, they said to each other, "What is it?" For they did not know what it was.
>
> Moses said to them, "It is the bread the LORD has given you to eat. This is what the LORD has commanded: 'Each one is to gather as much as he needs. Take an omer for each person you have in your tent.'"
>
> The Israelites did as they were told; some gathered much, some little. And when they measured it by the omer, he who gathered much did not have too much, and he who gathered little did not have too little. Each one gathered as much as he needed.
>
> Then Moses said, "No one is to keep any of it until morning."
>
> However, some of them paid no attention to Moses; they kept part of it until morning, but it was full of maggots and began to smell. So Moses was angry with them. (Exodus 16:4, 13-20, NIV, emphasis mine)

Once again, the kingdom imperative lies at the forefront of God's providing. The provision was a test of obedience—kings are to be obeyed at all costs. To fail to obey the king is to fail to honor that king. God provides for His army, but He requires His followers to do exactly as they are told.

More than this, the provision happened every day to ensure that they would have an ongoing, daily dependence on the God who would provide. The test was given to keep God in the center, and not on the edges, of the regular routines of life. The lesson is that God is the only treasure, the only true "food for the soul." Our needs must never be the center. Hoarding our resources only increases the focus on our need for more. Trusting God for our resources ensures that our needs are met but do not become our god. Dietrich Bonhoeffer spoke to this:

> Earthly goods are given to be used, not be collected. In the wilderness God gave Israel the manna every day, and they had no need to worry about food and drink. Indeed, if they kept any of the manna over until the next day, it went bad. In the same way, the disciple must receive his portion from God every day. If he stores it up as a permanent possession, he spoils not only the gift, but himself as well, for he sets his heart on his accumulated wealth and makes it a barrier between himself and God. Where our treasure is, there is our trust, our security, our consolation and our God. Hoarding is idolatry.[17]

Bonhoeffer was reflecting on Jesus' teaching about prayer, possessions, and treasure from the Sermon on the Mount, just a few verses past the Lord's Prayer in Matthew 6.

> Do not store up for yourselves treasures on earth, where moth and rust destroy and where thieves break in and steal. But store up for yourselves treasures in heaven, where neither moth nor rust destroys and where thieves do not break in or steal; for where your treasure is, there your heart will be also. . . . No one can serve two Masters; for either he will hate the one and love the other, or he will be devoted to one and despise the other. You cannot serve God and wealth. (Matthew 6:19-21, 24, NASB)

There is a temptation to focus our lives on the acquisition of wealth to make us secure. This temptation is sharp in Western societies where the ability to acquire wealth is much greater than in the survival societies of the third world. Still, even in poor cultures, it is difficult *not* to trust in material goods and possessions to ensure our future survival (or success). But the whole point of the Lord's Prayer is that our lives are to be centered not "on earth," but on the invasion of earth by heaven! Rather than asking heaven to guarantee our security, we are to live in such a way that the passing security of earth is rebuked by our God's providing! To trust in the security of things "here" is to deny the security of things "up there."

God must be our Master, and therefore must be trusted to meet our needs as we are about our Master's business. Daily bread comes from God's hands, not ours. Daily bread is a test to determine if we will obey our Lord.

PEN TO PAPER

1) Bonhoeffer's words are profound. Go back and reread them slowly and prayerfully. Take his main point and put it in your own words below:

2) Do your needs become your focus, or is the rule of God your focus as you talk to God about your needs? If your needs take center stage, you are worshipping a false god and need to renounce this immediately. If, on the other hand, you are attempting simply to walk with God and are trusting Him to provide, you are worshipping God rightly. If you are like most, you are "in the middle." Take a moment to ask God for a proper focus, to lay aside the too easy propensity to trust in the things of earth, and to recommit to the work of God.

3) Do you have any "idols" that need to go, any focus on material goods that must be renounced? If so, do it now, and ask God to help you start again.

PRAYER CHALLENGE

Today you will see or hear all kinds of advertising attempting to focus you on earth instead of heaven's provision. Each time you find yourself drawn to trusting earth's goods, recommit yourself to the kingdom of heaven and to God's supply of your legitimate needs. Commit to plan well for your future, but also to never making that plan the kingdom for which you live!

DAY 4

God supplies when we put the kingdom first.

There is no clearer word on our need for daily bread than the very material found just after the Lord's Prayer in Matthew's gospel. Jesus had been teaching about the radical nature of the kingdom of God, and about how the kingdom agenda must take center stage in all of our living. Let's listen to this very famous text that speaks to the issues of human need and God's rule in our lives:

> Therefore I tell you, do not worry about your life, what you will eat or drink; or about your body, what you will wear. Is not life more important than food, and the body more important than clothes? Look at the birds of the air; they do not sow or reap or store away in barns, and yet your heavenly Father feeds them. Are you not much more valuable than they? Who of you by worrying can add a single hour to his life?
>
> And why do you worry about clothes? See how the lilies of the field grow. They do not labor or spin. Yet I tell you that not even Solomon in all his splendor was dressed like one of these. If that is how God clothes the grass of the field, which is here today and tomorrow is thrown into the fire, will he not much more clothe you, O you of little faith? So do not worry saying, 'What shall we eat?' or 'What shall we drink?' or "What shall we wear?' For the pagans run after all these things, and your heavenly Father knows that you need them. But seek first his kingdom and his righteousness, and all these things will be given to you as well. Therefore do not worry about tomorrow, for tomorrow will worry about itself. Each day has enough trouble of its own. (Matthew 6:25-34, NIV)

When reading the Bible, it is always important to put the Scripture in its proper context. A good rule of thumb, on finding a "therefore," is to find out what it is "there for." In this case, the context is clearly the content of Jesus' prayer.

The chapter begins with the teaching that we should be "playing to the audience of one"—doing the things that God loves, knowing that only God should see them. The Father "who sees in secret" will reward us instead of people (Matthew 6:1). When we give, it is for God's eyes only (6:2-4). When we pray, it is for God's reward alone (6:5-6).

It is at this moment that we receive our introduction to Jesus' teaching on prayer. Jesus indicates that there is a way of praying that ensures that God hears our deepest heart since *he already knows what we need* (6:7-8). From this text it is clear that Jesus knew that they thought prayer was about having their needs met—human need alone! And so our Lord teaches the prayer that we are studying in which the Father and the kingdom come first (6:9-13)! All the rest of the chapter has to do with putting our asking into proper perspective. There is a word about forgiving to receive the Father's reward (6:14-15), fasting to receive the Father's reward (6:16-18), and then a word about putting heaven and heaven's reward ahead of everything on this earth (6:19-24). Based on all of that, Jesus says the "therefore" that leads into this section, which has as its main theme "Don't worry."

To focus on earth and earth's reward produces worry.

To focus on heaven and heaven's reward produces faith and confidence.

To focus on earth's goods ensnares us into seeking more goods.

To focus on heaven and heaven's reward frees us from basing our lives on that which will pass away. Once again, Bonhoeffer speaks well to this issue:

> Earthly possessions dazzle our eyes and delude us into thinking that they can provide security and freedom from anxiety. Yet all the time they are the very source of all anxiety. If our hearts are set on them, our reward is an anxiety whose burden is intolerable. Anxiety creates its own treasures and they in turn beget further care. When we seek for security in possessions we are trying to drive out care with care, and the net result is the precise opposite of our anticipations. The fetters which bind us to our possessions prove to be cares themselves.[18]

Why are our legitimate human needs put into the third line of the Lord's Prayer? It is because God would fill us with himself first and foremost, instead of with our goods and needs. God would direct us to the purpose of His kingdom's advance instead of the advancement of our own goals and purposes. God would call us to Himself and beyond ourselves!

God has called us to the true focus of our lives—the pleasure of the Father, heaven as our true home, God's kingly rule over all creation, God's righteousness in our lives, and the rebuke of worry over issues of necessary earthly existence—eating, drinking, clothing. The whole point of the Lord's Prayer and His teaching on daily bread is that *God knows our needs; our greatest need is that He be the center of our existence.*

Put need in the center and need becomes the god of our existence.

Put God in the center, and God takes care of the needs of our existence.

There is a sad "reward" if we get this one backward. If we put the needs of our lives, however legitimate, in the center of our existence, then anxiety replaces our faith.

Need has no personality except that of a parasite.

Need makes demands on the limited resources of our personality, and sucks out the peace, producing aloneness and alienation. To be cast on our own resources in seeking out more goods to fill up the legitimate needs of our lives only produces more need. It is a never-ending cycle that spirals down into a black hole of demand, leaving no room for fellowship with God.

That is the beginnings of hell, not heaven.

Our asking for provision must be our asking our King to take up His kingly rule. Then our King will supply our needs, beginning with our greatest need—to be in intimate fellowship with the God with whom we have to do.

The word of Christ here is to seek *first* the kingdom of God. It doesn't mean to seek *only* the kingdom of God. We are called (in fact, commanded) to ask when the issues of life press in and we need resources, food, money, friendships, time, hope, or love. These are the things that make life livable. The text implies that it is more than appropriate *to ask for* our legitimate material needs, *after* we have invested our focused energy on seeking first God's agenda. So we ask for bread, knowing that we are asking for the kingdom first. If the kingdom agenda supercedes bread for a season, we fast, we pray, we wait. The bread of life does take priority over the bread of the body. But God will feed us.

Pen to Paper

1) Go back and reread the passage from Matthew 6. Mark every reference to "worry" or "anxiety." Once that is done, try and summarize the point of this section into a couple of sentences.

2) The most often repeated command in the Bible surprises most people. It is the command "Don't worry" or its functional equivalents "Don't fret" or "Don't be anxious." If you could be completely candid with yourself (and God, of course!), what is your greatest worry? Reflect for a few moments and ask God to show you this:

Now ask how that worry could be given away to Jesus' Father. How could you "seek first the kingdom of God and his righteousness" with this issue?

3) Is there some issue of legitimate need—"daily bread"—that you are tempted to make the center of your life? Reread Bonhoeffer's words above and then name it below, and then replace that need focus by deliberately choosing to turn that one over to God. What are you to do with the need that presses in on who you are? Ask if it serves God's kingdom. If it does, then it is right to keep asking for the need to be met. If you are not sure, keep praying until your praying changes, for this might be God's way of meeting your legitimate need.

Prayer Challenge

Anytime you are tempted to worry about anything, decide now that you will deliberately ask if this need moves God's rule forward or takes you away from the Lord. If it moves God's purposes forward, keep praying for His will to be done. If it distracts, ask the Lord to show you how to drop the issue or change your praying. Let each moment of worry turn into a moment of prayer around the very thing over which you are concerned.

DAY 5

God commands us to ask!

A turning point in my life came when it became clear that I was disobeying God by failing to ask for necessary provision. I had been taught not to ask, but to get up and get whatever was needed by dint of effort and skill. Asking was foreign to my upbringing, even if the need was sharp. "If you pray for potatoes, put your hand to the plow!" went the saying.

While there was much to commend this saying against an attitude of laziness, there was little to commend it in terms of its focus on faith. This was just another way to say, "God helps those who help themselves," that we were the masters of our own destiny, that God didn't really intervene in human life. Beyond that, it was a subtle way of indicating that He didn't care. Yet notice the focus of Jesus' teaching on prayer and human need from Luke 11:

> Then Jesus said to them, "Suppose you have a friend, and you go to him at midnight and say, 'Friend, lend me three loaves of bread; a friend of mine on a journey has come to me, and I have nothing to set before him.' And suppose the one inside answers, 'Don't bother me. The door is already locked and my children and I are in bed. I can't get up and give you anything.' I tell you, even though he will not get up and give you the bread because of friendship, yet because of your shameless audacity he will surely give you as much as you need.
>
> "So I say to you: Ask and it will be given to you; seek and you will find; knock and the door will be opened to you. For everyone who asks receives; those who seek find; and to those who knock, the door will be opened.
>
> "Which of you fathers, if your son asks for a fish, will give him a snake instead? Or if he asks for an egg, will give him a scorpion? If you then, though you are evil, know how to give good gifts to your

children, how much more will your Father in heaven give the Holy Spirit to those who ask him!" (Luke 11:5-13, TNIV)

Once again, we are confronted with some of the essential threads of the Lord's Prayer. (In fact, this text occurs just after the shorter version of the prayer in Luke's gospel.) Here are found references to necessary provision—in fact, bread! Here is a reference to the "heavenly Father" who longs to provide from the storehouse of heaven.

And here, more than anywhere else, it is painfully clear that we must *ask*! In fact, the asking is to be persistent and consistent. This illustration is not instructing us to be pesky to the point of being a nuisance—filled with "shameless audacity," according to this rendering. No! Once again, this is not a direct correlation, but a contrast! God does not need to be "bugged" in order for us to get his attention and wear him down enough for him to deign to take pity on our awful situation. Rather, the point of Jesus' story here was that if legitimate human need could be met by harassing a sleeping neighbor in the dead of the night, then surely God has an ear to our persistent cry for help in time of need. A pestered human being who thinks you are a first-class pain can help you; surely God can do a whole lot better than this!

The point is that asking is needed! We are not simply to assume that because God knows we need the things of life, He will automatically supply them. Rather, God's *primary* concern is not to supply our needs, but to *deepen our relationship with him*, even around the central issues of life. And so, God has shaped the advance of the kingdom around our need to be in regular communication with him.

Jesus requires us to ask! This is not an option.

Jesus did not merely suggest a possible series of alternatives for us when times were tough. He commanded us to ask, and then ended his teaching by indicating that God was not an ogre setting us up for trouble or disappointment. Using another contrast, he made clear that even though we have sinful propensities ("you who are evil"), we have sense enough to determine that when those we love make legitimate requests we should answer them. By clear implication, God does far better than we do!

We have been given a command from our King to ask. Commands from kings must not be evaded or avoided. They are to be obeyed, or else we do not serve our king, but only ourselves. It is time for us to ask, expecting God to answer. He told us to do it. This was not generated out of our own thinking. It is best then to "Just do it!"

John Maxwell uses an acronym to sum up all three words in this material and gives some helpful pointers to assist us in our praying: The acronym is "ASK" for Ask, Seek, Knock.

ASK: Examine our needs to determine if the request is right in God's sight. To determine whether this is so, answer the following questions to determine if this is a fair request:

1. Is my request fair and helpful to everyone concerned?
2. Is my request in harmony with the Word of God?
3. Will it blend with my gifts?
4. Will it draw me closer to God?
5. What is my part in answering this prayer?

SEEK: When people seek, as Jesus directs us to do, they are asking with effort. This implies that He expects us to do our part even as we ask Him to do His. So when Jesus teaches us to pray, "Give us this day our daily bread," He doesn't mean that we are to sit back and expect God to rain down manna from heaven on us. . . . What Jesus means is, "Give us the opportunity to earn our bread." God does not give added resources to those who are lazy. . . . Prayer without action is presumption. . . .

KNOCK: When Jesus directs us to knock, He's asking us to be persistent! Keep on asking, keep on seeking and keep on knocking.[19]

PEN TO PAPER

1) Go back and reread the parable of the friend at midnight and the command of Jesus to ask, seek, and knock. Do you have any needs that are urgent enough to drive you to wake up a neighbor at midnight and demand an answer? What would they be?

2) Go back and review what it is that you listed in your needs, wants, and wishes from Day 2 of this week. Pick out three from the list that are the most important requests you would make of God. Examine each request using John Maxwell's ASK acronym and the questions he raises. Think through what you know about God's kingdom and how these requests "fit" the advance of God's rule below:

Request #1 _____
Why this is important to me as I serve the kingdom of God:

Request #2 _____
Why this is important to me as I serve the kingdom of God:

Request #3 _____
Why this is important to me as I serve the kingdom of God:

3) Name the boldest requests you ever made of God—those that would fit the words "shameless audacity." Were those requests answered? Why or why not?

Request: Answers:

_____   _____

_____   _____

_____   _____

PRAYER CHALLENGE

Today when a need arises that fits the category of daily bread, remember the command of Christ and ASK.

DAY 6

The power of corporate asking . . .

There are some issues in the life of faith which require more than just a request of a single believer. Daily bread for the people of the wilderness generation was given to *all* of the people, and not just a favored few. There are times when it is imperative to "test out" our asking for legitimate needs by sharing them with the larger faith community.

There are several advantages to this approach. The first is that this kind of asking moves us away from praying only about our personal concerns. It guarantees that we will at least *attempt* to discern whether our asking for the bread we need serves the kingdom agenda, or whether we are merely caught up in our own thinking. Beyond this, a second benefit is that fellowship grows out of tackling a thorny problem together with other believers. The old saying goes that "a problem shared is a problem halved." Thirdly, a different quality of power is released when it is clear that many (rather than just one) are agreed that God must intervene. When the many intercede for the power of God to move, and a prayer is answered, the faith of the many is made strong.

Jesus Himself was clear that there is a different level of prayer when the praying moves from one person to the many: "Again I say to you, that if two of you agree on earth about anything that they may ask, it shall be done for them by My Father who is in heaven. For where two or three of you have gathered in My name, I am there in their midst" (Matthew 18:19-20, NASB).

It is important to note that there are conditions found in this expansive prayer promise. The first is that there be a minimum of two believers in the Lord Jesus Christ who have taken the decision to ensure that their lives belong completely to the Lordship of their Savior. Given what we have learned about "the name" of Jesus in Week 2 of this resource, it is clear that to "gather together in the name" is to do far more than to merely gather for a prayer meeting. Rather it is to enter into the character and nature of Jesus Christ Himself, and to do this together. Sin issues must be dealt with, confessed, and surrendered; nagging troubles and doubts must be taken to the cross of Christ and left there; and fellowship around the things of God must take center stage. Once it is clear that the two believers are in fact both "in Christ" as far as they are aware, the second condition must be met: They must be agreed.

Both must be utterly convinced that God wants something done, and that this is not merely something that the two of them think would be helpful or "nice."

When believers gather in His very person, Jesus' power flows out of a sense of profound unity among the pray-ers—the unity named in John 17:11, 20-26, between Christ and the Father. Without this kind of agreement, the power of faith is weakened. The asking is not merely requesting that a need be fulfilled. Rather, this is an urgent appeal to the Lord of the universe that God Himself intervene around an agreed upon issue for the Lord's glory. It is filled with urgency, a demand, that this prayer *must* be answered, for the name and reputation of God Himself is at stake.

There is a profound truth that merits reflection. God has ceded His glory to us. What happens to God's people, then, has a direct bearing on God's own reputation. Our corporate walk as believers together reflects upon how the world perceives the power and the glory of God.

The ancient word spoken to Solomon at the dedication of the temple makes clear that corporate asking—based on a corporate recognition that the many need to turn to the Lord for help, with the many turning away from anything they know has wounded their walk with God—moves the very heart of God to enter into the human stream and answer the cry of those hearts.

> If I shut up the heavens so that there is no rain, or if I command the locust to devour the land, or if I send pestilence among My people, and My people who are called by My name humble themselves and pray and seek My face and turn from their wicked ways, then I will hear from heaven, will forgive their sin and will heal their land. (2 Chronicles 7:13-14, NASB)

Something like this happened in the state of Minnesota in 1877. The economy of the state was, for the most part, based on agriculture. The year before, grasshoppers had very nearly destroyed the Minnesota economy, eating up much of the crop, and leaving many very nearly destitute. Farmers, the backbone of the economy at the time, were quite worried. They believed that the same kind of plague would strike their state again and take out the wheat crop, bringing ruin to thousands of people who were already in desperate straits from the year before.

The situation was so very serious that the state governor, John S. Pillsbury, took the unusual step of proclaiming a statewide day of prayer and fasting. Pillsbury issued an edict that on April 26, 1877, every business, shop, school, and office close to seek the mercy of heaven to stop the grasshoppers from destroying the crop. Every man, woman, and child in the state was urged in that proclamation to ask God to prevent that terrible scourge from returning. On that April day all places of business, commerce, enterprise, and learning were closed. People abstained from eating and went to their churches or to their homes to seek God for their "daily bread" to be spared. The records indicate that a reverent, quiet hush fell over all the state.

The next day dawned bright and clear. Temperatures soared to what they ordinarily were in midsummer, which was very peculiar for April in that part of the country. Minnesotans were devastated as they discovered billions of grasshopper larvae wiggling to life. For three days the unusual heat persisted, and the larvae hatched out. It appeared that it wouldn't be long before they would start feeding and destroying the wheat crop.

On the fourth day, however, temperatures plummeted to well below freezing; that night a very harsh killing frost covered the earth. That frost was so severe that it killed every one of the grasshopper larva as surely as if poison or fire had been used. Grateful farmers never forgot that day. It went down in the history of Minnesota as the day God answered the prayers of the people.[20]

There is tremendous power in corporate prayer for daily bread. What it requires is a shared commitment and a mutual surrender to the Lordship of Jesus. It requires that the people of God be agreed and committed to continued agreement for the Lord to intervene.

PEN TO PAPER

1) Do you know of any issues in which there needs to be some kind of provision for God's purposes to unfold—purposes that are larger than just

yourself? Take a moment and record them below:

2) Is there someone that you could ask to pray with you for these issues to be brought to the Lord? Commit a name to writing and make a commitment to ask that person to join you in this prayer adventure.

3) Name the time when you will contact them and put a date and time on your calendar for the prayer time to occur.

PRAYER CHALLENGE

After you have had a chance to call your "prayer partner" and agree that you will pray about this issue, carve out some time to examine your life to see if there are any impediments to answered prayer. Are there any outstanding sin issues that need to be dealt with? Is there any strife between you and any other person that needs resolution? Is there an action step you need to take to prepare your heart to "gather in His name"? Take the step quickly, especially as the time for your praying together gets closer.

On your prayer day, perhaps you will need to fast. Fasting is simply abstaining from food in order to draw near to God. If you have never done this before (and you do not require regular meals for health purposes—as in the case of diabetes, etc.), the simplest fast is to skip one meal and use the time usually reserved for eating for prayer. Any time a hunger pang occurs, let it serve as a reminder to pray about the matter before you once more.

DAY 7

Christ Himself is the daily bread we need.

We have been living with the third line of the Lord's Prayer now for a week. The message that has come through our journey is that our most important needs must be subservient to God's agenda to accomplish His will on earth as it is in heaven. The need for "bread" in all its forms is legitimate—and legion. We must constantly be putting our agendas underneath our Lord's command to put his kingdom first. Here, prayer for daily bread finds its true reward—in knowing God.

There is one aspect of this request that needs to be sounded out for our understanding to be made complete. When all other needs have been satisfied and our hearts made full, the greatest need is for Christ Himself to be formed in all aspects of our lives. He is the bread we need for wholeness to come into our fractured existence.

In John 6 we find a series of scenes that underscore this reality. In the first scene, Jesus saw a large crowd in a wilderness area and realized there was no food to feed this gathering. Here the theme of bread and testing came together again. "He said to Philip, 'Where shall we buy bread for these people to eat?' He asked this only to test him" (John 6:5-6, NIV).

As it turned out the "test" was not merely a test of Philip's faith, but of the response of the crowd to the power of God. Jesus took five barley loaves and two fish and fed five thousand people with that meager supply. One would think that the response would be gratitude and a hunger for the things that Jesus would teach. Instead it turned into a demand for more of the spectacular, and a fleshly insistence that Jesus do things *on their terms*, instead of submission to the will of God, revealed in Christ.

> After the people saw the miraculous sign that Jesus did, they began to say, "Surely this is the Prophet who is to come into the world." Jesus knowing that they intended to come and *make him king by*

force, withdrew again to a mountain by himself. (John 6:14-15, NIV, emphasis added)

In the presence of a miracle of provision of daily bread, and in the very presence of God in human flesh, a gathering of five thousand Christ-seekers made the decision to manipulate the Lord of glory to become a king *according to their understanding* instead of serving the One who had granted them blessing on His terms.

Jesus had to withdraw His presence from their midst.

His presence will always withdraw when this occurs.

He will not be a puppet-king.

There is something demonic as well as holy in bringing our need for daily bread to God. If an answered prayer brings us closer to submission to His purposes, then the prayer has served its purpose—to focus on hallowing the Father's name, to advance the rule of God's kingdom and for His will to be done on earth as in heaven. Here the prayer for daily bread becomes an extension of "Your kingdom come."

But if answered prayer produces within us a manipulative yearning to see God "do it again," and He becomes a performer doing encores after the curtain comes down on the show, we enter the realm of demonic power instead of godly submission.

Demons seize hold in order to make others do their will.

Demons invade personalities to wrest control away from them.

Demons distract people from the kingdom agenda, promise fulfillment, and in the end remove human freedom.

Demonic power manipulates in order to control.

God's power invites us to come to Him and die with Him that He might accomplish the blessing of the many.

Jesus' ministry is focused on restoring what is lost, on returning people to fullness and to self-giving, that we might be able to choose Him, not based on manipulative demand, but on pure love. The crowd in John 6 didn't understand that the true bread was to know Christ Himself on *Christ's* terms.

In the second scene, the disciples (without the Lord) attempted to cross the lake and were caught in a storm. Christ came to them, walking on water; they received Him into their boat, and with Him present, they suddenly discovered they were where they needed to be. The presence of Christ, revealed on Jesus' terms and invited in, brought them where they needed to go.

In the third scene, the crowd was looking for Christ, but they did so in an off-center kind of way. Unable to make him their puppet-king, they tried to find Him where He was before. He wasn't there. Perplexed about where He went (and how He went there), they got into their own boats "in search of Jesus" (John 6:24).

In the next scene, the seekers found Him, and asked Him about how and when He got to the other side of the lake. Jesus revealed that their motives were egocentric, selfish, and self-gratifying. They had become focused on their physical needs instead of their need to keep the kingdom of God first. "Jesus answered, 'I tell you the truth, you are looking for me, not because you saw miraculous signs, but because you ate the loaves and had your fill'" (John 6:26, NIV).

The final answer of Christ to the seeking crowd (who really were seeking Jesus) was to teach them that He was the bread that would satisfy. When they asked for a miraculous sign (and told Him that Moses sent manna), His reply was to point to their need of a Savior, and their need to keep the kingdom first.

> "I tell you the truth, it is not Moses who has given you the bread from heaven, but it is my Father who gives you the true bread from heaven. For the bread of God is he who comes down from heaven and gives life to the world." . . . Then Jesus declared, "I am the bread of life. He who comes to me will never go hungry, and he who believes in me will never be thirsty." (John 6:32-33, 35, NIV)

God has commanded that we ask for daily bread. We do this as our third request in submission to the kingdom coming. If we focus on our hunger, we make Jesus a puppet-king by force. If we focus on knowing Christ in the midst of our need, Christ supplies us with Himself—and our needs are met.

There is no better illustration of this truth than the life and teaching of Dietrich Bonhoeffer. His teaching on its own is profound (we have been listening to him through this resource). When it is put in the context of his life, it moves from profound to magnificent. Bonhoeffer was a German national who deliberately chose to return to the madness of Nazi Germany in order to take a stand against the demonic power of the Führer. After the ascension of Hitler to power in 1933, he went on radio, lamenting and lambasting his own people for blindly following a leader who was nothing more than a "misleader." He took up a calling to lead a secret seminary in Germany and became the founder of the "confessing church," a group that held to classic Christianity but did not endorse the state church and its tacit approval of the government. Against this backdrop, he wrote *The Cost of Discipleship*, *Ethics*, and *Life Together*.

While teaching and writing he became aware of the underground resistance movement and spoke and preached against the Führer despite the fact that it could mean his death. The result was that he was arrested on the 5th of April, 1943, and imprisoned. He wrote letters and papers while in prison. Those papers were gathered and compiled into a volume of his last thoughts. On Sunday, April 5, 1945, just before the fall of the Nazi regime, after conducting a service of worship, he was taken out and executed—a man who believed in Christ and the call to love.

His final thoughts were reduced into a poem and turned into a hymn about three realities: humans, overwhelmed by sin, turning to God and finding in Him "bread for the soul"; God in search of us in Christ, dying for us on the cross; and finally, God redeeming us, giving us forgiven life, Christ Himself being the bread we need. Take a moment to reflect on this hymn:

Men go to God when they are sorely placed.
Pray Him for succour, for His peace, for bread.
For mercy, for them sinning, sick or dead.
All men do so in faith or unbelief.

Men go to God when He is sorely placed
Find Him poor, scorned, unsheltered without bread,
Whelmed under weight of evil, sick, or dead.
Christians stand by God in His hour of grief.

God goes to man when he is sorely placed.
Body and spirit feeds He with His bread.
For every man, He as a man hangs dead.
Forgiven life, He gives us through His death.
Dietrich Bonhoeffer, 1906-1945 (Versified by Rev. Walter Farquharson)[21]

PEN TO PAPER

1) There is much to think about after seven days of living with the prayer for daily bread. Perhaps the biggest concern lies in the difference between demonic power and godly submission. We have said, "Demonic power manipulates in order to control. God's power invites us to come to Him and die." In asking for our needs to be met, we need to make sure that we are ensuring that our needs come under the second, rather than the first. Think for a passing moment. What is the need that you ask to have met most consistently and regularly? Take a moment and record it here:

2) In asking for this request for this portion of "daily bread," are you drawn closer to God's kingdom, or taken farther away from Christ? Spend some time thinking about the outcome of bringing this request to God or having it answered. Then record your thoughts about whether you are drawn to Him through this.

3) Think about how each desire drives you toward the Lord or away from him. The ultimate prayer is that each desire (whether completed or unfulfilled) draw you closer to the kingdom agenda. The ultimate prayer is that your dying draw you closer to Christ than your living ever did, and that the effect of your dying achieve more for God's kingdom than your living ever did. That was certainly what happened in the life and death of Bonhoeffer. His words are covered in his sacrifices. Would you pray this way?

4) Take a moment now and put this line of the Lord's Prayer into your own words, bearing in mind what you have learned over this last week

PRAYER CHALLENGE

The most important prayer for daily bread is to find ourselves in the heart of Christ. When a desire for some need comes to you today (a hunger pang, a desire to pay your bills, a longing for friendship/laughter, the comforts of home after a long day), use that desire to ask Christ to fill your desire with Himself and thus to fill your life with Himself.

Week Six

YIELD YOUR SINS TO GOD

"And Forgive Us Our Debts . . ."

DAY 1

Forgiveness is the center of the gospel.

At the end of Week 5 we reflected on the words of Dietrich Bonhoeffer, speaking of our search for God and, in turn, of God's search for us. Take a moment and reread the words of the last verse of that hymn:

God goes to man when he is sorely placed.
Body and spirit feeds He with His bread.
For every man He as a man hangs dead.
Forgiven life, He gives us through His death.[22]

If you know the hymn, sing the words. If not, speak them aloud and ponder Jesus' death on the cross for us. Then take a moment to thank the Lord for His unspeakable gift.

Now let's take a moment to pray the Lord's Prayer. This time we will use the version found in Luke 11 (note that Jesus used this prayer more than once and, like us, adapted His teaching to each different context). This rendering is shorter—though the main outline is still very clear:

Father, thy name be hallowed;
thy Kingdom come.
Give us each day our daily bread.
And forgive us our sins,
for we too forgive all who have done us wrong.
And do not bring us to the test,
(but save us from the evil one [from the margin reading])
(Luke 11:2b-4, NEB)

If there is a center to the teaching of Jesus, it is that God is in the business of restoring, redeeming, and setting right what has been made wrong. Our Lord made abundantly clear that nothing was more important than God's call for us to be a people of forgiveness. This truly is an extension of the calling to be a people who pray, "Hallowed be Your name" and "Your kingdom come . . . on earth as in heaven." Tom Wright makes the case plainly in his short book on the Lord's Prayer. Speaking of our Lord's self-understanding, he refers to the incident in which Jesus spoke to a paralyzed man, declaring, "Take heart my son, your sins are forgiven" (Matthew 9:2 NEB). The crowd, of course, would have thought Jesus was making an extravagant claim. Jesus replied by healing him of his paralysis in front of the crowd. Wright's comments are insightful:

> Who does he think he is? They quite naturally asked. The obvious answer is: Jesus thinks he's the Kingdom-bringer. Jesus isn't just a "teacher"; he is making an *announcement* about something that is *happening*; and he is doing and saying things which explain that announcement and demonstrate that it's true. . . . Healings, parties, stories and symbols all said: the forgiveness of sins is happening, right under your noses. This is the New Exodus, the real Return from Exile, the prophetic fulfillment, the great liberation. . . .
>
> So Jesus went from village to village . . . announcing that the kingdom had arrived, that forgiveness of sins was happening, that God was transforming his people at last into the salt of the earth and the light of the world. And, wherever people responded to his call, he gave them instructions as to how they should live, as the new-Exodus people, the forgiveness-of-sins people. They were to live . . . as a cell of kingdom-people.
>
> In particular, having received God's forgiveness themselves, they were to practice it amongst themselves. Not to do so would mean they hadn't grasped what was going on. As soon as someone in one of these Jesus-cells refused to forgive a fellow-member, he or she was saying, in effect, "I don't really believe the Kingdom has arrived." The only reason for being Kingdom-people, for being Jesus' people, was that the forgiveness of sins was happening; so if

you didn't live forgiveness, you were denying the very basis of your own new existence.[23]

To be Jesus' people is to start with being forgiven, so that we might leave off the things that paralyze us. To be part of Jesus' countercultural community is to live out that kind of amazing forgiveness with all who sin against us.

There really are two parts to this understanding: The first part is that God forgives us; the second is that we forgive others.

To understand this reality, we need to recognize that to the Hebrew mind, anything said *once* by God was a "fact," though it could be altered. For example, Isaiah the prophet was told by God to warn King Hezekiah that he should set his house in order, for his death was about to happen. Hezekiah prayed, asking for a longer life. God spared him and he was given fifteen more years (see 2 Kings 20:1-7). Here a "fact" uttered by God was issued as a word of warning. Here prayer moved the heart of God and God changed the "fact."

Anything repeated *twice* was underscored in an urgent way; this would be an established fact that could not be altered, as when Pharaoh had two dreams and Joseph the patriarch interpreted the message for him. Joseph indicated that something repeated twice meant that God was at work and the matter would occur speedily (see Genesis 41:32).

Anything said *three* times was so profound that it was impossible to underscore it any further. In Gethsemane, our Lord prayed three times for a way other than the cross. God said no three times and Christ asked no further (Matthew 26:36-46). Paul prayed for a "thorn in his flesh" to be removed three times. God said no each time and Paul asked no further (2 Corinthians 12:8-9). Peter was told to reach out to Gentiles so that the gift of the Spirit might be given to them as well as to Jews and Samaritans. It required a threefold repetition to underscore how profound this message to him was (Acts 10:9-16). God's holiness was so profound that the Hebrew Scripture underscored it. God was not merely "holy." Nor was He the much more profound, "Holy, Holy." Rather, God is holy to the third degree, "Holy, holy, holy" (Isaiah 6:1-8). Now we come to the teaching of Jesus, and His radical message of profound forgiveness. Here we see how deep this message of forgiveness was to our Lord: "Now the tax collectors and 'sinners' were all gathering around to hear him. But the Pharisees and the teachers of the law muttered, 'This man welcomes sinners and eats with them'" (Luke 15:1-2, NIV).

The context is quite important. There were two groups: those with a tradition of absolute, scrupulous, meticulous obedience to the laws of God on the one hand; on the other were those on the edges of society—prostitutes, tax collectors, collaborators with the conquering power, the outcasts who were not welcomed by the "respectable." The first group didn't understand the message of Jesus' kingdom—radical forgiveness and the restoration of all that was lost. The second group, never welcomed into the company of the scrupulous, was astonished that they could be spoken to, let alone welcomed back. The meticulous were utterly uncomfortable in Jesus' presence. The outcasts were delighted to be near Him so that they might be restored.

Jesus was in the radical middle—He raised the standard of holiness from externals to the deepest heart, yet called the lost, the "written off," to a restored walk with God. Messiah spoke to both groups. He told three parables, all with the same point. In the parables, God Himself seeks the sinner and is delighted to restore the lost one; this is said not once, not twice, but three times.

Forgive. Forgive. Forgive.

Redeem. Redeem. Redeem.

Restore. Restore. Restore.

In the first parable, Jesus spoke of a shepherd searching for a lost sheep (sheep are not known for intelligence—the sheep is lost because it *wandered*).

In the second, He spoke of a woman who loses a coin and sweeps the house to find it. (The coin is lost because it got "*dropped*.")

The third is a parable directed at the two groups in verses 15:1-2: the scrupulous law-keepers and the fallen outcasts; these were the so-called "righteous" and those who knew they weren't. In a striking parallel, the parable contains two sons, a scrupulous law-keeper and a sinful, disrespectful outcast. God is pictured as a humiliated and scorned father who is shameless about his love for a son who would return to the fold. (Here, the sinner chose to *rebel*.)

> There was a man who had two sons. The younger one said to his father, "Father, give me my share of the estate." So he divided his property between them.

Not long after that, the younger son got together all he had, set off for a distant country and there squandered his wealth in wild living. After he had spent everything, there was a severe famine in that whole country, and he began to be in need. So he went and hired himself out to a citizen of that country, who sent him to his fields to feed pigs. He longed to fill his stomach with the pods that the pigs were eating, but no one gave him anything.

When he came to his senses, he said, "How many of my father's hired men have food to spare, and here I am starving to death! I will set out and go back to my father and say to him: Father, I have sinned against heaven and against you. I am no longer worthy to be called your son; make me like one of your hired men." So he got up and went to his father.

But while he was a long way off, his father saw him and was filled with compassion for him; he ran to his son, threw his arms around him and kissed him.

The son said to him, "Father, I have sinned against heaven and against you. I am no longer worthy to be called your son."

But the father said to his servants, "Quick! Bring the best robe and put it on him. Put a ring on his finger and sandals on his feet. Bring the fattened calf and kill it. Let's have a feast and celebrate, for this son of mine was dead and is alive again; he was lost and is found." So they began to celebrate. (Luke 15:11-24, NIV)

Tom Wright makes clear that the parable could have been called the "Parable of the Running Father." For an old man in the ancient Middle East to run and reaccept the son who shamed him would be equivalent to the Prime Minister of England opening Parliament in a bathing suit (see Wright, pp. 49-50). This was an unabashed embrace of the ones who would return to their senses after sinning horribly and wounding many.

To be a servant of King Jesus, then, is to be a "forgiven forgiver."

It is to adopt a lifestyle of fearless forgiveness.

The message didn't end with the lost son restored, however. It ends with the meticulous brother appalled at the mercy of his father who would "receive sinners and eat with them." The posture for him would be folded arms, an angry scowl, and a scathing rebuke of the milquetoast, jelly-spined father as he gazed down his nose in contempt at such moral ineptitude. He is conscious of no personal sins, asks for no pardon, upholds his consistently meticulous lifestyle of law-keeping, and refuses to embrace the lost, holding forth his unclaimed rights. The word at the end of the parable underscores the message again: "But we had to celebrate and be glad, because this brother of yours was dead and is alive again; he was lost and is found" (Luke 15:32, NIV).

There is no room for anything other than a hearty embrace of God's forgiveness. This is the point of the fourth line of Jesus' prayer: forgive us our sins, as we forgive those who sin against us.

PEN TO PAPER

1) Go back and reread the last paragraph of Tom Wright's words about being kingdom people. Record what this might mean for you as a person, and for your church fellowship as a community. Then pray it into existence.

2) Now review the parable from Luke 15. Who are you in this text? The older brother, the younger brother, the servants on the side, the "foolish father," or someone watching from above? Tell why you think so.

3) Do you feel "lost" because you wandered, were dropped, or rebelled? If so, take a moment to turn to the Lord who would forgive and simply confess your deepest heart. Note that the younger son didn't just come back. He came back knowing he deserved nothing. He expected nothing and planned on taking nothing. Then he received everything. Take your time with this. Tell the Lord what you did—write whatever detail is in your heart, hiding nothing; tell Him you deserve nothing and simply be

still. God will send grace. Then God would have you receive forgiveness.

4) Which group feels welcome in your church—the meticulous, the scorned, or those in the radical middle of the Lord? Who might those people be? Name them and pray for each one in turn. What do they do? Where do they live? How can we love them?

The meticulous legalists:

_____

_____

The scorned sinners:

_____

_____

Those in the radical middle (embracing and restoring the fallen):

_____

_____

PRAYER CHALLENGE

For a servant of King Jesus, the calling is to be a "forgiven forgiver." To reject that God has forgiven you or to fail to forgive another is to abandon the kingdom of God. Take a moment and think on this reality.

Begin your day with a plan: anytime an old wound returns to memory, pray a blessing on the one who wounded you. Be specific. Be extravagant. End your prayer time with thanksgiving that God has shifted the center from justice required to justice fulfilled—from requiring perfection, to being perfect Himself, and enabling us to forgive, forgive, forgive.

As you feel led, pray the Lord's Prayer as you now practice it. When you come to the "forgive" line, choose the highest blessings you can imagine for the ones who have ruined everything and made you suffer. Refuse to be bound by yesterday's transgressions—yours or another's.

DAY 2

Forgiveness isn't easy, but it is required.

"Make every effort to live in peace with all men and to be holy; without holiness no one will see the Lord. See to it that no one misses the grace of God and that no bitter root grows up to cause trouble and defile many."
(Hebrews 12:14-15, NIV)

It is more than possible to miss the grace of God. The key is connected to what it means to forgive from the deepest heart, or merely to tolerate behavior and "stuff it" until it explodes into a bitter rage. Failure to forgive leads to a growth in negative inner grief. The old saying goes "Bitter or better."

Bitterness is nothing more than old unforgiveness.

Bitterness is what grows from a seed of injustice, planted and watered in the garden of what-might-have-been. When nurtured, it brings forth fruit. This fruit, fully mature, tastes sweet at first bite, but it turns the inner being sour with a harsh and biting deep despair.

Jesus told us to forgive.

More than this, He commanded us to pray for our forgiveness based on how we extend it to others! He leaves no room for yesterday's sins and the grudges we nurse from old offenses. The kingdom is here and it means mercy! It stands for release from past wounds—suffered from those who sinned against us—based on the blood of His Son.

It is sobering to listen to the words that follow immediately after our Lord taught us to pray this prayer: "For if you forgive others for their transgressions, your heavenly Father will also forgive you. But if you do not forgive others, then your Father will not forgive your transgressions" (Matthew 6:14-15, NASB).

Forgiveness is such a kingdom priority that our Lord made sure we understood this by adding an addendum to the prayer. The thrust is that if we receive mercy, we are to extend it. Receiving forgiveness must grow us to become so like Christ that we extend it to others freely.

There is no clearer picture of bitterness than a tale told by Paul Brand and Phil Yancey in their book *Fearfully and Wonderfully Made.*[24] It is a medical story with a bitter twist, of an amputation that came back to bite the injured.

Amputation is a last resort and not always a positive success. Very often amputees experience something called phantom pain—a memory of the nonexistent limb lingers in the brain. Amputees "feel" what is no longer attached to them. Invisible toes curl, imaginary hands grasp things, a "leg" feels so sturdy a patient may try to stand on it. Sadly, the experience can include pain. Doctors watch helplessly, because the part screaming for attention doesn't exist. Brand and Yancey tell of a man who experienced pain like that—a medical school administrator named Barwick.

Barwick had a serious and painful circulation problem in his leg but refused to allow amputation. As it grew worse, Barwick grew bitter. "I hate it! I hate it!" he would mutter about the leg.

At last he relented and told the doctor, "I can't stand it any longer. I'm through with the leg. Take it off." And so surgery was scheduled immediately. And here is where the story becomes bizarre.

Barwick asked the doctor, "What do you do with amputated legs?"

"Do a biopsy and explore them a bit, but we usually incinerate them."

Barwick made a grotesque request: "I would like you to preserve my leg in a pickling jar to install on my mantel shelf. Then as I sit in my armchair, I will taunt that leg, 'Hah! You can't hurt me anymore!'"

Barwick was able to pull some strings and have his way. Sadly, though, Barwick, thinking he would be the victor, wound up the loser. The man had phantom limb pain of the worst degree. The wound healed, but he could "feel" that leg swelling, cramping, hurting, and there was no relief. He had hated that leg with such intensity that the pain-memory lodged permanently in his brain, haunting him. Barwick made a plan not merely to remove the pain, but to shake his fist at it for the rest of his days.

To fail to forgive leads us down a similar path—we shake our fist at yesterday's wounds and injustices, only to discover that we are haunted by the phantom pains of someone's former sin against us.

Jesus tells us to make a plan to be better, and He will grant us our request. What pleases the Lord is when we *keep short accounts* instead of *keeping score*. Jesus would say to us that conflict must never be left unresolved. He said, "Forgive us our debts *as* we forgive our debtors." There is no more difficult line in the Lord's Prayer. There is no deeper calling in the kingdom than to live out this line, and to learn and relearn what it is both to receive and to experience grace. His point is plain: We can live our lives in the *torment of unforgiveness* or in the *freedom of forgiveness*. The key to this truth lies in chapter 18 of Matthew's gospel. Matthew 18 is about getting our relationships right, even if it is utterly expensive—up to and including figurative amputation:

- Verses 1-4 start off with a question about who is the greatest in God's kingdom. Jesus answers that children and the humble (those who trust God like children trust parents) are the greatest.
- Verses 5-9 turn into a word of warning, a woe. The warning has to do with sinning against other people, especially the young, the innocent, and the new believer. There will be a severe judgment if a "little one" is made to sin because of our actions. Better to lose an arm than use it to hurt another and earn hell!
- Verses 10-14 indicate that the heavenly Father will seek and save any little ones who become lost. The context implies that they have been wounded by someone who made them stumble. These have the Father's love set on them to win them back.
- Verses 15-18 are words to the faith community. The point here is never to let the sins of the community get that far, never to let an offender be allowed to wound anyone, let alone a "little one." We are commanded to discipline and correct each other. We are to make sure that offenders are corrected, first *privately* (one to one) then *semi-publicly* (one plus one or two others) and finally *openly* (the congregation—made up of house groups—likely twelve families or less) so that no one is allowed to hurt another in the name of God. After three strikes, you're out! To fail to hear the cry of the church to stop the awful behavior means that the gospel has been rejected, and the one still wounding others is no longer treated as a Christ-follower, but as a self-server. This seems severe, until we get to a parable about restoration.

We have just learned that a threefold repetition was as far as the Hebrew mind would go. Jewish custom was to forgive up to three times, and then to be done. Peter decides to be magnanimous, and double the number and add one more. "Then Peter came and said to Him, 'Lord, how often shall my brother sin against me and I forgive him? Up to seven times?'" (Matthew 18:21, NASB).

Jesus answered him with the impossible—seventy-seven times (or seventy times seven—both are absurdly high), to make his point, told a parable of the kingdom with a King and a call to forgive.

> Therefore, the kingdom of heaven is like a king who wanted to settle accounts with his servants. As he began the settlement, a man who owed him ten thousand talents was brought to him. Since he was not able to pay, the master ordered that he and his wife and his children and all that he had be sold to repay the debt.
>
> The servant fell on his knees before him. "Be patient with me," he begged, "and I will pay back everything." The servant's master took pity on him, canceled the debt and let him go.
>
> But when that servant went out, he found one of his fellow servants who owed him a hundred denarii. He grabbed him and began to choke him. "Pay back what you owe me!" he demanded.
>
> His fellow servant fell to his knees and begged him, "Be patient with me, and I will pay you back."
>
> But he refused. Instead, he went off and had the man thrown into prison until he could pay the debt. When the other servants saw what had happened, they were greatly distressed and went and told their master everything that had happened.
>
> Then the master called the servant in. "You wicked servant," he said, "I canceled that debt of yours because you begged me to. Shouldn't you have had mercy on your fellow servant just as I had on you?" In anger his master turned him over to the jailors to be tortured, until he should pay back all he owed.
>
> This is how my heavenly Father will treat each of you unless you forgive your brother from the heart. (Matthew 18:23-35, NIV)

Jesus was using currency to make His point: a "denarius," a "talent," 10,000 talents, and 100 denarii. A denarius was a laborer's daily wage (enough to feed a family for a day). One talent was 6,000 denarii—twenty years' wages. Translating numbers from culture to culture is difficult. However, insert your wage to make the point:

1 talent = 20 years' wages
10 talents = 200 years' wages
100 talents = 2,000 years' wages
1000 talents = 20,000 years' wages
10,000 talents = 200,000 years' wages

Just so we understand the point, we need to know that no one in the Middle East had that kind of money. In fact, no one in the Roman Empire did either. The gross domestic product of Galilee, Idumea, Judea, and Samaria was 900 talents. The sum Jesus was picturing was eleven times greater than all of the money in ancient Palestine!

The king wanted the gross domestic product of the Roman Empire back! The man could not repay (no one could). He pleaded for time to repay, threw himself down, and begged for mercy. The king looked down and saw the pathetic misery of this creature; he was "filled" with compassion. The Greek is hard to translate. It could be rendered, "His bowels brimmed over with compassion." Every part of the anatomy of that king was filled with mercy. He forgave the debt—more than a king's ransom.

To shift this to the gospel of the kingdom, the blood of God the Son has been spilled. The King did not have enough goods to render justice, so He became one of us and let Himself be killed—a King for a king's ransom. Our debt was paid.

What should this inspire in us except wonder, gratitude, and awe? It should fill us with a resolve to live out what we have received. But what did this man do? Like bitter Barwick, he shook his fist at his pickled leg. He resolved never to be in that position again, found one who owed him pocket change, seized him by the throat, and demanded repayment. Instead of extending the very grace he had just received, he ruined another's existence and threw him into debtor's prison! He had a healing but chose to fix on the bitter wound.

What did the king do? In 18:34 the king handed over the ingrate to torment, until he should pay back his king's ransom. The application of the story is sobering. "My heavenly Father will also do the same to you, if each of you does not forgive his brother from your heart" (Matthew 18:35, NASB).

This says that *the heavenly Father* will hand over the ungrateful unforgiving to the tormentors!

It is now more than clear that in the kingdom parables we have two kingdoms at war. There is the kingdom of God and the shadow kingdom of the false ruler Satan until he is overthrown.

So then who are the tormentors that God hands us over to if we do not forgive? Possibly this means we are handed over to:

1) Guilt that destroys
2) Sinful grief
3) Bitter despair or
4) Some form of demonic attack

The two-kingdom contrast implied by the two realms at war points to some kind of demonic attack. Since the prince of darkness uses each of the tools in the list above, perhaps it is God saying to the devil, "This one won't follow me. He is yours until he repents and forgives from the heart."

Here is Jesus' point. God is ever willing to extend grace and healing. It is expensive. Sometimes it is severe, but He will pay the cost Himself. In gratitude, we are to receive it, and from that experience of grace, we are to extend it to others. Failure to extend forgiveness is to be forever locked into the grief of our yesterdays.

Do we want mercy? God gives it, based on one condition: We must decide once and for all that the past will be over and done, that those who have wronged us will no longer be the object of our hatred. We will no longer encompass them in the harbor of our bitterness. We will tell God that they are off our hook, and that as far as we are concerned, we wish them no ill and will allow no thinking to poison our relating to them, or our believing, our hoping and our love.

Forgiveness is:

1) acknowledging that someone has ruined your life,
2) declaring to God (and to them if possible) that as far as you are concerned you will not seek retribution, nor will you treat them as their sins deserve
3) choosing to let him off of your hook for God to do with him as He sees fit. Finally this leads to a last step:
4) praying blessing on them, as Christ commanded.

PEN TO PAPER

1) Take a moment to reread the parable of the unforgiving debtor. Reduce the main point of the story into a sentence. Record that here.

2) Are there people in your life who truly hurt you? Does it still come back to haunt you with anger? If not, rejoice. If so, make a plan to forgive. Record the memories that return in the space below.

3) Now reread the four steps of forgiveness named above at the close of the teaching section.

   a. Take one of the memories and name the fact that the person, situation, group, etc., truly did injure you and you paid.
   b. Declare to the Lord that you will absorb their sin (this is what forgiveness does) and bear the cost of their injuring you.
   c. Picture the cross of Christ. Deliberately place this pain-memory on it and tell the Lord you will not pick it up again. (Anytime the memory returns, return to this picture of the sin against you dead on the cross.)
   d. Choose to pray a blessing that will make the person who sinned against you more like Christ. (If she stole from you, pray that she would receive generosity. If she lied, that she becomes utterly truthful. If she manipulated a situation at your expense, pray that she becomes forthright and fair.) Bless her with this prayer every time you remember her and ask God to fill her with His presence.
   e. Close your prayer with thanksgiving that God has had mercy on us and saved us for Himself.

PRAYER CHALLENGE

This kind of praying can lead to many memories of past injustices. Each time one of these comes to mind, jot it down so that you can take it to the cross when you are able. Then practice praise that God is calling you to wholeness. Deliberately thank Him. Use a psalm or sing praise with each memory. God is healing your soul. Thank Him.

DAY 3

Even the most evil of sins against us can be forgiven—
and God can use them as a platform for His purposes.

Mark Twain used to say that there is at least one thing in favor of the practice of prayer—we can't lie while we pray.

And yet we want to do so. There are some painful things in our lives that we don't want to name because the hurt is too profound. Perhaps we can't bear to face our issues because it will take too much energy; perhaps the pain was so very grievous that it is simply easier not to gaze upon the things that caused us so much hurt, even when we know that we were or are the victims and not the ones who should have suffered.

Yet the teaching of Scripture is clear. To "stuff it" is not to forgive it. It is to let it fester. Hidden wounds grow worse rather than better. Old, old wounds grow much, much worse. This is the "bitter root" named in the Hebrews reading yesterday.

One spring, there was a section of the back garden of our home that was very difficult to reach. Rather than dig out a particular weed, I topped the thing. It was so hard to reach that I just let the matter go. About two months later, while meditating on the idea of the "bitter root" and working in the garden, I noticed a huge weed in that same section of garden. This time, despite the fact that I had to pick my way through a bunch of obstacles, I took a shovel and a hose to soak the soil and worked around that root. It took quite awhile. Instead of a quarter-inch across and three inches long (as it would have been two months before), it was a taproot, fully three inches thick and about eight inches deep, with fibrous roots extending out in many directions. I placed another weed about the size of what that root would have been two months before over my heart and noticed it was small enough to extract with little effort. Then, placing the larger root there, it became clear that it was larger than my physical heart and would have taken up a lot more space. Pulling it later, rather than earlier, is much harder work.

There is a solution to bitter unforgiveness. The solution is to choose to forgive and to ask God to buy the injury back, even if it is awful. In fact, it is possible for someone else's sin against us to be a beginning of something profound and powerful. Our Lord taught this in the Sermon on the Mount, just before he taught the Lord's Prayer. Though the word "forgive" is not in this context, it is the plain point of the material. In fact, Jesus would have us go *underneath* and *through* any attack of evil by extending grace and mercy, even to those who would wound us profoundly. Listen closely to this word:

> You have heard that it was said, "An eye for an eye and a tooth for a tooth." But I say to you, do not resist an evil person; but whoever slaps you on the right cheek, turn the other to him also. . . . Whoever forces you to go one mile, go with him two. Give to him who asks of you, and do not turn away from him who wants to borrow from you. You have heard that it was said, "You shall love your neighbor and hate your enemy." But I say to you, love your enemies and pray for those who persecute you, so that you may be sons of your Father who is in heaven; for He causes His sun to rise on the evil and the good, and sends rain on the righteous and the unrighteous. For if you love those who love you, what reward do you have? Do not even the tax collectors do the same? If you greet only your brothers, what more are you doing than others? Do not even the Gentiles do the same? Therefore you are to be perfect, as your heavenly Father is perfect. (Matthew 5:38-48, NASB)

Mahatma Gandhi, a young lawyer looking to begin a new life, moved from the desperate conditions of life in the Indian subcontinent to South Africa. There he participated in the Boer War as a medical orderly during the battle of Spion Kop, outside of Durban (sharing the field with an unknown named Winston Churchill—future leader of the British Empire—and another named Louis Botha, the first Boer Prime Minister of the new South Africa). There he realized that war, fighting, and killing were all utterly senseless. He also realized that a "colored" Hindu such as he was would never have a future in South Africa; so he returned to India. Back on his native soil, he read these amazing words from the Sermon on the Mount. He was so very astonished that such teaching should exist that he decided to find the people who believed that these words were true and should be lived. He was greatly disappointed when he went to a Christian church and was turned away because of his turban and his race. Yet this teaching pervaded all he did in the years to come. He adopted a lifestyle of nonviolent resistance (later imitated by Martin Luther King Jr.) that led to India's freedom from British rule (and America's black civil rights movement). His greatest disappointment was that he met no one who lived out these words of Christ our Lord.

Had he met Betsy and Corrie ten Boom, his disappointment would have vanished away.

Corrie and her family, working with the Dutch resistance, sheltered Jews during World War II in their home in Holland to save them from the Holocaust. The Nazis arrested her and her entire family and sent them off to concentration camps. Corrie and her sister, Betsy, were imprisoned together at Ravensbruck inside Germany. There they witnessed and endured unspeakable violence and despair, very nearly starving to death. Betsy was beaten by a Nazi guard, weakening her already sickly frame so that in the course of time she grew weaker and finally died.

Corrie grew sick at heart.

Yet Betsy had always prayed for God to bring good out of horrible evil. She prayed for her guards and that the atrocities of the camp could be used by God as a platform for something beautiful for God. Her words to her sister, Corrie, carried her through the remaining years of her life. Betsy had a vision from God; she "saw" the prison barracks painted green with growing plants and flowers to heal the soul. Then she turned to her sister and told her to tell the world a message from the Lord: "We must tell people what we have learned here. We must tell them that there is no pit so deep that [God] is not the deeper still. They will listen to us Corrie, because we have been here."[25]

Betsy died shortly thereafter. Corrie was released through a "clerical error." She returned to Holland, was liberated by the Allied Forces, and grew strong again. After the war, someone donated some concentration camp barracks and she painted them green, put gardens in them to heal the soul and so began a ministry of love and healing to her former enemies. She went often to speak in the shattered remains of Germany, carrying the message that her sister Betsy told her just before she died.

There was one moment that was definitive for Corrie ten Boom. She had gone to Germany to preach the gospel of forgiveness. Listen to her words:

> It was at a church service in Munich that I saw him, the former S.S. man who had stood guard at the shower room door in the processing center at Ravensbruck. He was the first of our actual jailers that I had seen since that time. And suddenly it was all there—the roomful of mocking men, the heaps of clothing, Betsie's pain-blanched face.
>
> He came up to me as the church was emptying, beaming and bowing. "How grateful I am for your message, Fraulein," he said. "To think that, as you say, He has washed my sins away!"
>
> His hand was thrust out to shake mine. And I who had preached so often to people . . . of the need to forgive, kept my hand at my side.
>
> Even as the angry, vengeful thoughts boiled through me, I saw the sin of them. Jesus Christ had died for this man; was I going to ask for more? "Lord Jesus," I prayed, "forgive me and help me to forgive him."
>
> I tried to smile. I struggled to raise my hand. I could not. I felt nothing, not the slightest spark of warmth or charity. And so again I breathed a silent prayer. "Jesus, I cannot forgive him. Give me your forgiveness."
>
> As I took his hand, the most incredible thing happened. From my shoulder along my arm and through my hand a current seemed to pass from me to him, while into my heart sprang a love for this stranger that almost overwhelmed me.
>
> And so I discovered that it is not on our forgiveness any more than on our goodness that the world's healing hinges, but on His. When He tells us to love our enemies, He gives, along with the command, the love itself.[26]

When we think we cannot forgive, God can do it through us. What it takes is a decision to choose His highest and to invite our Lord into our weaknesses. Then He can forgive through us. He can also use our former despair as the starting place of care for untold people who are in desperate need of the mercy of our God.

Corrie learned to bless those who cursed her, to pray for those who despitefully used her, and through this process, learned that forgiveness is not only required but enabled. She learned that there was "no hole so deep that God was not the deeper still."

Can you forgive the ones who caused you such despair that you do not wish to face the pain?

PEN TO PAPER

1) Take a moment to reread the passage from Hebrews at the beginning of yesterday's lesson. Then reread the account of the weed in the garden from the start of today's lesson. Are there old injustices that you have "stuffed" within the inner being? It is time to release them to the Lord for His redemption. He can take something awful and turn it into something beautiful. Take five minutes to reduce to writing the things that bind you to yesterday, the wounds that are painful to face, let alone to heal. Record them here:

2) Corrie's words about forgiveness can help us with our despair. Listen to them again: "It is not on our forgiveness any more than on our goodness that the world's healing hinges, but on His. When He tells us to love our enemies, He gives, along with the command, the love itself."[27] Now take the events you have listed above and ask the Lord for the power to be able to forgive. You cannot do it yourself. Ask Him to do it through you. Return to the four steps we have used to walk in forgiveness and go through each event named above with those four steps.

3) Now ask God to take the injustices you have experienced and to turn them into something beautiful for God. Thank Him for His grace and His power to deliver and transform us into His image. End by praising Him, whether doing so is easy or requires work.

Prayer Challenge

Anytime an old injustice comes to mind today, ask God to turn it into a ministry opportunity. Ask God to transform it into a calling to bless and heal. Choose to do good when evil is done. Ask God how you can go *underneath* and *through* any unclean sin against you, so that God may be glorified through your actions.

DAY 4

Forgiveness is not forgetting.

This issue has confused many a believer for many a year. "Forgive and forget . . ." Yet the woman who lost her job due to the manipulations of another can't forget, especially when she has to pay the rent from savings and doesn't have enough to feed the children. Though she chose not to treat the one who wounded her as he deserved, the memory doesn't fade. In fact, it is "in her face" with every bill she receives.

Rev. Dale Lang raised a responsible, other-centered teenaged son. He was standing in the hallway of his high school in Taber, Alberta. A young man in a trench coat entered the school with a hidden rifle and opened fire, killing the lad as he was getting ready for school. Lang went into the school the very next day and stood on the spot where his son was killed, calling people back to the school in the name of his Lord. He refused to accept that despair could destroy the clean work of the school; he refused to allow the death of his teenaged son to destroy his ability to believe in the goodness of God.

But he cannot forget.

There is a famous text that speaks of the hope of the New Testament era. The keeping of the Law of Moses as a basis for the forgiveness of sins was always difficult. The sinful human heart simply could not sustain a steady walk with God that never fell into transgressions (whether by plan or through a slip arising from weariness). In fact, rendering sins as null and void in the sight of God was always expensive—it required the shedding of blood, an animal life for the human one. More than this, God, anticipating the sins of the nation, set apart the family line of Aaron the priest specifically to pray against God's own anger falling on the children of Israel during those times when they would. Yet even Aaron's sons did not treat God as holy and were destroyed for attempting to manipulate the Lord's presence with "strange fire" (Leviticus 8-9 for their ordination; 10:1-7 for the death of two of Aaron's sons).

Generations later, the prophet Jeremiah heard a word from God about a new beginning for His people and for the world. Instead of an outer observance of a legal code, God would do a different kind of work, an inner work of the Spirit which would make the first agreement with His people so obsolete that it would forever thereafter be called "old":

> "Behold the days are coming," declares the LORD, "when I will make a new covenant with the house of Israel and with the house of Judah, not like the covenant which I made with their fathers in the day I took them by the hand to bring them out of the land of Egypt, my covenant which they broke, although I was a husband to them," declares the LORD.
>
> "But this is the covenant which I will make with the house of Israel after those days," declares the LORD, "I will put My law within them, and on their heart I will write it; and I will be their God, and they shall be My people. They will not teach again, each man his neighbor and each man his brother, saying, 'Know the LORD,' for they will all know Me, from the least of them to the greatest of them," declares the LORD, "for I will forgive their iniquity, and their sin I will remember no more." (Jeremiah 31:31-34, NASB)

This word from Hebrew Scripture (the "Old" Testament to Christians) is the hope of the New Testament, the hope that God will work on us from the inside out, instead of us working to please God from the outside in. Here, God stamps His Word on our interior being. Through God's actions (and not merely our failed attempts at human achievement), God Himself makes it possible for us to know Him. It is the last part of 31:34 that gives us such hope. All the sins and transgressions that created a barrier to intimacy between us and God are removed by *God's* decision to choose to forgive.

We quote this text and, longing to emulate the Lord's example, say, "If God forgets, so should we."

Sadly, we have taken a figurative rendering of truth and tried to make it literal. God forgave a lot of sins in biblical history. Yet we know about them. We know about Israel's sin of worshipping the golden calf (though God forgave them through the prayer of Moses in Exodus 32). We know of the adultery of King David and Bathsheba (though they both repented and

God forgave). We know of the sins of the patriarchs, the prophets and the apostles—though God forgave. It is recorded for us in the public chronicle that we have come to call the Bible.

It wasn't forgotten. It was *recorded*—under the inspiration of the same God who chose to "remember their sin no more."

What occurred was that God *did not treat them as their sins deserved*. God chose to mend their ruptured relationship with Him through forgiveness of their sins; then God gave them a new start (though often the consequences of their sins made future life difficult).

To forgive, then, is not to forget.

In fact, it isn't even to trust.

If some employees steal from your cash register you may choose not to prosecute. You may in fact decide to forgive them—and not treat them as their sins deserve. The police will not be called. You will not allow their names to be besmirched by reporting the incident to a local newspaper. You may not even ask for the money to be returned. You may tell them that they will not be charged and they are free to go.

But this doesn't mean that they should immediately be put back on the till. In fact, the incident may cause the company to reassess the way that accounts are monitored, the screening methods of the Human Resources department, and whether those employees would be able to continue at all.

To forgive is not to forget. Rather it is to get to the place in which we choose to accept that someone else has ruined our lives. As Christ did, we no longer hold it to their account, but pay the cost ourselves, trusting that God will redeem our losses in some way that we cannot even begin to imagine. Neil Anderson has developed a succinct summary of what forgiveness is and is not. We would do well to listen to him as we ponder what it means to pray "forgive us our debts as we forgive those who are indebted to us":

> *Forgiveness is not forgetting.* People who try to forget find they cannot. God says He will remember our sins "no more" (see Hebrews 10:17), but God, being omniscient, cannot forget. Remember our sins "no more" means that God will never use the past against us (see Psalm 103:12). Forgetting may be the *result* of forgiveness, but it is never the *means* of forgiveness. When we bring up the past against others,

we are saying we haven't forgiven them.

Forgiveness is a choice, a crisis of the will. Since God requires us to forgive, it is something we can do. But forgiveness is difficult for us because it pulls against our concept of justice. We want revenge for offenses suffered. But we are told never to take our own revenge (see Romans 12:19). You say, "Why should I let them off the hook?" That is precisely the problem. You are still hooked to them, still bound by your past. You will let them off your hook, but they are never off God's. He will deal with them fairly—something we cannot do.

You say, "You don't know how much this person hurt me!" But don't you see, they are still hurting you! How do you stop the pain? You don't forgive someone for their sake; you do it for your sake, so you can be free. Your need to forgive isn't an issue between you and the offender; it's between you and God.

Forgiveness is agreeing to live with the consequences of another person's sin. Forgiveness is costly. You pay the price of the evil you forgive. You're going to live with those consequences whether you want to or not; your only choice is whether you will do so in the bitterness of unforgiveness or the freedom of forgiveness. Jesus took the consequences of your sin upon Himself. All true forgiveness is substitutionary, because no one really forgives without bearing the consequences of the other person's sin. God the Father "made Him who knew no sin to be sin on our behalf, that we might become the righteousness of God in Him" (2 Corinthians 5:21, NASB). Where is the justice? It is the Cross that makes forgiveness legally and morally right: For the death he died, He died to sin, once for all" (Romans 6:10, NKJV).

How do you forgive from your heart? You acknowledge the hurt and the hate. If your forgiveness doesn't visit the emotional core of your life, it will be incomplete. Many feel the pain of interpersonal offenses, but they won't or don't know how to acknowledge it. Let God bring the pain to the surface so He can deal with it. This is where the healing takes place.

Decide that you will bear the burden of their offenses by not using that information against them in the future. This doesn't mean that you must tolerate sin; you must always take a stand against sin.

Don't wait to forgive until you feel like forgiving; you will never get there. Feelings take time to heal after the choice to forgive is made and Satan has lost his place (Ephesians 4:26-27). Freedom is what will be gained, not a feeling.

As you pray, God may bring to mind offending people and experiences you have totally forgotten. Let Him do it even if it is painful. Remember, you are doing this for your sake; God wants you to be free. Don't rationalize or explain the offender's behavior. Forgiveness is dealing with your pain and leaving the other person to God. Positive feelings will follow in time; freeing yourself from the past is the critical issue right now.

Don't say, "Lord, please help me to forgive," because he is already helping you. Don't say, "Lord, I want to forgive," because you are bypassing the hard-core choice to forgive, which is your responsibility. Stay with each person until you are sure you have dealt with all the remembered pain—what they did, how they hurt you, how they made you feel (rejected, unloved, unworthy, dirty).

You are now ready to forgive the people on your list so that you can be free in Christ. Those people no longer have any control over you. For each person on your list, pray aloud:

Lord, I forgive _____ for
_____.[28]

PEN TO PAPER

1) It is now time for us to do justice to this requirement of our Lord. It is time to forgive. You can do this alone. Some will need another they trust to "talk this through." Whether alone or with a godly friend, take a one-hour block of time and find a place in which you will not be interrupted. Spend some time praising God. After settling into His presence, ask God to bring to mind the people you need to forgive. Write their names below. Follow the steps outlined by Anderson and Mylander above. Remember all the detail, and in the presence of God simply say:

"Lord, I forgive _____ for _____. I take them off of my hook and trust them to Yours for whatever will bring grace to their lives. Redeem their lives, even as I trust You to buy back what I have lost through their sin. In Jesus' name. Amen."

PRAYER CHALLENGE

It may be that during your day, you will find yourself remembering something that someone did, even years ago. Refuse to serve the old wound by revisiting it. Rather, anytime an old sin-wound returns to memory, simply say, "Lord, I forgive _____ for what he did. It hurt. I suffered. I will not ask them to pay me back in return. Bless them instead. Thank You for your power to redeem."

DAY 5

God forgives the deepest sins, and uses the memory to call us to new life.

There are some godly people who simply don't believe that God could ever forgive them for the sins they have committed. *The victims of my sin were so kind and unsuspecting*, these people reason. *The losses they suffered were so horrible. The sins committed were so awful, so hurtful. And it is all my fault! I planned it that way! God's forgiveness is for another, not me! God could never use me for His glory without tainting His glory.*

If we were studying Hebrew Scripture, we could turn to the story of King David and Bathsheba, and the way the godly king fell as he gazed upon a woman having a bath on the rooftop next door (one wonders why she bathed on a rooftop next to the king's balcony). Not only did they commit adultery, but David attempted a cover-up with liquor and a ruse. When the cover-up failed, David arranged to murder the faithful husband using the highest offices of the land—the head of the armed forces of the godly nation.

The husband died on the field of battle. David married the widow in an appearance of providing for the aggrieved woman.

It had the sweet savor of gentle compassion to all the world.

It stank in the nostrils of God.

David was confronted by a prophetic word from the seer Nathan.

He could have had Nathan killed too. Instead he repented, turned to the Lord, acknowledged his sin, and entered into a fast, seeking God for the life of the child born of the adulterous union. That child did in fact die.

And then God redeemed, and though David's life was filled with trouble after this foolish action, his fellowship with God was restored, and his calling to lead the nation, though wounded, survived, so that a child from the same union would become a forerunner of the birth of the Messiah.

Adultery.

Worse yet, this was adultery with a loyal friend's wife. The husband had fought beside him when his life was in peril.

A failed cover-up.

Murder in the first degree.

A mask of "righteous" provision for a grieving widow.

Prophetic public denunciation.

And redemption.

What was horrible and awful was redeemed so profoundly that God's provision for our salvation was found in the way he bought back David's and Bathsheba's sin. (See 2 Samuel 11-12 for the whole account. See also the genealogy of our Lord in Matthew 1—especially 1:6—to see that David's second child with Bathsheba was the forebear of Christ, and a forerunner of our hope.)

Perhaps you have committed adultery. Perhaps you've lied to cover your tracks. Maybe you have used your position in the church or the community to mask your awful lifestyle. You may even have committed murder. It is unlikely you have been to the highest corridors of power in the land and used the military to accomplish your dirty work. But even if you have, God is not a stranger to your iniquity. He knows it all. If you don't come clean, God will arrange for it to be revealed in the proper time. He will not be mocked.

And if you repent, God will restore your broken relationship.

The only thing that Jesus can't heal is the cover-up.

So what is covered?

There is a message here. We are to give God even the things we believe can never be forgiven. Don't tell me you can't accept this. Don't be an absolute fool! He commands us to ask. So ask!

"In this manner, therefore, pray: . . . Forgive us our debts . . ." (Matthew 6:9, 12, NKJV).

Perhaps you know the story, but it bears repeating. This fellow had tasted three years of intimate friendship, of sharing the road, of seeing and doing miracles, of even walking on water. The man's name was Simon, son of John. Jesus called him Peter. Better yet, he would have known his name meant "Rocky."

He was the leader of the three and the twelve and would become the cornerstone of the early church. The case could be made that he was Jesus' best friend. And yet, at the Last Supper, these words were spoken of him:

"Simon, Simon, Satan has asked to sift you as wheat. But I have prayed for you, Simon, that your faith may not fail. And when you have turned back, strengthen your brothers" (Luke 22:31-32, NIV).

Once again we see two spirits at work: God's and Satan's. We also see the conviction of our Lord in the power of prayer. He really did pray for Simon. In His prayer ministry for His friend, Jesus "saw" what was coming and how it would try Peter's heart to the bitter edge. He perceived the spiritual warfare over the soul of this leader, God's Spirit and the enemy's vying for his eternal destiny. Jesus sought God's intervention in his life. Peter makes a solemn declaration out of his deep love for his Master and Messiah. "But he replied, 'Lord, I am ready to go with you to prison and to death.' Jesus answered, 'I tell you, Peter, before the rooster crows today, you will deny three times that you know me'" (Luke 22:33-34, NIV).

Shortly after this word of prophecy, Jesus was betrayed by Judas Iscariot in the Garden of Gethsemane. Peter attempted to save the Lord. He picked up a sword and cut off the ear of a man named Malchus. The Lord stopped him, healed the ear, and submitted to the arrest.

Peter *tried* to keep his word. He followed the Lord after his arrest.

Then it happened around a charcoal fire.

Smell has a particular effect upon memory. A fragrance associated with a memory has the effect of "stamping" that memory into the deepest recesses of the mind. Anytime that smell would recur, so would the memory.

In ancient Palestine, almost every meal happened over a charcoal fire.

> The girl at the gate said to Peter, "Aren't you also one of the disciples of that man?"
>
> "No, I am not," answered Peter.
>
> It was cold, so the servants and guards had built a charcoal fire and were standing around it, warming themselves. So Peter went over and stood with them, warming himself. (John 18:17-18, GNT)

Given how he had defended the Lord with a sword and been stopped, perhaps Peter was going "undercover" to seek for some way to save him. He was, after all, right in the courtyard. Meanwhile, Jesus was being tried before Annas and Caiaphas. He was sent from one to the other bound and tied up like a criminal. He likely passed through the courtyard where Peter was attempting to hide.

> Peter was still standing there keeping himself warm. So the others said to him, "Aren't you also one of the disciples of that man?"
>
> But Peter denied it. "No, I am not," he said.
>
> One of the High Priest's slaves, a relative of the man whose ear Peter had cut off, spoke up. "Didn't I see you with him in the garden?" he asked.
>
> Again, Peter said, "No"—and at once a rooster crowed. (John 18:25-27, GNT)

Mark 14:71-72 tells us that he didn't merely deny Him; he denied Him in a fit of rage, so fervently that he swore an oath while he was doing it.

We have learned about the Hebrew mind and the threefold repetition. Something said once was a fact, but it could be altered. Something said twice was a sealed fact that could not be changed. A threefold denial was to deny Him to the uttermost—so profoundly that there would have been no way back.

Peter wept bitterly. He had denied the Lord of glory at His hour of deepest need, after three years of intimate friendship.

It is no wonder that Peter decided to return to his old way of life. Every time someone cooked a meal, he would have caught the fragrance of the charcoal and remembered his shame. Three times a day, every day, walking down every street in every village all around the world, he would smell the charcoal and despair.

He used to be a fisherman, and a good one. He had been called while he was fishing. He had caught a miraculous catch of fish and begged the Lord to leave him because he was an awful sinner (see Luke 5:1-11). Now he *knew* it was true. His sins would not be forgiven. He would just go back to yesterday.

And so he went back. Being the leader he was, he took six other disciples fishing. They caught nothing—that is, until the stranger told them to do what Jesus had said to Peter once before: to throw out his nets for a catch after they came up empty.

There were so very many, like that time before.

And now he smelled the fish and remembered. Once before, in a sinking boat filled with stinking fish, he named his stinking sin to one who was so holy that it scared him (Luke 5:1-11). The Lord had told him that he would no longer catch fish, but *people* that day. And every time he smelled fish he remembered. Listen to what happened:

> The disciple whom Jesus loved said to Peter, "It is the Lord!" When Peter heard that it was the Lord, he wrapped his outer garment around him (for he had taken his clothes off) and jumped into the water. The other disciples came to shore in the boat, pulling the net full of fish. They were not very far from land, about a hundred yards away. When they stepped ashore, they saw *a charcoal fire there with fish on it and some bread.* (John 21:7-9, GNT, emphasis added)

There was that smell of the charcoal fire. There was that smell of the stinking miraculous catch of fish—his calling to catch people. There was the fragrance of the charcoal fire covered by the fragrance of the catch. There was the smell of stinking sin . . .

Then an incredible act of mercy was given to Peter. All the threads of miracle, calling, shame, and redemption come together from the one whose nature it was to forgive, who would call him to proclaim the kingdom by being a "forgiven forgiver." Jesus called him again, this time over a charcoal fire, with a miraculous catch and a call to sacrifice. And this time Peter would know he was loved to the uttermost. It was given three times over that fire, once for each denial.

> After they had eaten, Jesus said to Simon Peter, "Simon, son of John, do you love me more than these others do?"
>
> "Yes, Lord," he answered, "you know that I love you."
>
> Jesus said to him, "Take care of my lambs."
>
> A second time Jesus said to him, "Simon, son of John, do you love me?"
>
> "Yes, Lord," he answered, "you know I love you."
>
> Jesus said to him, "Take care of my sheep."
>
> A third time, Jesus said, "Simon, son of John, do you love me?"
>
> Peter became sad because Jesus asked him the third time, "Do

you love me?" and so he said to him, "Lord, you know everything; you know that I love you."

Jesus said, "Take care of my sheep." . . . Then Jesus said, "Follow me!" (John 21:15-18, 19, GNT)

Peter's denial became a matter of public record. It became the basis for his future ministry. He would be a "forgiven forgiver," one who would proclaim that God was merciful, who could forgive the deepest denial, even denial to the uttermost. God's calling was deeper than the deepest denial. Betsy ten Boom would have said, "There is no hole so deep that God is not the deeper still."

And now every time that Peter would smell a charcoal fire he would remember his shame *and* God's mercy. And every time he ate fish (likely once a day or so), he would remember the threefold call to serve God's people.

His forgiveness became the basis for his future ministry.

And so can yours!

Do not deny the Lord's calling on your life to redeem your sin.

David learned that lesson.

So did Peter.

So must we.

Give God your deepest despair, and let it become the foundation of your calling to "tend my lambs."

PEN TO PAPER

1) Is there sin in your life so deep that you believe that the Lord cannot use you ever again? Confess it to the Lord right now. Ask Him by divine appointment to buy back the broken threads of your despair and to weave them into a magnificent calling that surpasses anything you could ever have imagined. Don't say, "It's impossible." Ask Him to redeem. Use whatever language you can. Let Him redeem.

2) Now ask God to call you afresh. What calling would you ask God for in your highest imagination? Dream big! Ask the Lord to work in your life again and to use your shame as a platform for His grace to be put on display forever. Ask Jesus to pray for you that your faith fail not. And when you have turned again, strengthen your brothers.

Prayer Challenge

One of the principle teachings of the Bible is that God has redeemed our fallen race. Adam's sin meant that there was no part of human life that wasn't touched by human sin—all parts of our being are tainted with the iniquity of our first parents. But Jesus' entrance into the human condition as a human being, born of Mary, means that there is no part of human experience that cannot be redeemed. All of God came into all of humanity. And there is no sin so deep that God is not deeper still. Ask God's Spirit to buy back each sinful inclination. Today, anytime a sinful thought comes to mind, turn back to this prayer, that God would use this sinful attitude, practice, or inclination as a platform for His goodness.

DAY 6

A different kind of "debt."

We have been journeying through the Lord's teaching on the forgiveness of our sins. We have also been examining what it means to forgive others the wrongs that they have done to us. It is clear that Jesus was teaching us about what we owe others. In fact, there are several words used to send the message about what "sin" is. Different renderings of the prayer focus on what it means to pray this prayer. The three most common words are "debts," "trespasses," and "sins." They each hold a slightly different nuance.

To "trespass" is to cross ground that doesn't belong to us, or that we have no right to cross. This involves a deliberate act of recognizing that someone else's space is there and it doesn't belong to us. We cross it just the same, violating someone else's domain. Take a moment and think through what it means to do this. Whose ground have you crossed? Name it and confess this to God.

To "sin" means "miss the mark" or to "fall short." The term originally came from archery. To fail to hit the target was to "sin." This is when we attempt to live for God but fail to achieve the Lord's righteous standard of living. This means that we simply are unable to do what God would have us do, even though we tried. It includes not only crossing someone's territory, but simply failing to be focused on goodness. It includes the things we have done and the things we have failed to do. Take a moment and reflect on what it means to "miss the mark" in your own life. Confess whatever comes to mind and offer this to God.

To be "indebted" is to owe another. This may refer to sinning against someone, and owing him a debt because your actions cost that person something. But the word doesn't have to refer to a sinful act. There can be people to which we simply owe a debt. The following story illustrates the principle.

Perhaps you have seen the famous etching called "Praying Hands" by Albrecht Dürer. There is a famous story behind the work of art. Around the year 1490 there were two struggling artists named Albrecht Dürer and Franz Knigstein. They were good friends who were both poor and had to work to sustain themselves. They were also attempting to train as artists in their spare time after working long hours doing manual labor. The result was that they simply couldn't do both.

In desperation, the two friends decided to cast lots to decide which one of them should carry on doing manual labor. The other would go on to develop as an artist, and then they would reverse roles, with the new artist supporting the one who had worked. As it turned out, Albrecht won the toss, and Franz took up extra work to support the two of them. The first went off to spend time with famous artists and to hone his skills in the hope of being able to return and help his friend.

In time, Albrecht returned to spell off his friend. He had become a successful artist and could now afford to send his friend to school. But to his horror, Albrecht discovered that the heavy manual labor had ruined his friend's hands forever. Franz would never become an artist now. What he had done was forfeit his future out of loyalty to his friend.

One day, Albrecht found Franz on his knees. His hands were clasped in prayer, gnarled yet offered to God in loving sacrifice. Hurriedly, Dürer sketched the moment and produced the etching that generations have come to admire as the "Praying Hands."

They were hands of love, hands of sacrifice—and they "speak" to us of the debt of love and the call to prayer.

There was no sin issue between these two friends, yet Albrecht "owed" Knigstein and would be indebted to him for the remainder of his life.

"Forgive us our debts" may have nothing to do with sin at all. In fact, it may have everything to do with loving sacrifice by others so that we might succeed. Mothers and fathers sacrifice for their sons and daughters. Unknown soldiers fought and died so that we might have our freedom. Philanthropists have given so that untold and unknown thousands might receive mercy through medical advances, fellowships for poor students, and work opportunities. Take some time now and reflect on what you owe. Commit it to writing below and thank God for the sacrifices of those who gave for your hope.

Now reflect on this passage from Scripture:

A Pharisee invited Jesus to have dinner with him, and Jesus went to his house and sat down to eat. In that town was a woman who lived a sinful life. She heard that Jesus was eating in the Pharisee's house, so she brought an alabaster jar full of perfume and stood behind Jesus, by his feet, crying and wetting his feet with her tears. Then she dried his feet with her hair, kissed them, and poured the perfume on them. When the Pharisee saw this, he said to himself, "If this man really were a prophet, he would know who this woman is who is touching him; he would know what kind of sinful life she lives!"

Jesus spoke up and said to him, "Simon, I have something to tell you."

"Yes, Teacher," he said, "tell me."

"There were two men who owed money to a moneylender," Jesus began. "One owed him five hundred silver coins and the other owed him fifty. Neither of them could pay him back, so he canceled the debts of both. Which one, then, will love him more?"

"I suppose," answered Simon, "that it would be the one who was forgiven more."

"You are right," said Jesus. Then he turned to the woman and said to Simon, "Do you see this woman? I came into your home, and you gave me no water for my feet, but she has washed my feet with her tears and dried them with her hair. You did not welcome me with a kiss, but she has not stopped kissing my feet since I came. You provided no olive oil for my head, but she has covered my feet with perfume. I tell you then, the great love she has shown proves that her many sins have been forgiven. But whoever has been forgiven little shows only a little love."

Then Jesus said to the woman, "Your sins are forgiven."

The others sitting at the table began to say to themselves, "Who is this, who even forgives sins?"

But Jesus said to the woman, "Your faith has saved you; go in peace." (Luke 7:36-50, GNT)

PEN TO PAPER

1) Go back and reread the text above. Just be still before it and write down your impressions—thoughts, words, questions, ideas. What is the account saying?

2) Now go back and read it aloud again—listen. Who are you in the account? Simon, the woman, our Lord, or an observer? What is your perspective on what happened?

3) Record now what you "feel" as you read the text.

4) End your time by reflecting on what you owe. And thank God.

PRAYER CHALLENGE

Note today when you receive something where someone else has labored. Every time you become aware that you have received, thank God.

DAY 7

Living forgiveness as a lifestyle . . .

Martin Luther was the one who reclaimed a truth which had long lain fallow on the field. By teaching Paul's Epistle to the Romans, he realized that he could never justify himself before God. His sins were too numerous to count. It was a great relief to him to discover that God was the one who would justify him—all he had to do was to accept the sacrifice of Christ by faith. And so Luther taught "justification by faith," the release of the consequences of our sins in God's sight. Of course, this is what it means to be a "forgiven forgiver."

Luther went on to remember Paul's emphasis on baptism—that our old body of sin is killed on the cross and buried in our baptism. The thought was that we "drown the old man" in baptism.

Still Luther found that though he took his sins to Christ regularly, they kept returning to his heart and mind. He is quoted as saying, "It's true we drown the old man in baptism—but he swims! He swims!"

Isn't that our experience as well? We confess a sin and discover ourselves in the same one the next day. Or we are sinned against and do not want to forgive again. Our sense of justice is appalled that we should be the ones to suffer and be forced to bear the whole thing over again.

This one strikes close to home. Forgiving isn't something I do easily. In fact, it is something I don't really want to do, because it costs to forgive. It costs when someone hurts me or someone I love, and it doesn't seem fair.

I remember a time like this. Someone was saying things about me that simply weren't true, and it hurt! Every time an attempt was made to try and mend the damage it got worse. The worst thing about it all was not what people were saying. It was the interior battle—the interior rage, the sense of wrongness surrounding every detail, spilling over into everything else, including family life. The hardest part was the sense of absolute helplessness to be able to repair the damage; there was also the shameful sense within that

I didn't want to forgive. Rather, I wanted vindication!

One night I found I couldn't sleep. My mind was racing, justifying my actions, fearing the next meeting to attempt to iron things out, expecting failure instead of success. I didn't know where to turn. And so I cried out to the Lord to show me something from His Word that would heal my soul. I found myself wandering downstairs to my home library. There I picked up a copy of an old book that had been given to me by a godly, prayerful, gentle man. The book was dog-eared, underlined, and written over all throughout. The title was *Love, Acceptance and Forgiveness* by Jerry Cook. I couldn't put the thing down. Page after page spoke of the need to forgive, even if the offenders didn't "get it." Conviction rose within my deepest heart that this was what I needed to do—yet I longed for a word from the Bible.

Then Cook quoted this text:

> If you love those who love you, what credit is that to you? For even sinners love those who love them. If you do good to those who do good to you, what credit is that to you? For even sinners do the same. If you lend to those from whom you expect to receive, what credit is that to you? Even sinners lend to sinners in order to receive back the same amount.
>
> But love your enemies, and do good, and lend, expecting nothing in return; and your reward will be great, and you will be sons of the Most High; for He Himself is kind to ungrateful and evil men. Be merciful, just as your Father is merciful. Do not judge and you will not be judged; and do not condemn, and you will not be condemned; pardon and you will be pardoned.
>
> Give, and it will be given to you. They will pour into your lap a good measure—pressed down, shaken together, and running over. For by your standard of measure it will be measured to you in return. (Luke 6:32-36, NASB)

Here again we see the reciprocal focus of this line of the Lord's Prayer. "Forgive us as we forgive others." But this text takes it a step further. To forgive is to deal with past offenses and to put them into God's hands. Here, Jesus tells us to adopt a lifestyle of expecting nothing at all, even when a return is due.

In other words, undercut the need to forgive by expecting nothing! If we expect nothing, when someone sins against us, we won't need to forgive, because nothing was owed to us in the first place.

This led to an interior battle. I wanted to expect something in return! Life works that way. If kindness is offered, we expect kindness in return. If grace is offered, we expect a gracious response.

James Houston describes something of this battle within:

> We will find prayer a dangerous experience if we are unwilling to change. To pray is rather like joining an underground resistance movement in an enemy-occupied country. We fight back in prayer to overthrow the kingdom of darkness with the light of the gospel.
>
> The problem is that the darkness is not simply all around us, but inside us too. So prayer becomes a weapon that can painfully turn in on us. Prayer opposes everything in us that is false, evil and sinful. Prayer attacks all the indifference and moral complacency, all the conceit and selfishness within us. Prayer assaults our spiritual apathy and dryness. Because of this, prayer is constantly the means we can use to reassess our values and objectives before God.
>
> Through prayer, we receive Christ's grace to question ourselves, to bring our lives up to the line of his teaching. Prayer changes us more than we would expect, or want. Accepting this is also the grace of Christ in us.[29]

That word to "expect nothing in return" worked its way into my soul. When I went to meet the one who was speaking things about me that I never said, it served as an anchor to the soul. I was able to listen and receive. In time I was able to forgive.

The goal of this line of the Lord's Prayer is that our lives are kingdom lives, living our forgiveness even before it is needed.

PEN TO PAPER

1) Go back and read the gospel passage above. When you get to the part in which Jesus begins to give us commands about how we should live

("But love . . ."), underline each command. Take some time to put those commands into your own words here:

2) How does this word affect you? Are there those who are a constant source of trouble for you? What would Christ have you do with them?

3) Now reread the section from James Houston. Do you find darkness within? What would God have you do in the practice of prayer? Are there any commitments that come to you from this material? How would God have you think, live, and believe?

4) Now the breadth of the meaning of this line of the prayer is before you. Paraphrase what this line has come to mean to you after seven days of living with this prayer.

PRAYER CHALLENGE

Someone will sin against you today, and you will want to retaliate in some sense of the word, whether by thought, word, or deed. Commit the following to memory and attempt to live this thought out when you have been wounded by the actions of another: "But love your enemies, and do good, and lend, expecting nothing in return; and your reward will be great, and you will be sons of the Most High; for He Himself is kind to ungrateful and evil men" (Luke 6:35, NASB).

Week Seven

ENGAGE THE ENEMY

"And Do Not Lead Us into Temptation . . ."

DAY 1

Jesus believed not only in "evil" but in an "evil one," and so must we.

"Jesus was called to throw himself on the wheel of world history, so that, even though it crushed him, it might start to turn in the opposite direction."
—Albert Schweitzer

W e have been journeying through the Lord's Prayer, attempting to understand what Jesus meant by the words and phrases of His praying. Now we come face-to-face with our Lord's understanding of temptation, sin, evil, and the evil one.

To begin our time, let's pray the prayer as we have begun to understand it anew. To assist you in your praying, printed below is the translation that appears in the Good News Bible. Pray this slowly and reverently; insert your thoughts and hopes as you now understand this prayer. Pray it aloud and then sit quietly, letting its meaning enter into your thinking and believing. Ponder any fresh insight that you gather from this rendering.

> Our Father in heaven:
> may Your name be honored;
> may Your kingdom come;
> may Your will be done on earth as it is in heaven.
> Give us today the food we need.
> Forgive us the wrongs we have done
> as we forgive the wrongs that others have done to us.
> Do not bring us to hard testing, but keep us safe from the Evil One.
> [For Yours is the kingdom, and the power and the glory for ever, Amen.]
> (Matthew 6:5-13, GNT)

Does this translation help you pray the prayer more effectively? How does it help you? Record that here:

This translation captures the essence of the intent of the prayer when it comes to facing the tempter and his power: "Do not bring us to hard testing, but keep us safe from the Evil One."

We have been living with the idea that our Lord did not deal with "evil" in the abstract. To pray for the kingdom to come was to pray for the powers of evil to be cast out. But even a cursory reading of the gospels makes clear that our Lord, the apostles, and the early church did in fact believe in the existence of not only evil, but an "evil one" called the devil, Satan, the Accuser, and the tempter (among other titles). We have also seen that many of the parables of the kingdom and Jesus' clear teaching of the kingdom in fact refer to this reality as their bedrock assumption. There is a Holy Spirit associated with God's kingdom rule and there is an unclean spirit, the devil, associated with the false rule of the world; his presence is to be cast out.

When Jesus was accused of casting out demons by Beelzebub, the ruler of demons, He replied that kingdoms divided against themselves do not stand (i.e., Beelzebub would be foolish to disperse power to work against his own purposes). He said this: "But if I cast out demons by the Spirit of God, surely the kingdom of God has come upon you" (Matthew 12:27, NKJV).

In teaching His famous parables of the kingdom, Jesus spoke of a sower and the seed. The seed was the Word of God sown into the hearts of people. In interpreting the passage, our Lord made clear that there was another power at work, opposing the work of God's Word and the advance of His kingdom: "Therefore hear the parable of the sower: When anyone hears the word of the kingdom, and does not understand it, then the wicked one comes and snatches away what was sown in his heart. This is he who received seed by the wayside" (Matthew 13:18-19, NKJV).

He also spoke of a world in which a good farmer sowed good seed in good ground, but of an enemy who sowed bad seed among the good. Here is how our Lord explained that teaching:

He who sows good seed is the Son of Man. The field is the world,

the good seeds are the sons of the kingdom, but the tares are the
sons of the wicked one. The enemy who sowed them is the devil,
the harvest is the end of the age and the reapers are the angels.
(Matthew 13:37-39, NKJV)

Certainly the account of the temptation of our Lord makes clear that
He was utterly convinced of supernatural reality—the Holy Spirit, heaven's
power, angels, and demons.

When He had been baptized, Jesus came up immediately from the
water; and behold, the heavens were opened to Him, and He saw
the Spirit of God descending like a dove and alighting upon Him.
. . . Then Jesus was led up by the Spirit into the wilderness to be
tempted by the devil. . . .
Then the devil left him, and behold, angels came and ministered
to Him. (Matthew 3:16-17; 4:1, 11, NKJV)

When Jesus came to the conviction that it was time for Him to die for
our salvation, He and the crowd surrounding Him at the time were given a
gift—a powerful voice from heaven indicating that God would glorify His
name through Jesus' death. As we saw on Day 7 of Week 2 of this adventure,
Jesus then spoke an interpretive word to the crowd who heard the voice: "Jesus
answered and said, 'This voice did not come because of Me, but for your sake.
Now is the judgment of this world; now *the ruler of this world will be cast out.*
And I, if I am lifted up from the earth will draw all peoples to Myself'" (John
12:30-32, NKJV, emphasis added).

As was stated in Weeks 2 and 3, by now it must be clear that to pray this
prayer is to enter into the field of battle, to partner with God in reclaiming
our fallen world, wresting it away from the false ruler of darkness and
returning it to God the rightful King. The enemy's weapons are hatred, strife,
evil, despair—anything that produces distraction from God's purposes. The
weapons of the believer focus on God's kingdom, are empowered by God's
Spirit, and are made active through the prayer ministry of the church. They
are such things as loving, serving, praying, helping, healing, obeying God's
inner promptings, and reclaiming goodness in the midst of despair. According

to the apostle Paul, the main weapon in the battle is "truth," both the truth of the gospel and Jesus Christ who Himself is the truth (see Ephesians 6:14 and John 14:6).

This is a kingdom of God/kingdom of Satan battle, and Christ "set the future into motion." He turned death inside out and started to turn the wheels of history in the opposite direction when He rose from the dead. Because He did that as a human, He began to reverse the fall of man with the rising of the first new man (setting up a rising from the dead for all who turn to Him). Jesus began this process by entering the human stream as a second (and last) Adam, reclaiming from all false rule and rulers, everything lost through the fall (and subsequent death) of the first Adam. Paul summarizes this teaching in his first letter to the Corinthians:

> But now Christ is risen from the dead. . . . For since by a man came death, by Man also came the resurrection of the dead. For as in Adam all die, even so in Christ all shall be made alive. But each one in his own order: Christ the firstfruits, afterward those who are Christ's at His coming. Then comes the end, when He delivers *the kingdom* to God the Father, when He puts an end to all rule and all authority and power. For He must reign until He has put all his enemies under his feet. (1 Corinthians 15:20-25, NKJV, emphasis added)

When we began praying this prayer, we invoked the power of God to deliver us from bondage. We upheld His name as hallowed and immediately prayed for the power of God's kingdom rule to overtake and vanquish the evil found on earth. What is now more than abundantly clear is that God is working *through our praying* to cast out all evil, all wicked influence, and even the evil one himself in order to replace all of these with His own benevolent rule of justice, grace, mercy, and peace. By praying "your kingdom come," we declared war on the forces of darkness and allied ourselves with God. Now it is important for us to recognize that in this fallen world, evil is real because there is an evil one. To reclaim this fallen world, we need to be guided—and guided through tests and trials that will threaten our walk with God. Hence the next line of the prayer: "Lead us not into temptation, but deliver us from the evil one . . ."

PEN TO PAPER

1) There are really two realities found in this next line of the prayer. The first is that God is leading us—and He is doing so in a world that is utterly fallen, filled with sorrow, sin, and death. The second is that there is an enemy opposed to the work of God who has a personality and a plan to destroy us, and who has already lost the decisive battle for the dominion of the planet. Everything that formerly belonged to him began to be reclaimed for God through the resurrection of Christ. Take a moment now and record a time when you sensed that you were guided, led by God.

2) Now reflect on a time when you were convinced that you were being led by God, but encountered "interference" that seemed to arise out of nowhere. What did you do when this occurred? Did it occur to you that the "evil one" was attacking, attempting to prevent your clean walk with God? Why or why not?

3) Jesus believed in the supernatural realm. The prayer assumes this reality as basic to the fabric of the universe. Pray to understand that this is reality, and not some mere human construct to give meaning to meaninglessness. Then pray for God's solution to this—the infilling of the human heart with all the powers of heaven—His Holy Spirit. Ask to be baptized (immersed) in His very nature. God will use this to defend you and lead you.

PRAYER CHALLENGE

As you go through the day today, take the GNT translation of the line we are studying with you: "Do not bring us to hard testing, but keep us safe from the Evil One." Repeat it anytime you sense distraction from God's purposes or a temptation to sin or despair. Know that God is with you, even during times of severe testing, and that He can bring release to us by guiding us through His Word and Spirit.

DAY 2

God leads us into Christ, who was led into temptation for us, so that we can experience God's deliverance.

Perhaps the hardest part of the prayer of our Lord to understand is the phrase that is rendered as follows: "Lead us not into temptation . . ."

Now why would God lead anyone into temptation? Is He not the God who delivers us from it? Doesn't the Bible tell us that God tempts no one? "Let no one say when he is tempted, 'I am being tempted by God'; for God cannot be tempted by evil, and He Himself does not tempt anyone" (James 1:13, NASB).

Many are the explanations, and none of them are entirely satisfactory. Some writers simply choose not to deal with the specific language of the prayer, but to move on to the different kinds of temptations that one faces; they choose not to grapple with the reality that Jesus Himself was led *into* temptation by none other than the Spirit of God. Having received the empowerment of the Spirit of God at His baptism, He experienced being led by the same Spirit into severe trial: "Then Jesus was led up by the Spirit into the wilderness to be tempted by the devil" (Matthew 4:1, NASB).

The language of Mark's gospel is very strong, implying that Jesus was compelled, required to enter into Satanic confrontation (with the aid of angels throughout the trial): "And immediately the Spirit *impelled* Him to go out into the wilderness. And He was in the wilderness forty days being tempted by Satan; and He was with the wild beasts and the angels were ministering to Him" (Mark 1:12-13, NASB, emphasis added).

Perhaps the best clue lies in understanding the ministry of the Spirit, and the fall of humanity. The ministry of the Spirit began afresh in Jesus and continued in the outpouring of the Spirit on the church at Pentecost. Having received the anointing of the Spirit at His baptism (power for His ministry), the powers of the next age, Jesus was enabled to enter into His Messianic mission to retake the planet from the usurper who had stolen it away from our first parents.

This mission then was unique to Christ alone.

Jesus' experience of being "led into temptation" cannot be ours—at least not in the singular way that Jesus' purpose required. Rather, He experienced being led into the presence of the tempter as "the Primordial Man"—the Second Adam, to reclaim what had been lost by the first. He was led into that battle so that He could obtain His first victory against the false ruler of this world. All this was so that we would not have to be taken there and suffer utter defeat!

The temptation of our Lord was specific to Jesus' calling; Jesus' anointing with the Holy Spirit was to equip Him to encounter and defeat the false spirit-power of Satan's kingdom forever. Once again we have God's kingdom versus the devil's rule, the Holy Spirit against the false spirit. Here the Spirit of God was given to *lead* Jesus, and in the process He encountered and entered into His unique mission—to confront and defeat Satan and his control of our fallen world. Because Jesus did this, we are enabled to pray that we not have to face what He did.

Bonhoeffer goes so far as to indicate that there are only two temptations in the Bible—the temptation of our first parents and the temptation of Christ. The first temptation was a disaster for our race, the second was our salvation:

> As in Adam's temptation all flesh fell, so in the temptation of Jesus Christ all flesh has been snatched away from the power of Satan. For Jesus Christ wore our flesh, he suffered our temptation, and he won the victory from it. Thus today we all wear the flesh which in Jesus Christ vanquished Satan. Both our flesh and we have conquered in the temptation of Jesus. Because Christ was tempted and overcame, we can pray: Lead us not into temptation. For the temptation has already come and been conquered. He did it in our stead.[30]

Bonhoeffer's thesis is that when we are enticed to sin, it is the "Adam in us" that is exposed to sin; the result is that we fail "in Adam." When the enemy attacks us as Christian believers, he does so to attack the Lord Jesus in us, but loses every battle when the believer finds his or her identity "in Christ," in who Christ is. When we sin, our old nature is exposed—Satan's attack is revealed, and God is glorified in that we are shown how we need to turn to our Redeemer, to "throw ourselves upon the Word of God." When we have victory, it is only because we are already "in Christ" in the first place. In either case believers are thrown upon not their own resources but God's Word, which calls us back to life in Christ. Thus all temptation loses its ultimate power. God is always the victor. We are drawn either (1) to a need for the grace of Christ due to our fall or (2) to rejoice because we have received a victory over sin because we were in Christ.

The center of this petition, then, while it includes the battle with temptation to sin, centers on the prayer for us to be *led* and *delivered*; we are led by the Lord and we experience victory against the forces of darkness. "Lead us . . . and deliver us from the evil one."

While we face temptation in a fallen world, we do so as those who have a Redeemer, a Victor who came that we might be empowered to face the things that destroy, and find our hope in Him. Insomuch as we are in Christ, His power flows to our aid. Inasmuch as we are "full of ourselves," He cannot aid us, for our resources come to an end. There is a good word in Hebrews that speaks of how Christ comes to help us.

> Seeing then that we have a great High Priest who has passed through the heavens, Jesus, the Son of God, let us hold fast our confession. For we do not have a High Priest who cannot sympathize with our weaknesses, but *he was in all points tempted as we are, yet without sin*. Let us therefore come boldly to the throne of grace that we may obtain mercy and find grace to help in time of need. (Hebrews 4:14-16, NKJV, emphasis added)

The point of all prayer is *relationship* with God. Even when we face the tempter's power, it is possible to discover that we are driven toward the Lord who would fill us with His power. We can identify with His mission. In the midst of that identification, we can receive "mercy and . . . find grace to help in time of need."

PEN TO PAPER

1) Take a moment and reflect on what it means to be "in Christ." Record below what it means to be so identified with Jesus that we think His

thoughts after Him, sense His life flowing with ours, and discover His power when confronted with a temptation.

2) Reread Bonhoeffer's words above. What do they mean to you? Paraphrase his main point here.

3) Pray this line of the prayer with a comma inserted to clarify the intent:
   a. "Lead us, not into temptation, but *deliver* us from the evil one . . ."

   b. Repeat it several times until you find yourself thinking of the specific temptations that come against your clean walk with God. Pray for release from satanic attack.

   c. Then render thanks to God.

Prayer Challenge

You will be tempted today. The greatest temptation is not merely to cross a line that we know we should not cross. The greatest temptation is to rely on ourselves alone as we face the tempter's challenge to cross that line.

When tempted, remember the word from Hebrews that is addressed to us when we are needy and helpless: "Let us therefore come boldly to the throne of grace, that we may obtain mercy and find grace to help in time of need" (Hebrews 4:16, NKJV).

Commit this text to memory, and turn to Christ for grace and mercy to remain "in Him" rather than to be distracted out of Him. Ask Him to deliver you from evil, knowing His power to do it, each time a temptation comes to you.

DAY 3

Tempted in all points, the Risen Christ can help us by His Spirit's leading us to the Word.

Perhaps one of the most important truths to know is that to feel tempted is *not* to be guilty of sinning. In fact, the closer our walk with God is, the more frequent and the sharper the temptations will be. It is better to want to do evil but not do it, than to meet some temptation unawares, have no resistance, and stumble into sin without putting up a fight! Jesus was tempted sharply and had an occult experience *right in the middle of seeking God in a holy fast* (Satan appeared to Him and asked Jesus to worship him)— yet He had no sin. He simply didn't do the evil that was offered to Him. Still, He had to deal with the temptations on a regular basis, even as we do.

Richard Foster gives sound advice that at first reading sounds unusual:

> We should learn to pray, even while we are dwelling on evil. Perhaps we are waging an interior battle over anger, or lust, or pride, or greed or ambition. We need not isolate these things from prayer. Instead we talk to God about what is going on inside that we know displeases him. We lift even our disobedience into the arms of the Father; he is strong enough to carry the weight. Sin, to be sure, separates us from God, but trying to hide our sin separates us all the more.[31]

The point is the same as has been given throughout this resource. God wants a *relationship with us.* This means that we have need to speak to Him, *even in the middle of sharp temptation,* in difficult circumstances, and in those times when we are contemplating doing something awful. The only way to access the resources of heaven in our fight against sin is to speak with the Lord in the middle of the fray. Jesus did this. He was in constant communication with the Father. And God gave Him what was needed to stand His ground through His entire life.

Now let's focus on what our Lord did when He was sorely tempted. Yesterday we heard the writer of Hebrews tell us that He was tempted in all points of life, yet He lived His life without sin. We are given a window into this in the account of the temptation. There have been several times we have listened to this text in this resource (most noticeably in Week 3, Day 3). However, we haven't examined the *nature* of the temptations of our Lord (note that there are two spirits in this material and the unclean spirit speaks of his "kingdoms"). Let's reexamine that text now:

> As soon as Jesus was baptized, he went up out of the water.
>
> At that moment heaven was opened, and he saw the Spirit of God descending like a dove and lighting on him. And a voice from heaven said, "This is my Son, whom I love; with him I am well pleased."
>
> Then Jesus was led by the Spirit into the desert to be tempted by the devil. After fasting forty days and forty nights, he was hungry. The tempter came to him and said, "If you are the Son of God, tell these stones to become bread."
>
> Jesus answered, "It is written: 'Man does not live on bread alone, but on every word that comes from the mouth of God.'"
>
> Then the devil took him to the holy city and had him stand on the highest point of the temple. "If you are the Son of God," he said, "throw yourself down. For it is written:
>
> "'He will command his angels concerning you,
>
> and they will lift you up in their hands,
>
> so that you will not strike your foot against a stone.'"
>
> Jesus answered him, "It is also written: 'Do not put the Lord your God to the test.'"
>
> Again the devil took him to a very high mountain and showed him all the kingdoms of the world and their splendor. "All this I will give you," he said, "if you will bow down and worship me."
>
> Jesus said to him, "Away from me, Satan! For it is written: 'Worship the Lord your God, and serve him only.'"
>
> Then the devil left him, and angels came and attended him. (Matthew 3:16-4:11, NIV)

There are several things to note about this passage:

The first is that Jesus *received the Spirit of God* to empower His ministry (He was already born of the Spirit directly through His virginal conception), *and was driven to face the accuser.* To be filled with the Spirit does not mean that we will never be troubled by temptation again. In fact, it may mean exactly the opposite. As we enter into Jesus' ministry (we do not have a ministry of our own—we simply enter into what God wants done in Christ), we will also, like Him, have to face the enemy of our souls, attempting to do to us what he tried to do to Christ—to cause us to act apart from the Lord, and only with our own resources.

Secondly, note that the point of the attack was the point of the revelation! Jesus was given a magnificent word that God was pleased and that He was the much loved Son. With this word of assurance given to Him, the enemy attacked Christ by saying, "*If* you are the Son, *prove* it!" When the enemy of our souls attacks, he will take on the things that are precious. He wants to destroy *the relationship* that God is building with us.

Thirdly, Christ was tempted three times (i.e., tempted to the uttermost), and in three different ways:

1) He was attacked at the very most basic level—*physically.* He had endured a forty-day fast. He had a legitimate need to eat. The enemy attempted to compel Jesus to produce food from rocks to satisfy His needs apart from God's leading.

2) He was attacked at the level of *the soul* (the emotions, mental faculties, and the will). The devil asked Jesus to do something that God would not endorse in order to *make God prove Himself,* on Satan's terms! He even quotes a Scripture text to make this sound biblical (isolated texts can seem to point to a thing to do, but they must be weighed against all Scripture principles—God never commanded anyone to attempt suicide to test out whether one could be saved by angels).

3) He was attacked at the level of *the spirit* (the intersection point in every person for heaven's influence to be brought to bear). Here, the devil threw off all pretense. He revealed who he was and showed Jesus everything he had the power to offer (all *the kingdoms* of the world and their glory) in order to obtain the worship of the Second Adam.

Christ was tempted in all points like us, yet without sin. He was tempted (1) physically, (2) emotionally, and (3) spiritually. We will be tested at all three levels as well.

There was one consistent defense that our Lord used. Filled with the Holy Spirit's power, confronted by the false spirit's power, He quoted the Spirit-inspired Scripture, relying on the Word. (From the Bible we know that Jesus' mind was saturated with biblical truth.) It is striking to notice that He didn't merely rely on the Word in His thinking alone. He quite literally "spoke it aloud," addressing the area of temptation and speaking directly to the tempter about it, using Scripture as His guide to throwing off satanic attack.

Notice that He had been (1) filled with *the Spirit* and He used (2) *the Word*. This was done (3) in the context of *praying against the temptation of an evil spirit*. Both of these together—the leading of the Spirit and the power of the Word—come together to direct us in our battle with temptation and the evil one, especially in the context of prayer. They are never to be separated. The apostle understood this when writing of dealing with satanic attack: "And take the helmet of salvation and *the sword of the Spirit*, which is *the Word of God, praying* always with all prayer and supplication *in the Spirit*" (Ephesians 6:17-18, NKJV, emphasis added).

In order to succeed against the powers of darkness we will need an attitude of reverence toward the Word of God. We must make a plan to learn it, read it, memorize it, and when confronted by any trial from the tempter to separate us from our relationship with God, to speak the Word aloud in our praying to defeat the influence of evil. As we immerse ourselves in the Word, the Spirit of God will direct us into *speaking it* against the temptations we encounter.

PEN TO PAPER

1) There is much to consider here. Reread Richard Foster's comments above. Do you speak to the Lord when you are contemplating doing something wrong?

2) Does it help you to know that sinless, perfect Jesus, the Son of God and

God the Son, had an occult experience while seeking the Father's will? What does this say about temptation and when it can occur? What are we to do when we are doing something godly and find ourselves attacked?

3) Think for a moment now of how you specifically are tempted. Jesus' method was to quote a Scripture passage that directed Him (and rebuked the attacker) into the right course—back into fellowship with God. Jesus used three Scriptures to keep Himself rooted in His relationship with God. Commit these three to memory, and when you sense a distraction away from the Lord, quote each one.
   a. Physical temptation: "Man does not live on bread alone, but on every word that comes from the mouth of God" (Matthew 4:4, NIV).
   b. Emotional temptation: "Do not put the Lord your God to the test" (Matthew 4:7, NIV).
   c. Spiritual temptation: "Worship the Lord your God, and serve him only" (Matthew 4:10, NIV).

PRAYER CHALLENGE

Sometime today, perhaps at lunch or as you are preparing for bed, pray the Lord's Prayer as you now understand it. Give a season of time (three to five minutes) to each of the five movements that we have studied, until you sense you have completed this.

DAY 4

We can escape the tempter's power with Jesus' power and a plan.

There is a tempter, and there is the tempted.

A little better than two hundred years ago, four men stood atop a grassy knoll overlooking the North Atlantic. They saw a ship's light glowing through the stormy night sky. One man paced back and forth, leading a horse with a lighted lantern tied to its nodding chin. Soon, a short distance at sea, the vessel would undergo shipwreck and be pounded to pieces by the roaring waves, losing life and cargo to the deep—or to the scavengers.

You see, the four men would go out when the storm had passed and salvage what was left of the ship—this was how they made their living. They lived at Nags Head—a village not too far from Cape Hatteras, North Carolina; and they had a plan to destroy cargo vessels so that they could plunder them. Not far from that spot there is an island that runs up and down the coast, forming a protective barrier against the sea. This underwater shelf of sandy dunes, the Diamond Shoals, has been nicknamed "the graveyard of the Atlantic." The rotting remains of at least 2,300 ships can be found trapped among those shoals—most of them trapped by accident. Some of them were brought there by the treachery of four men and a horse.

Listen to Charles Durnham's description of their treachery:

> With a lighted lantern fastened to the head of an old nag of a horse, the men of Nags Head . . . went out on stormy nights to draw ships onto Diamond Shoals. On a promontory overlooking the ocean, the horse was led back and forth, up and down. And often, on the seaward side of Diamond Shoals, a ship's pilot, standing at the helm, searching for a passage up the coast, would see the bobbing light and take it for the stern light of a ship that had found safe

passage. The helmsman would spin the wheel and follow. Within minutes the ship was aground on the shoals. If there was time the crew took to the lifeboats. If there was not time, it was all the same to the wreckers.

Next morning, the wreckers came out in dories to inspect their latest prize. With luck there would be ship's timber for houses, new utensils and dishes, perhaps even silver-plate for their home and money for their purses. It was a profitable business. Even now visitors to Nags Head will see old houses built and furnished with plunder taken by the wreckers so long ago.[32]

The tempter has a plan.

His desire is to bring us to shipwreck.

His desire is to plunder what is ours for his own purposes, using our legitimate needs and desires to draw us out of safety and into his trap. He cares not whether we live or whether we die. His desire is our ruin.

We need to know that his plan is for our ruin in order to plunder us.

We need a plan as well.

We need to be aware of his principal tools and make a plan to come through to victory. There is wise counsel from a companion of our Lord on this matter—the apostle John has written about the three areas of temptation we face and of how to overcome them.

> Do not love the world or the things in the world. If anyone loves the world, the love of the Father is not in him. For all that is in the world, the lust of the flesh, the lust of the eyes, and the pride of life—is not of the Father, but is of the world. And the world is passing away, and the lust with it; but he who does the will of God abides forever. (1 John 2:15-17, NKJV)

Notice that the apostle writes about our need to love. We either love God or love something else. We have to decide that our love will be focused on God and the things God loves. He also speaks of lust. Lust and love are interrelated possibilities; they "push the same buttons" in our being, but they do so from different sources and have entirely different outcomes.

Though both appear as a guiding light, their outcomes are quite different: the first is a lighthouse that guides us to safety while the second is the horse of Nags Head, with its promise of freedom, and the outcome of the shipwreck of our souls.

Love (God-honoring love) is rooted in freedom; it chooses to seek the best for the object of our care and sacrifices to bless the other.

Lust is rooted in compulsion and is choice transformed by twisted manipulation into an insatiable demand. It seeks only the satisfaction of its selfish desire and cares nothing for the object of its desire.

It is clear that they are not the same; yet the potential for either lies within the breast of every human—historically, including our first parents, our Lord in His earthly humanity, and now, us.

Before we go further it is important to make clear that desire is legitimate, a part of what it means to be fully human. A desire may in fact be something that serves God's kingdom, such as the dedicated longing of the cancer researcher to find a cure for the leukemia that killed his baby sister. A lust is desire gone awry—something that dominates a human soul; it controls and destroys, as the raging lust of the sex offender who wants to ravage an innocent to sate his yearning for utter domination.

Every human is tempted—it is the common lot of every disciple (as it was of our Lord). In a church in which I served, the teens were doing a Bible study on temptation. In a brainstorming time, various temptations were named aloud and placed on the whiteboard; then the points of attack were identified and discussed to help those teens in their walk with God. At the end of the discussion, God's heavenly reward was put forward as the final outcome for the one who was victorious.

A teenaged girl was struggling to understand. Finally she "got it." A light went on in her soul and she said this: "Let me get this straight. *We're not safe until we're dead.* Is that right?"

Right indeed!

We will be tempted, at times sorely tempted. What will determine the outcome is where our love lies. If we love what God loves, the tempter's power will lose all power. If we do not choose (in advance) to love what God loves, the tempter will put before us one or all of the above three things, and will succeed in luring us away from Christ our Lord; like a moth drawn to a burning candle, we will move toward what we think is glory and find ourselves afire in flame.

The *lust of the flesh* is to be dominated by our physical (and usually legitimate) appetites. It includes such basic things as food, drink, the desire for sexual satisfaction, physical rest, or even exercise.

The *lust of the eye* is the domination of our senses by things that are beautiful, regardless of whether this is a mountain vista, a walk in the desert dawn, a piece of artwork, or an attractive member of the opposite sex. One fellow told me he called this "eye candy."

The *pride of life* is the domination of a person's existence through excessive ambition, focused on ego gratification. Ultimately this is to reject God and become the master of one's own destiny. The final estate is that this person is his or her own god!

In each case, the temptation begins with the twisting of something good toward some other purpose. With the first form of temptation, eating and drinking are necessary. Existing to gratify our senses *alone,* however, is tantamount to false worship. Paul speaks of people "whose end is destruction, whose god is their belly, and whose glory is in their shame—who set their mind on earthly things" (Philippians 3:19, NKJV).

Now we shall examine the second area: There is nothing wrong with enjoying beauty. There is something terribly wrong in the hoarding and the possessing of beautiful things (or people) to gratify an insatiable urge for more.

The third temptation directs us toward self-worship. There is nothing wrong with a desire for excellence. There is something terribly wrong when excellence is turned into perfectionism to point to our own personal "pride of achievement."

It is striking to compare the list in 1 John to the temptations of our first parents and then of the Lord as our Second Adam.

> The three lusts—of the flesh, of the eye and of ambition— correspond to three psychological responses Eve gave to the primal satanic temptation. "The woman saw that the tree was good for food (the lust of the flesh) and that it was a delight to the eyes (the lust of the eye), that the tree of life was to be desired to make one wise (the pride of life) (Gen. 3:6).

They also call to mind Satan's three-pronged attacks on our Savior: "Command this stone to become bread" (the lust of the flesh). . . . "Throw yourself down" (the pride of life). . . . The devil took him up and showed him all the kingdoms of the world in a moment of time. . . . "It shall all be yours" (the lust of the eye and the pride of life) (Luke 4:1-15).[33]

The Bible says two things about these realities. The first is about temptation and the second about the tempter.

When it comes to temptation, the Word is unequivocal:

Run!

If it pulls at your soul, and you find that it distracts you from God's kingdom, get out of there. Don't attempt to "be strong" in yourself and stand on the edge of the precipice. Move away from it, and put up a fence. Establish a marker on the spot and use it to warn others that this is the thing that trips you up every time. This is not a matter of prayer; it is one of obedience. "But you . . . flee these things" (1 Timothy 6:11, NKJV).

A sex therapist who had many god-fearing (and struggling) men in his practice once told me that the simplest way to assist someone besieged with sexual addictions was to ask him what his "triggers" were—the things that caused him to think about and, in the end, to do, the things that he wanted out of his life. Then, he would make a simple plan to avoid the triggers. One fellow was instructed to walk one block west, instead of in a straight line, to work. One block west had no pornographic signs posted on the way. The straight line went by three porn shops.

On the other side of temptation is a plan to walk with God. Paul said to Timothy, not only to run *away*, but to run *toward*: "But you, O man of God, *flee* these things [i.e., temptations], and *pursue* righteousness, godliness, faith, love, patience, gentleness. Fight the good fight of faith, lay hold on eternal life, to which you were also called" (1 Timothy 6:11-12, NKJV, emphasis added).

Paul gave Timothy a positive word—make a plan to choose what is good. Here we come to the root meaning of the word "disciple." A disciple is one who disciplines his or her life around a practice. In the case of Christian believers, it is the practice of godliness. We must have a systematic plan to learn such things as prayer (you are doing that with this resource), service (i.e., dedicate a time each week when you help the poor), hospitality (invite someone into your home for a coffee), giving (practice budgeting and giving a percentage of your money away), biblical study (do daily Bible reading, and join a small group for study together), worship (go to church), forgiveness (bless the ones who wronged you), etc.

Let's be absolutely clear: We are *saved* by grace. Nothing can be added to our salvation by our own efforts.

Yet we *grow* by the practice of godly disciplines.

Instead, we *grow weak and ineffectual* without them.

Jesus practiced them. So should we.

He commanded us to teach everyone to obey all that he taught us (Matthew 28:20).

The Bible also gives us a word about the tempter: We are to *resist* him.

Tell him to leave. Command him to go with a strong word of command. Jesus did this. So also did those who learned from our Lord. Listen to Peter's counsel:

> Be sober, be vigilant; because your adversary the devil walks about like a roaring lion, seeking whom he may devour. *Resist him*, steadfast in the faith, knowing that the same sufferings are experienced by your brotherhood in the world. (1 Peter 5:8-9, NKJV, emphasis added)

James, the brother of our Lord, has a similar word: "Submit yourselves, then, to God. *Resist the devil*, and he will flee from you. Come near to God and he will come near to you" (James 4:7-8, NIV, emphasis added).

How does one resist the devil? Turning is the answer.

Turn *away* from the temptation you are facing.

Turn *toward* the God who loves you.

While you are turning, tell the enemy of our souls to leave. Tell him with your words, and tell him with your actions.

Give him no quarter. Make no allowances for the practice of sin in your life. If there are rats congregating around your broken trash can, eliminate the rats; then, repair the trash can, or more rats will return! Break off the relationships that weaken your faith. Build relationships that strengthen your walk with God.

Live "in the world, but not of it." And God will be pleased.

PEN TO PAPER

1) How are you tempted in each area:
   a. The lust of the flesh

   b. The lust of the eye

   c. The pride of life

2) With each temptation, there is a way of escape. Go back and write down
   how you will avoid each temptation. Share that plan with your spouse or
   your prayer partner. Pray for God to lead you away from your personal
   "triggers" and that you be led into "deliverance from evil."

PRAYER CHALLENGE

Put your plan into action today. Plan to avoid the "triggers" that set you up for
trouble. Plan to "run" if you stumble over one or more of them today. Pray in
earnest the words of our Lord, "Lead us—not into temptation—but deliver
us from the evil one."

DAY 5

We can receive power against temptation by praying as Jesus taught us.

Perhaps this seems obvious, but in being led by the Lord in a fallen world and confronted with temptation, we can find release from the trouble or trial by asking God to save us from it. Asking for release from temptation, or for power to overcome it, however, must not be cavalier or flippant. Rather, the asking for release is intense and profound. It assumes a battle posture and a fight just before us. It assumes we are in the midst of God's calling to reclaim earth for Christ, who will in turn give it back to God the Father.

We have already examined the account of our Lord at prayer in the Garden of Gethsemane. Yet there is one aspect related to this prayer that bears examination: Jesus saw the human weakness of His three closest friends on earth—Peter and James and John. He saw the weakness, He knew that there was trouble coming upon them, and He longed to give them direction and help to overcome.

His longing for human companionship in a time of intense sorrow was profound. He asked them to "watch" with Him—to pray *with* Him—or at least to remain *beside* Him. My hunch is that something more was happening. He wanted to teach them the way through the trial. Surely it is clear that He was praying, and He didn't want to pray alone. Yet it is striking to notice that even in this extreme situation, Jesus attempted to teach them what they needed to be doing. To the last, He was a masterful teacher, even at His darkest hour.

Sadly, they simply couldn't do it. They were overcome with physical weariness. Listen closely to the words of our Lord to them: "Then he returned to his disciples and found them sleeping. 'Could you not watch with me for one hour?' he asked Peter. 'Watch and pray so that you will not fall into temptation. The spirit is willing, but the body is weak'" (Matthew 26:40-41, NIV).

Jesus here gives us a profound key to His own ability to endure. His prayer life *enabled Him to receive* what was needed to endure the temptations He would undergo in the midst of completing His calling. Through this kind of praying, God's power was given and He received grace to overcome. In His case the temptation was to crack under horrific violence, or to deny His calling as He was to be brought before governors, kings, jeering and violent soldiers, a whip of cords, a mocking crowd, and a pain-filled death. Luke tells us that God heard His request and gave Him the strength He needed to follow through with His mission, as a direct result of His intercession:

> And He withdrew from them about a stone's throw, and He knelt down and began to pray, saying, "Father if You are willing, remove this cup from Me; yet not My will, but Yours be done." Now an angel from heaven appeared to Him, strengthening Him. And being in agony he was praying very fervently; and His sweat became like drops of blood, falling down upon the ground. (Luke 22:41-42, NASB)

Jesus had been warned. He knew His time had come. He needed strength not to turn from His awful burden, but to do what was needful. He knew the answer—and that was to seek God in the midst of the trial. He must pray that He not fall into the temptation to turn from His calling. He wanted to teach the disciples the same. God sent an angel in response to His prayer to stay focused on God's kingdom—for God's will to be done through His dying. He could not allow even His very human desire to live (ordinarily the right outcome—He had evaded death before) to obstruct His mission.

To pray for the kingdom to come was not (and never will be) "easy believism." This was not a cheap and painless intercession such as we see in too many of our prayer meetings. This was someone who knew He must die, and who needed strength not to evade His calling.

Let us be clear. Prayer is no kindergarten exercise for the faint of heart. Prayer is an encounter with the power of God, and with God Himself; this God we serve is no tame or doting celestial grandfather who projects benevolence on all who deign to speak with Him. Rather this is an Almighty Sovereign who has an agenda to save the world. He is magnificent love and severe holiness at the same time. His agenda is to overthrow evil at the very deepest root. To get us to the place in which this can be done, He will lead us into our calling. Our calling to proclaim Christ and to resist evil in all its forms may make us sweat profusely and find no comfort *except in knowing that we are being and doing exactly as God commands.*

The book of Hebrews tells us that this kind of praying was not only related to Jesus' prayer in Gethsemane, but was the manner that Jesus prayed all His earthly life. The writer is very bold. He indicates that Jesus' life was in fact His training ground for His ultimate sacrifice. He *trained* to be God's High Priest. This is what the writer of Hebrews was saying when he said that Jesus had some things to learn.

> In the days of His flesh, He offered up both prayers and supplications with loud crying and tears to the One able to save Him from death, and He was heard because of His piety. Although He was a Son, He *learned obedience* from the things which He suffered. And having been made perfect, He became to all those who obey Him the source of eternal salvation being designated by God as a high priest. (Hebrews 5:7-10, NASB, emphasis added)

In Gethsemane Jesus was training His disciples in how to pray.
This time they didn't pass the test.
Jesus did.

To learn to endure requires time with God. Without this time with God, our resources will reach an end, and the enemy will succeed in distracting us from God's direction.

To pray is to discover one's life calling.

In the midst of one's calling, to pray is to receive strength from God to remain in the power of the Lord, and to stay faithful to the course.

He tells us to *pray* with the specific goal that we not stumble and fall as we are doing our God-given assignments. By this, Jesus meant that God's Word to us would cause us to struggle, rethink, wrestle, groan, weep, shout, and finally come to peace with our calling. And this type of praying is for us as we pray alone—and as we pray together.

The temptation about which our Lord prayed in this passage was not some small peccadillo (though He never did any of those through His entire life). Rather He was admonishing the disciples to pray lest they miss the calling of

God on their lives.

He knew the cross was looming before Him.

He knew the cost of following His Father's will.

He knew that a divine encounter would send the resources of heaven to them in advance of the temptation.

He received it as a result of His fervent intercession.

They fell asleep and denied their Lord.

But God redeemed—and we are thankful.

PEN TO PAPER

1) We are hardly used to expressions of extreme emotion in praying. However, it is far more common than most allow. Has there been a time when you were drawn into some form of profound intercession, and you were weeping, shouting, or crying out to God for His intervention?

2) What is the calling on your life? And what is the temptation you face in light of your calling?

3) Pray! Pray that you both know what God desires and that you have the strength to do it and not be deflected from it.

PRAYER CHALLENGE

You may be aware that God is calling you to something, but it is a struggle. When you set apart your time to pray, do not be afraid to express deep emotion, or to admit that what you want and what God wants through or in you are not identical. Pray until your heart and mind are aligned with whatever purpose God might have for you. Then, stand your ground.

DAY 6

We need to use the armor of the Lord to remain steadfast against the enemy—and that is to "put on Christ" Himself every day.

There can be no discussion about prayer against evil and the evil one without a mention of the spiritual armor of Ephesians 6. But before going to this famous passage, it is imperative to indicate that this is not the only place that the apostle used this kind of imagery. In fact, he was not the first to indicate that God's armor was to be worn to battle evil. The prophet Isaiah spoke of the coming Messiah who would be filled with the power of the Spirit. This Messiah would be clothed in "spiritual armor" and use those weapons to destroy evil forever:

> The Spirit of the LORD will rest on him—
> the Spirit of wisdom and of understanding,
> the Spirit of counsel and of power,
> the Spirit of knowledge and of the fear of the LORD. . . .
> With righteousness he will judge the needy,
> with justice he will give decisions for the poor of the earth.
> He will strike the earth with the rod of his mouth;
> with the breath of his lips he will slay the wicked.
> Righteousness will be his belt
> and faithfulness the sash around his waist. (Isaiah 11:2, 4-5, NIV)

Here it is clear that the rule of the coming Messiah would include the destruction of evil forever. He would do it by being clothed with the power of the Spirit of the living God (the word for Spirit here is *ruah*). His weapons would consist of Word (the rod of His mouth—His divine utterances) and Spirit (the breath [*ruah*] of His lips), and this would lead Him to establish righteousness and faithfulness as His completed dress.

As a good Jew, Paul would have known this promise of the coming Messiah.

He taught that our hope was to find our complete identity in this Messiah—who was revealed to him as Jesus of Nazareth on the Damascus Road. When writing to the Thessalonians, he told them to leave *off* drunkenness and evil behavior, and he used (in his earliest epistle) an image of bodily armor; they needed to put something *on*. "But since we belong to the day, let us be self-controlled, putting on faith and love as a breastplate, and the hope of salvation as a helmet. For God did not appoint us to suffer wrath but to receive salvation through our Lord Jesus Christ" (1 Thessalonians 5:8-9, NIV).

The point here is that to resist evil behavior was to daily "clothe oneself" with a suit of armor—in this case, faith and love as a breastplate—to cover the heart, and hope as a helmet—to fill our thinking and believing—all around the person of Jesus Himself and His salvation.

The second time that Paul uses the image of armor is found in his most famous epistle—the book of Romans. Here he is telling people not to give themselves over to sin, but to "clothe themselves" with Christ. Then he tells them that to do this is to put on spiritual armor.

> The night is nearly over; the day is almost here. So let us put aside the deeds of darkness and *put on the armor of light*. Let us behave decently, as in the daytime, not in orgies and drunkenness, not in sexual immorality and debauchery, not in dissension and jealousy. Rather, *clothe yourselves with the Lord Jesus Christ*, and do not think about how to gratify the desires of the sinful nature. (Romans 13:12-14, NIV, emphasis added)

The contrast in the material is of:

- Night and day,
- Deeds of darkness and armor of light,
- Behaviors of sin or a deliberate self-clothing of the believer with the Lord Himself.

The point is just this—the armor we are to put on is none other than the Lord Jesus Christ Himself. In a daily exercise, we are to deliberately choose to center our thinking, our behaving, our living, our decision making, our interactions with people, our everything—by placing ourselves within a garment, the Lord Himself.

In other words, we are to be "Jesus with skin on." Better yet, we are to hide ourselves in Jesus' own skin and let Him do the walking while we live inside. We are to be "in Christ." The enemy only has power over us when we are not.

That is one of the principle themes of the book of Ephesians—the place we usually go to in order to read about the "armor of the Lord." It is important to note that the book is entirely concerned with a two-spirit contrast—with the battle of the believer who is filled with the Spirit while he or she abides "in Christ" and the enemy's desire to subvert our walk with God by causing us to sin and to step outside of who Christ is. The book is not individualistic—that is, its primary concern is not about how an individual believer can stand strong (although there is much here for the individual to apply).

Rather, the main point of the book is that God is about to buy all of creation back from the powers of darkness and sum up all things in Christ (Ephesians 1:10). God did this incredible thing through embarrassing the demons. He has embarrassed them (called "principalities and powers" in this book) by creating a whole new species of human.

According to Ephesians, anyone who comes to Christ is no longer Jewish or Gentile (whether that "Gentile" is a Hungarian textile worker, a South Asian engineer, an Amazonian tribal, an African diamond miner, an English lord— or any other kind of human). All races have ceased to exist in God's sight, as He has created a new human race—a people who passed through the cross, who were joined together by the call of God and were jointly, as a new people together, filled with the Holy Spirit to create a new home in which God dwells by the Spirit (2:11-22). The book is entirely focused on Jesus' Spirit forging out a profound unity of humans, who together can be filled up with all the fullness of God (3:1, 14-21). This new race together—made up of an impossible mixture of former enemies—attests to how everything will be summed up in who Jesus is. Every layer of society is commanded to mutually submit to each other—husbands and wives, parents and children, masters and slaves (5:21-6:9). This unity, so unbelievable that it causes the world to be astounded—and the principalities and powers dumbfounded at God's hidden wisdom (3:8-12)—is so profound that it leads the world to believe. It becomes the basis for Paul to ask for prayer that he be enabled to preach the gospel boldly.

This is the background for the battle motif at the end of the book. The enemy of our souls wants believers to abandon their position "in Christ." He especially wants us to abandon our position of being "in Christ—together" as the temple of the Spirit/the new race. Satan wants us to no longer submit to each other, to no longer forgive each other, to no longer encourage each other. In a word, to stop being united in Christ. If he can destroy the unity of God's people, he can stop the advance of God's kingdom altogether. So the apostle tells the recipients of this letter to stand strong, not in their own resources, but in God's Messiah through the experience of Word and Spirit—to be "in Christ" and to be "in Christ—together." Let's listen to the apostle teach us once again:

> Finally, be strong in the Lord and in his mighty power. Put on the full armor of God so that you can take your stand against the devil's schemes. For our struggle is not against flesh and blood, but against the rulers, against the authorities, against the powers of this dark world and against the spiritual forces of evil in the heavenly realms. Therefore put on the full armor of God, so that when the day of evil comes, you may be able to stand your ground, and after you have done everything, to stand. Stand firm then, with the belt of truth buckled around your waist, with the breastplate of righteousness in place, and with your feet fitted with the readiness that comes from the gospel of peace. In addition to all this, take up the shield of faith, with which you can extinguish all the flaming arrows of the evil one. Take the helmet of salvation and the sword of the Spirit, which is the word of God. And pray in the Spirit on all occasions with all kinds of prayers and requests. With this in mind, be alert and always keep on praying for all the saints. (Ephesians 6:10-18, NIV)

The goal is to be "strong in the Lord" and not "strong in ourselves." The full armor is the armor of an army, not merely of an individual. We put it on individually, but we put it on so that we can do battle *together*. There is an army of unclean spirit-forces attacking the people of God. We are to wage this war as a unit, not as solo warriors with no commander and no camaraderie.

This requires that we not only seek out fellowship with other Christians but also insist on the promotion of mutual submission to Christ as the Holy Spirit leads us. To fail to do so is to reject the gospel—and to set ourselves up to be destroyed. An army standing its ground has a much better chance against an advancing army than a single soldier against a legion.

Notice that all of the pieces of armor have some sort of relationship with the truth of the gospel. We have:

- *The belt of truth*—the truth of the gospel. This is both knowledge *about* God and, since our Lord is truth incarnate, the "truth that is in Jesus" (see 4:21). Note that all the rest of the pieces of the armor are in some way attached to and held together by this belt.
- *The breastplate of righteousness*—truth known in the heart and lived out in "right living"
- *Shoes of preparedness*—truth in action, "walked out"
- *The shield of faith*—truth known together (body covering shields joined together for battle to stop the archers from picking off each warrior alone), held out to deflect the lies of the enemy thrown at us,
- *The helmet of salvation*—truth believed in the mind and diligently applied through the renewal of the mind by the Word and the Spirit (1:13-14; 4:23), and
- *The Spirit's sword*—truth proclaimed by the believer.

It may be that a final piece of armor is "prayer in the Spirit" (though this is not entirely clear). What we do know is that in this two-spirit battle, prayer is the action that undergirds the placement of each piece of the armor, shapes the unity of the Spirit, and holds it in place. Note that it is prayer in the Spirit—God directing our prayers to be "in Christ," and not just us "praying a list" (though one method of prayer is to make a list and pray it through).

The enemy simply wants us to step out of being "in Christ." He does it by subverting truth, undermining unity, and isolating Christians. To defeat the powers of darkness, then, we need a plan to know the Word, fellowship with other believers, and eliminate the prideful idea of a "solo warrior."

What is your plan?

PEN TO PAPER

1) Review the pieces of the armor of the Lord. Deliberately pray each piece into place as you complete this lesson.

2) Now, name your congregation—the place you are called to be with the people of God. Pray for the people you know. If you don't know anyone well, make a plan to join a small group in which you can, and then pray for the members of the group. Pray principally for their unity and for their calling to follow the Lord with their armor on—as God leads them to love others into God's kingdom rule.

3) Now pray "in the Spirit"—as the Spirit of God prompts you—giving you an idea, a person in your heart, a sin to confess, a calling to consider, a person who needs a visit. Pray about each item and then make a plan to obey the prompting you receive.

PRAYER CHALLENGE

The enemy will try to deflect you from a fearless commitment to unity with other Christians, especially around joining forces with them in prayer. Commit to do nothing until you have prayed with other believers. When you are tempted to just "go it alone," remember that to reject unity with other believers is to separate yourself from Jesus Christ Himself. Plan to bless others and join a church fellowship.

DAY 7

God's power can deliver us from the evil one.

There was a time when I didn't really believe that they existed. Then the reality became clear.

I was walking down a hallway in high school and heard a believing Christian teenager singing a snatch of a hymn: "I've been washed in the blood of the Lamb . . ."

I had been raised "old school." If a girl was in trouble, you went to her defense. Yet as I heard this girl humming and singing gently as she passed me in the hall, rage rose up within me and I wanted to stop her, to do anything to prevent her singing about that!

I was appalled, horrified at myself, that such an innocent thing as a girl singing gently as she walked down the hall could provoke such a strong reaction (inner rage at the mention of "the blood of the Lamb").

You need the background to understand this story.

I had been investigating the claims of Christ. Many of my brother's friends had become Christians, and their behavior changed. The changes were significant enough for many, including myself, to notice. Then I kept meeting Christians who seemed different. I was both attracted to their faith and repelled by it at the same time. In fact, I could say "Christ," and "God," but could not use the name "Jesus" or mention "the blood." Those words would catch in my throat and would stop there.

The story is long, but suffice it to say that after some months, I wound up in a living room with a gathering of other teenagers, listening to a British evangelist, steeped in the teaching of Methodism. He preached a standard Methodist sermon (I later discovered that he used John Wesley's "The Marks of the New Birth" as his outline). He gave an invitation to respond to the gospel, and despite the battle within, I found myself at the front—before anyone else responded. After some time, many more responded to the invitation, and the evangelist began placing his hands on others and praying for them, beginning with the person closest to him. I looked up to watch him as he prayed. Each time he did, something seemed to happen to the one being prayed for—gentle peace would be given, joy, tears, laughter, these things and more happened as he prayed.

He came to me last of all—perhaps because I was the first up.

I'll never forget the moment.

I was expecting the man to place his hands on my head as he had done with all the others. Instead he did something that caught me completely by surprise. He pointed his finger into my abdominal area and said, "Get out! In Jesus' name, get out!"

I looked down at his finger, and I saw or perceived his hand "glowing" with a gentle light. And all around my abdomen there was an inky black cloud which was moving with the upward motion of this man's hand.

The evangelist kept saying, "Get out! Now! Begone and leave this young man! In Jesus' name!" and his hand kept getting higher as the black mist rose.

I watched as long as I could, until the man's finger was at the base of my throat. Then I tilted my head up, and out of my mouth flew this black misty "thing"; it went right through the wall.

Suddenly I was surrounded by a brilliant, radiant light that shone with such radiance that it outblazed the sun. Yet it didn't hurt to look upon that light.

Then that light came into my interior being! I was filled with absolute, rapturous joy, and I stood to my feet! I cried out Jesus' name! Then I knew He was inside my deepest heart, and I could say His name and accept the gift of His blood to cover my sins.

I had been "delivered from the evil one."

This should come as no surprise to those who have read the gospels with fresh eyes. Jesus was an exorcist. He regularly cast out unclean spirits, and this was linked to His teaching ministry:

> They went into Capernaum; and immediately on the Sabbath He entered the synagogue and began to teach. They were amazed at His teaching; for He was teaching them as one having authority, and not as the scribes. Just then there was a man in their synagogue with an unclean spirit; and he cried out, saying, "What business do we have with each other, Jesus of Nazareth? Have You come to

destroy us? I know who You are—the Holy One of God!"

And Jesus rebuked him, saying, "Be quiet, and come out of him!" Throwing him into convulsions, the unclean spirit cried out with a loud voice and came out of him. They were all amazed, so that they debated among themselves, saying, "What is this? A new teaching with authority! He commands the unclean spirits, and they obey Him." Immediately the news about Him spread everywhere into all the surrounding district of Galilee. (Mark 1:21-28, NASB)

In addition, He taught His disciples to do the same, linking power over demonic forces with the proclamation of the kingdom. After choosing the twelve, He sent them out with a mandate: "And as you go, preach, saying, 'The kingdom of heaven is at hand.' Heal the sick, raise the dead, cleanse the lepers, cast out demons. Freely you received, freely give" (Matthew 10:7-8, NASB).

The message that is given to us is that the apostles had mixed results. They sometimes succeeded in this matter: "They went out and preached that men everywhere should repent. And they were casting out many demons and were anointing with oil many sick people and healing them" (Mark 6:12-13, NASB).

In one case, their failure is recorded for our learning. A boy was having seizures that were demonic in origin (Jesus distinguished between physical healing and demonic oppression); yet the disciples seemed helpless to cast out the demon. Jesus rebuked the mixed faith of those involved in the action, cast out the unclean spirit, and later gave the disciples the following instruction: "When He came into the house, His disciples began questioning Him privately, 'Why could we not drive it out?' And He said to them, 'This kind cannot come out by anything but prayer'" (Mark 9:28-29, NASB).

Demonic reality is real, not only in the places that are uneducated, poor, and steeped in witchcraft. Demons exist not only in ancient times, or in superstitious or primitive cultures, but today, among the cultured and the well-to-do, as well as among the rich, the middle-class, and the poor. They attack people, attempt to destroy them, and they do so by wresting control of who they are away from the person so besieged.

But Jesus can bring release—He can "deliver . . . from the evil one." Jesus' power is much, much stronger! It is accessed by faith, believing prayer (sometimes extended seasons of prayer—and from time to time, fasting), and walking in the power of the Holy Spirit. One of the principle tasks of proclaiming the advance of God's rule is the casting out of the usurper powers that destroy.

Most Western Christians live in a state of "arms-length" or "suspended" belief (which amounts to unbelief) about this aspect of Jesus' ministry; we are uncomfortable at the idea of the existence of demons (and their God-honoring counterpart—angels). We attempt to find a natural or physical interpretation for neurotic or deviant behavior (or for miracles as God grants them), even when medicine, science, or common sense cannot explain the events of life. There are times when a supernatural explanation is the obvious solution. Now, while neurotic behavior may in fact be rooted in such things as an abusive background, a failure to take responsibility for sin, or a medical condition (and this must be weighed and considered in every case), dismissing the demonic from our thinking robs the church of a crucial aspect of the ministry of Jesus.

Read the gospels with a highlighter and underscore the incidents like these and you will be astonished to see how very frequently Jesus did things like this. Jesus verbally rebuked diseases, leprosy, and demons. He commanded sickness directly, and spoke forthrightly to Satan when the unclean spirit attempted to use Peter's voice to distract him from his mission (Matthew 16:23). Read the text and see that Jesus didn't speak to Peter at all, but to the demonic power using his voice.

Richard Foster calls this kind of praying "Authoritative Prayer." In fact, he devotes a chapter to this toward the close of his book on prayer (it would be wise to refer to its entire contents before attempting this type of praying). He tells a story of this kind of praying that undergirds its reality:

> Some years ago I met a distinguished-looking woman . . . in Santa Barbara, California. I shall call her Gloria. . . . I remember the refined dignity with which Gloria carried herself. "Sophisticated," I thought to myself. . . . But the story she told . . . was anything but sophisticated. Gloria had suffered from six months of intense affliction from the evil one. . . . Six months earlier, while on a week-long silent retreat, Gloria, suddenly . . . experienced acute stomach pains.

"I doubled over in agony," she told me. "Then I felt a presence: a horrible, awful presence. I began weeping profusely. I felt unbelievably heavy . . . as though I was carrying a cross. Then I saw a monstrous thing. It was huge, dark, ugly. It spoke with a gravelly voice, like an animal. The impression came to me, 'The devil is trying to eat me up!'"

Bent over in pain, Gloria laboriously made her way to the chapel. She sprinkled herself with holy water, and prostrated herself on the floor, saying, "I will worship only God." There . . . she fell asleep. . . . When Gloria awoke, she felt somewhat better. . . . She received Eucharist and then went to bed. . . .

In the middle of the night, however, she was yanked awake. "My body was jerking so violently," she told me, "that I feared my neck would break. All I could think of was, 'The devil is trying to destroy me!'" She staggered down the hall and pounded on the door of the priest. . . . Unsure of what to do, he called one of the sisters, . . . and together they sat up with Gloria until the darkness subsided somewhat. "I know they thought I was mentally ill," Gloria confided. "What else could they think?"

"The episodes . . . have continued now for six months." Gloria was sharing with me in a straightforward . . . manner. "Then in your lecture on prayer, you warned of spirits that are opposed to the way of God. . . . Please, can you help me?" . . .

[I] knew I was in the presence of someone who was completely rational. I sensed that the afflictions Gloria had been experiencing were from the enemy of her soul. . . . I said . . . "Yes, I can help you." . . .

Placing my hands on Gloria's head, I prayed with all the authority and tenderness I could muster. I ordered the darkness—whatever it was—to leave and to go into the strong arms of Jesus. Gloria began weeping—a deep, inward weeping accompanied by huge sighs. I invited the peace and the love of God to enter her, filling every aspect of her mind, body, and spirit. And the darkness left. The peace came. Together we sat in perfect silence, sensing the flow of grace and mercy.[34]

Foster went on to relate that ten years later, "Gloria" had never had a return of that darkness.

Our calling is to imitate our Master. There is power in the authority that Jesus has given to us. But we must use it by *speaking* when we are under God's anointing to do so (an important component of prayer ministry). Foster names seven important principles of doing this kind of praying, paraphrased in this section below:

1) Don't look for a demon in every pain. "A pain is a pain is a pain." Instead use this authority to correct everyday issues like eating habits, sexual fantasies, and fears and failures. (Command them to obey the Lord's Word.)

2) Don't put on some special voice. "If the power of God is present, then we do not need any special effects, and if the authority is absent, then all the gymnastics in the world will not make up for the deficiency."[35]

3) It is common to experience unusual anointing of the Holy Spirit for specific ministries. Wait for the anointing of the Spirit to increase, cover ourselves with the blood of Christ, and seal ourselves into His cross.

4) Deal firmly with evil, but deal gently with people.

5) Don't use this kind of prayer as a substitute for godly spiritual disciplines.

6) When praying against an evil presence in another, do this kind of prayer ministry with others.

7) Act humbly as you learn and grow.[36]

PEN TO PAPER

1) Take a moment to record your impressions of what happened when Richard Foster prayed for "Gloria." What struck you from that account?

2) Did you notice? When she experienced satanic attack, Gloria didn't address the evil or tell it to leave. Search the Scriptures and you will discover that whenever evil is fought against, it must be told directly to go. Jesus never asked the Father to rebuke a demon for Him. The apostles and the early church commanded evil to leave. Make a commitment that when an evil thought or propensity comes into your mind, you will command it to leave, using Jesus' name. Let's practice. You have an area of consistent weakness. Simply tell that area to obey Jesus. Say it aloud. Take unforgiveness as an example. You have forgiven a person a dozen times, yet the memory of that sin still haunts you. Declare that you serve Jesus this way: "Spirit of bitter unforgiveness—begone in Jesus' mighty name!" Pick your area and do it right now. Record your impressions below.

3) Now, review the learning of the last seven days. Based on what you now know about sin, evil, temptation, and God's power, paraphrase this line of Jesus' prayer:

PRAYER CHALLENGE

Today you will find that your thinking is a mix of clean and unclean thoughts. When an unclean thought enters your thinking today, do not entertain it. Rather, rebuke it in Jesus' name. Tell it to leave and give it no quarter. Then declare the opposite will be so in your thought life today.

Week Eight

REJOICE IN GOD'S VICTORY

"For Yours Is the Kingdom . . ."

DAY 1

Prayer ends as it begins—with God.

Dr. George Buttrick wrote a classic work on the nature of prayer. In it, he attempted to capture the intent of Jesus' teaching on prayer by doing a free rendering of the Lord's Prayer. Here is how he words the text that we have been studying for the last six weeks:

Our Father, whose dwelling is Light,
> May thy Nature be revered—on earth as it is in heaven . . .
> May thy Kingdom come—on earth as it is in heaven . . .
> May thy will be done—on earth as it is in heaven . . .
Give us our bread, day by day.
> Forgive us our debts, we forgiving our debtors.
Grant that we fail not in the time of testing,
> But deliver us from the Evil One.
(Thine is the kingdom, the power and the glory, forever). Amen.[37]

Buttrick's conviction was that the *three* introductory lines (and not merely the usual two) are parallel and therefore each modified by "on earth as it is in heaven"—a fresh perspective on this prayer. Take some time now to simply pray the prayer using this rendering. Take your time, praying whatever comes to mind as you seek God and God's rule through this model. Take ten minutes now and center yourself on praying this form. Record any new perspectives from this that come to you from it.

Now we come to the climax of the prayer. The early church knew that it was inconceivable for the prayer to end with "deliver us from the Evil One." And so this doxology was inserted and became part of the later manuscript tradition. It isn't found in our earliest copies of Matthew or Luke, nor is it in the best manuscripts available to us. However, it was already a well-known conclusion to the prayer very early in the history of Christendom, finding its way into the prayer practices of the church within a hundred years of Jesus' day.

However, given the way that Jews prayed in the time of Christ (and throughout their history), it is beyond belief for the prayer to end in anything other than an ascription of praise to God. Listen to how King David ended his prayer as people donated to the temple that his son Solomon would build (and note the parallels to the conclusion of the Lord's Prayer):

> David said, "Blessed are You, O LORD God of Israel our father, forever and ever. *Yours, O LORD, is the greatness and the power and the glory* and the victory and the majesty, indeed everything that is in the heavens and the earth; *Yours is the dominion*, O LORD, and You exalt Yourself as head over all. Both riches and honor come from You, and You rule over all, and in Your hand is power and might; and it lies in Your hand to make great and to strengthen everyone. Now therefore, our God, we thank You, and praise Your glorious name." (1 Chronicles 29:10-13, NASB, emphasis added)

Certainly the Psalms, both those penned by David and those from other authors, would regularly make a practice of declaring God's victory or requiring those hearing them read to do so:

> Ascribe to the LORD, O sons of the mighty,
> Ascribe to the LORD glory and strength.
> Ascribe to the LORD the glory due His name;
> Worship the LORD in the majesty of holiness.
> (Psalm 29:1-2, NASB [2b is the marginal reading])

Here the psalmist would tell his soul (when worshipping alone) or he would instruct the throng of believers gathered for worship that ascribing praise to God was an act of the will—something that we choose to do as a part of our prayer life.

The apostle Paul would end his prayers with praise. Perhaps the clearest example of this is the very long prayer-report of Ephesians. The case can be made that the first three chapters of that book are functionally three prayers forming, in reality, a single prayer unity—with teaching and sacred memory inserted into the praying!

- Ephesians 1:3-14 is a *prayer* of blessing (theologically packed and Trinitarian)
- 1:15-23 is the report of Paul's *prayer* for the Ephesians for the power of God to fill them
- 2:1-22 is *sacred memory* of their conversion (formerly dead in sins, made alive, recreated as a new race of former Jews and Gentiles to become a home in which God dwells corporately by His Spirit)
- 3:1—the *prayer* taken up again, only to be interrupted by
- 3:2-13—the *sacred memory* of his role in Gentile conversions, and of how this new race is on display to the principalities and powers
- 3:14-19—Paul now completes his *prayer* for the church begun in 3:1 (the new race, the temple in which God dwells) to be filled with God's power, His Spirit, and His love—being filled to the fullness of God Himself. This sets up
- 3:20-21: *A concluding doxology, ascribing praise* to the God who has done these wonders. Listen to this doxology—a "word of praise" (that is what doxology means), and once again, note the similarity to the ending of the Lord's Prayer:

Now to Him who is able to do far more abundantly beyond all that we ask or think, according to *the power* that is at work within us, to Him be *the glory* in the church and in Christ Jesus to all generations *forever and ever*. Amen. (Ephesians 3:20-21, NASB, emphasis added)

Regardless of whether we have the exact words of our Lord, we have the common intent of Judeo-Christian prayer recorded here; the concluding material in Jesus' prayer resounds with the same themes as the prayer itself—

that God's kingdom, God's power, and God's glory are what prayer—and most especially this prayer—is all about.

Here is what we have done then in praying through the first five movements of this model of our Lord:

- We have praised God with the specific intent that God's name be glorified.
- We have declared allegiance to God's kingdom rule, and prayed specifically for God's will to be done, naming our heartfelt issues before the Lord, and conforming them to God's directives and the leading of the Holy Spirit. Through this action we declared war on the forces of darkness and aligned our wills with God's to retake our fallen world back from the usurper.
- We have asked for provision to be given so that we could follow through with the battle to see God's kingdom reshape the fallen world into God's creation again.
- We have taken away the ground our enemy would use to attack us by making a clean breast of our sins, asking God to forgive our own, and choosing to treat others not as their sins deserve, but as grace has forgiven us.
- We have raised up our protective shields (the Lord Himself) over our hearts and our unity, taking our stand against darkness and despair—and we have seen victory in God directing our steps.

Now comes the time when (to conclude our praying) we need to speak aloud what we have received and to reaffirm that God is the King we serve. Do you remember how it was rendered in *The Message*?

You're in charge!	(Yours is the kingdom)
You can do anything you want!	(Yours is the power)
You're ablaze in beauty!	(Yours is the glory)
Yes. Yes. Yes.	(Forever and ever! Amen!)

The point is more than clear. To pray effectively requires ending as we began, by ascribing praise to God for His kingdom rule, by reaffirming God's power to accomplish whatever He wants in our lives, and by asserting that God will get all the credit, in all that we think, say and do.

PEN TO PAPER

1) Read the ascriptions of praise from the passages listed above. Read them aloud until those words become your own. Record what this "ascription of praise" did in your soul.

2) Take a moment and record the mighty things that God has done, in you, your church, your home, your small study group, anywhere. Begin by recognizing that God has brought you to Himself and saved you from certain destruction. Name them all and then thank God for each thing that He has done.

3) Now pray the last line of the Lord's Prayer as Peterson has rendered it above.

PRAYER CHALLENGE

Today is a day to remember what God has done—and to celebrate it! Each time a memory of God's power or intervention comes to mind, thank Him. Tell Him that His is the kingdom, the power, and the glory. If you are musical (or even if all you can do is "make a joyful noise"), sing the doxology with every thankful memory:

> Praise God from whom all blessings flow.
> Praise Him all creatures here below!
> Praise Him above, ye heavenly hosts!
> Praise Father, Son, and Holy Ghost! Amen.

DAY 2

Jesus redefined power forever. We are to celebrate
Jesus' ability to empower us to serve.

We have spent much time in this resource examining and praying through Jesus' teaching on the kingdom of God. We know that it most certainly involves God becoming the undisputed ruler of our lives and of the world around us through the action of His Spirit. What we have been learning is that the power of the kingdom is made active through the prayer ministry of the church.

But we can see from the concluding doxology that it is important for us to examine what the Lord and the early church understood by the two remaining concepts found in this prayer—"power" and "glory." Jesus redefined these terms through His life and His example.

"Power" is understood as the ability or the enablement to accomplish or to do. There is raw power—material in its nature—and there is spiritual power, and they simply are not the same. Buttrick's comment on prayer, kingship, and power put this into perspective:

> Jesus is the King of mankind through prayer. "King" is . . . the [one] who can, the [one] who is able. Kings were once a democratic choice. They earned the crown by consent through *demonstrated power*. We have strange notions of power. A transcontinental plane has a wingspread of one hundred feet, a length of sixty feet, a weight of twelve tons, and its engines can hurl it through the air. . . . It is a token of power. But if the plane carries a man who has just learned of his mother's death, the plane has no power to mend his broken heart. Earth's power is very helpless power. But Jesus had real power—"power over all flesh, that he should give eternal life." Other men spoke and their words died with their echo: Jesus spoke the same words, and they shook the world. . . . He . . . only . . . can

lift our transitory flesh into an eternal light. He is Prophet, Priest and King, because his days were hid in prayer.[38]

Here "power" is defined not as some sort of sheer force, but as the ability to mend a broken heart, as the capability to transform our experiences of death into the hope of life. It takes little imagination to extend that to the power of the Lord's Spirit to take our sins and transform them into opportunities, to take our faults and to use them so that His reputation for goodness is expanded. Certainly in the life of our Lord, His power was made evident in the accomplishment of the miraculous. And yet this power flowing through Him was put to use to *serve* others, especially the poor, the helpless, and the hopeless. His power was not put to use to aggrandize Himself, or to draw the adoration of the masses at His own innate ability to "do." And the key to this power was the fact that Jesus' days were saturated with prayer.

The disciples needed to be retrained in the nature of power. When a Samaritan village rejected His presence, due to His Jewish focus on Jerusalem, the disciples wanted to use God's power to *over*-power them. They understood power as sheer force rather than God-honoring deliverance and enabling help. As happened more than once, they were serving the Lord and misunderstanding His mission and power.

> When His disciples James and John saw this, they said, "Lord, do You want us to command fire to come down from heaven and consume them?" But he turned and rebuked them, [and said, "You do not know what kind of spirit you are of; for the Son of Man did not come to destroy men's lives, but to save them."] And they went on to another village. (Luke 9:54-56, NASB)

This lesson didn't come easily to the disciples. When they were talking about Jesus as King, and the coming kingdom of our Lord, He needed to reteach them that the fundamental understanding of power used by the world (to overpower so that the conquered should serve the conqueror) was diametrically opposed to God's rule of power—which was to send power to raise others up.

And there arose also a dispute among them as to which one of them was regarded to be greatest. And He said to them, "The kings of the Gentiles lord it over them; and those who have authority over them are called 'Benefactors.' But it is not this way with you, but the one who is the greatest among you must become like the youngest, and the leader like the servant. For who is greater, the one who reclines at the table or the one who serves? Is it not the one who reclines at the table? But I am among you as one who serves. You are those who have stood by Me in My trials; and just as My Father has granted Me a Kingdom, I grant you that you may eat and drink at My table in My kingdom. (Luke 22:24-30, NASB)

It is interesting to note that Jesus didn't discourage the disciples from desiring to be first or even to be the greatest. Rather He *redefined* how to accomplish it and the outcomes that being first or greatest would bring. Jesus still believed in the exercise of power, but it was not to be used for personal achievement or to establish a believer as one in whom pride of place was unmatched. Jesus does "the great reversal" and makes the lowly the high and the high the lowly.

Jesus' power is given to *empower*.

To declare "Yours is the power" is to declare that all the world's systems of personal achievement, the maximization of self-interest, or sitting on top of the heap to control others is contrary to God's kingdom. It is to be repented of and rejected as earth-bound and doomed to extinction. To use the language of James, this kind of wisdom is "earthly, natural, demonic" (James 3:15, NASB). In fact, it is to be overturned and forever abandoned as the way of the world and not of God.

Jesus' power is the abandonment of power in order to release it.

His "powerlessness" even unto death produces resurrection.

God does not depend on the "latent power of human potential" or our innate ability to achieve. In fact, when Peter went back to fishing after considering himself a failure, he still caught nothing. It was only by obeying the word of Christ to cast out his nets when he felt that he had nothing left to offer that he caught anything at all—and the catch at Jesus' invitation was astonishing (John 21:6; see also Luke 5:1-11).

He bids us come, but it is not a "come to Me and you will be a better person." It is a word to deny ourselves, an invitation to relinquish the control of our existence and to put our "everything" at God's disposal. It is a word to join the Lord and to "die with Christ."

That is the utter rejection of the human potential movement, and of our culture's obsession to maximize our self-interests. We don't merely attempt to improve our lives to become better people. We kill them off until all that we are is utterly abandoned to God. This is "dying with Jesus." We live then, only when God raises us to God's purposes and not our own.

There is a strange paradox with God's power. When we turn our lives over to Christ to "come and die with him," we discover that God can work through us in a remarkable way. He calls us to "disciple" ourselves and those we meet. We do, in fact, make use of our human resources—but only after the center of our existence has been rendered dead and buried, when it is completely reoriented and is utterly different. We do this at God's command.

When we pray, "Yours is the power," we are saying "we have no power—we are powerless unless you raise us up!" We are declaring that God's power is the best power, the most amazing power, the most humbling manifestation of grace we could ever know. We are committing our lives afresh to God flowing through our lives on God's terms.

Will you turn your power over to Him?

PEN TO PAPER

1) Take a moment to think through how we use the word "power." Write down your thoughts simply as they come to you.

2) Now reread Buttrick's words about the contrast between God's power and human power. What kind of power was Buttrick ascribing to Jesus? What was the source of that power?

3) Review the passages about the use of power from the ministry of Jesus. What was Jesus' power to do as it flowed through the disciples? What did they need to do to accomplish things the "Jesus way"?

4) What do you pride yourself on being "able to do"? Take a moment and list the things that you do well. Then, in an act of love, give them all to Christ. Submit all of your "power" to the power of Christ. Decide to use those gifts or endowments only to serve others.

PRAYER CHALLENGE

Today you will encounter many a situation in which you can use your abilities to accomplish something. Today, as you are going about your necessary business, tell the Lord that this power you are using (to think, plan, organize, build, tear down, study, travel, etc.) is in submission to His purposes. Ask Him to show you how to channel your power into service.

DAY 3

Jesus' power was released through submission. If we say
"yours is the power" we mean "ours is the submission."

There was a time when I thought that Jesus' power was automatic. I
believed that since He was the Son of God and God the Son that
He could, for example, simply walk on water whenever He chose
to do so; it was a settled conviction that the healing ministry of Jesus would
occur whenever He chose to do so. A closer examination of the life of Christ
shows that He gave up that prerogative when He entered the human stream of
existence. "Therefore Jesus answered and was saying to them, 'Truly, truly, I
say to you, the Son can do *nothing* of Himself, unless it is something He sees
the Father doing; for whatever the Father does, these things the Son also does
in like manner'" (John 5:19, NASB, emphasis added).

This is not the only text in which this teaching is found. He repeats this
a few verses later. "I can do *nothing* on My own initiative. As I hear, I judge;
and My judgment is just, because *I do not seek My own will*, but the will of
Him who sent Me" (John 5:30, NASB, emphasis added).

Certainly Jesus' prayer at Gethsemane makes clear that, at least once,
He did not *instantly* do every thing that the Father spoke to Him. There
He found Himself struggling to obey the clear will of the Father, and took
time to pray it through. Three times He asked for the will of the Father to be
altered. And three times He received the answer "no." He had to choose to
do the thing that the Father wanted, and the choice had to be deliberate and
clear. "My Father, if it is possible, let this cup pass from Me; yet not as I will,
but as You will" (Matthew 26:39, NASB).

Still, the idea that Christ had to submit to the Father to perform His
miracles seems alien to many who hold to classic Christian faith. Examine
His ministry though, and it becomes clear that His was not a ministry
of self-will, but of prayerful discernment. He recognized that the Father
was doing something. Then Jesus would willingly obey as He entered His

Father's work. This applies not only to His words, but also to those instances in which He did the miraculous:

> One day He was teaching; and there were some Pharisees and teachers of the law sitting there, who had come from every village of Galilee and Judea and from Jerusalem; *and the power of the Lord was present for Him to perform healing.* (Luke 5:17, NASB)

Here the context makes more than clear that Jesus performed a miracle of healing. However, Luke went to great pains to record that in this instance, God's power was present in some kind of tangible way. Those who were participating in the event—either those observing to "check Him out," those receiving Jesus' prayer and therefore being healed, those who were friends or relatives of those being healed, or those learning the ways of the Master by watching (as the disciples most certainly did)—had an unusual sense that "something was afoot," that God's power was present in a unique manner. The old Puritan writers used to call this "the manifest presence of God."

While those times of "anointing" or "unction" are rich and profound, it has an implication. This means that there were times and seasons in which the power of the Lord was *not* present to perform healing—even in the ministry of our Lord and Savior.

Jesus didn't heal automatically, or even when He had a whim to do so, based on a need of the moment. He did not have an "intrinsic" or "built-in" supply of power rooted in who He was as the Son of God. Rather, He obtained access to divine empowerment by *the practice of prayerful submission.*

Many have asked, "If Jesus was in fact God in human flesh, why did He have to pray?" The reason is simple. When He entered the stream of human existence, He "emptied himself, taking the form of a bond-servant" (Philippians 2:7, NASB). The apostle had just explained that Jesus "did not regard equality with God a thing to be grasped" (Philippians 2:6, NASB). He gave up the divine prerogatives of intrinsic power and omniscience.

He could only know what the Father *told* Him, and in fact, did not know many things (e.g., "But of that day and that hour no one knows, not even the angels of heaven, *nor the Son*, but the Father alone" [Matthew 24:36, NASB, emphasis added]).

He could only *do* what the Father *showed Him.* This explains why He hesitated to heal the Syro-Phoenician's daughter and was surprised by the faith of the centurion. Jesus was given a mandate, a calling, and a plan. But it required constant communication with God the Father through Spirit-inspired praying. He was given His ministry on a "need to know" basis.

Even though He was in essence the Son of God, He relinquished all rights, all privileges, and all power to become utterly and completely human, to identify with us so completely that something as alien to God as death might be His common lot with us.

This has implications for our praying, "Yours is the power."

Based on the above, it is clear that *Jesus had to pray to find out what God the Father wanted.*

He (like us) had to pray to access the resources and the power of heaven. Jesus, of necessity, based on His self-humiliation in becoming a human, was *required* to seek for "the kingdom to come and the will to be done on earth as it is in heaven"—just like we do. And when the Father spoke a hard word requiring submission to a greater will, He, just like us, had to *choose* to submit. Jesus was and is the model of our ability to access the power of God. Just like Him, we can receive what the Father has for us through the only means available to Him and to us—submission to the divine will, as God speaks to us in the two-way communication called "prayer."

And when the tasks of the day were done, and God had moved through His existence in a sovereign, powerful way, the prayer ends by declaring that "the kingdom, the power, and the glory are Yours!"

This declaration makes clear that *God* did it by *God's* power, and that Jesus' power was the power of submission.

To declare "Yours is the power" is to announce in an act of personal alignment with God's movement: "Ours is the submission!"

Henry Blackaby and Claude King have made this teaching more clear in our day by indicating that instead of running programs based on our desire to "help God's work get done" we are far more likely to succeed if we simply "find out where God is working and join Him there."

Do you want to be a servant of God? Find out where the Master is, then that is where you need to be. Find out what the Master is doing, then that is what you need to be doing. . . . When I am in the middle of the activity of God and God opens my eyes to let me see where He is working, I always assume that God wants me to join Him.[39]

This principle is found in the lives of the many that have walked with God to do His work throughout the history of the Christian church. It is illustrated by an incident from the life of Hudson Taylor, a nineteenth-century pioneer missionary to China, and the founder of the China Inland Mission. He was one of the first to abandon the idea of using mission societies as a means to export and promote Western culture in the name of the gospel; instead he would preach the gospel within the culture he was attempting to reach, living, dressing, and eating as the local people.

When Hudson Taylor was just beginning his work in China, he took a trip from the city of Swatow to Shanghai to get his medicines and equipment. It was his plan to return to Swatow and work with a Scottish missionary there. When he arrived in Shanghai he discovered that all was lost—the warehouse with all his supplies had burned to the ground. Nothing could be salvaged from the wreckage.

This was serious blow. Taylor was unable to comprehend why God would allow such an awful thing when his every intention was only to serve the poor and share his faith. After some thought he took the decision to walk to the city of Ningpo. Though he had little money with him, he determined to purchase some supplies from another missionary there and then to take a canal boat back to Swatow. He journeyed along the canals, preaching the gospel as he travelled.

At the end of the canal system, Taylor hired some baggage carriers and soon outdistanced them, finally waiting through a long hot afternoon for them to catch up. It was then that he discovered the reason for their delay. They were hopelessly addicted to opium—and unreliable. This gave him no choice except to dismiss them. He did, keeping the leader, whom he delegated to hire more workers. The trouble was that the leader was unreliable as well. He never showed up, having stolen Taylors bags and their contents.

Reaching a point of exhaustion, he went to an inn, and after paying for a room, found it infested with rats and insects. After an awful night, he pressed on to the coast, and came to another city, in need of a solid night's rest. Since he was a foreigner, no one would help him; in fact, he was shadowed by the local police. At length a young man offered to help, and escorted him through the city trying to find someone to give him a place to lay his head. They trudged together until one in the morning when his so called "guide" abandoned him. Taylor wound up on the steps of a temple, trying to stay awake. Three thugs in the shadows waited for him to fall asleep, so that they could rob him of his few possessions. Taylor stayed awake that night only by singing hymns and repeating Bible verses. Sometime in the night, the three thieves gave up in disgust and Taylor caught a little rest.

When day dawned, Taylor found his "guide" from the night before demanding an outrageous fee for his services. At this point, Taylor exploded in rage, taking the man by the arm and physically shaking him, until the fellow left him alone. Utterly dispirited, and weary to the bone, he started to retrace his steps back to Shanghai. For eight long miles, Taylor dragged himself along, complaining to God and in spiritual rebellion. He demanded to know why this had happened to him. He wondered if God had abandoned him completely.

Suddenly it dawned on him that he had been the problem. All through the painful journey, he simply had not asked God what to do. He had done it himself. He had not asked for guidance, or protection. He was so focused on his troubles, that he hadn't thought to ask God for His wisdom. He just made up his mind and did what he thought best. Taylor's journal records that, as he went along, he confessed his utter prayerlessness to God, and asked the Lord to forgive him. As he did this, Taylor's heart was "flooded with a glorious sense of the presence and forgiveness of Christ." The control passed from Hudson Taylor to the Lord Jesus Christ where it truly belonged.

Then Taylor discovered that his trial was actually a mercy. He arrived in Shanghai and was given a letter that was waiting for him. It contained a check for the exact amount of money needed to cover his expenses and the purchase of the needed medical supplies. Then he learned that during his arduous journey there had been terrible trouble in Swatow. He would have arrived just in time to be imprisoned. In fact, that may have led to his execution. Through that awful series of events, God actually spared Taylor from even more trouble that he had experienced.[40]

Taylor learned to live out the phrase, "Yours is the power." Through it he learned that "ours is the submission."

PEN TO PAPER

1) Read Luke 5:17 above. Note that the power was not automatic. What did this mean for Jesus and His ministry? What does it mean for us in our praying?

2) Hudson Taylor quickly learned that even "doing ministry" can get in the way of walking in God's power. He discovered that "God's work, done God's way, will never lack God's supply." What this requires is submission to the Lord's work—not doing our own ideas "for God," but rather being sent "by God." Henry Blackaby's teaching that we "find out where God is at work and join Him there" has become a helpful watchword. Where is God at work around you? How can you join Him?

3) Pray for an anointing of "the power of the Lord" to come upon you. And when you discover God's power at work, submit to what God is doing, then decide that you will declare when the day is done, "Yours is the power—forever!"

PRAYER CHALLENGE

God wants to manifest His power through you. Be sensitive to the fact that God is at work around you. When you sense the Lord is at work, join Him there.

DAY 4

To declare "Yours is the power" is to recommit ourselves to
God's rule as against the unclean spirit's rule. By our submission
to His movement, Jesus' power in and through us
"embarrasses the demons."

God's power and God's glory are both intrinsically joined to the movement of God's Spirit. We have seen that there is a clear link between God's kingdom and God's Spirit, and that God desires that our walk in the Spirit cast out evil powers: "But if I cast out demons by the Spirit of God, then the kingdom of God has come upon you" (Matthew 12:28, NASB).

We have also seen that when the disciples spoke with the resurrected Lord about the Holy Spirit (i.e., the Spirit who makes holy), they immediately asked about the coming kingdom of God. Jesus then told them to focus on the gift of the Spirit as the beginning of God's kingdom rule. Notice how He refers not just to the presence of the Spirit, but to the "power" that they will receive:

> So when they had come together, they were asking Him, saying, "Lord, is it at this time You are restoring the kingdom to Israel?" He said to them, "It is not for you to know the times . . . but you will receive power when the Holy Spirit comes upon you." (Acts 1:6-8, NASB)

There is an extended passage of the New Testament that speaks about the Spirit of God, the power and the glory of God given to believers, revealed in God's people, and demonstrating God's glorious purpose. This passage contains teaching about unclean spirit-beings and our former life of despair under the false rule of the "prince of the power of the air." It also indicates our magnificent destiny by way of contrast with our awful past. It is Ephesians 1:17 to 2:7. Here is my own rendering of the material:

[I pray] that the God of our Lord Jesus Christ, the Father of glory, would give you the Spirit who brings wisdom and revelation concerning the knowledge of himself, that he would give you enlightened inner eyes so that you might know the hope to which he has called you—[that hope consists of] the treasure of the glory of his inheritance among those he has made holy, and the ever-expanding immensity of his power toward us who believe. This power corresponds with the exertion of the strength of his might which God exerted in the Christ when he raised him from among the dead and seated him at his right hand in the sphere of the heavenlies, far above every form of rule, authority, power and dominion—above every power that can be named—not only in this age, but also in the next. And God placed all things under his feet, and gave Christ to be head over all things on behalf of the church, his very body, which contains the fullness of him who fills all things in every way.

Now you were dead in your transgressions and sins. Formerly you lived in them, walking according to this World-Age, according to the ruler of the domain of the atmosphere—the spirit which is even now working among those characterized by disobedience. All of us used to be among them, conducting ourselves in line with the compulsions of our flesh, completing the desires of the flesh and the mind. We, just like the rest, were children of wrath by nature.

But God—being wealthy in mercy, because of his enormous love with which he loved us (even when we were dead in our transgressions)—made us alive together with Christ (you have been saved by grace). He co-raised and co-seated us in the sphere of the heavenlies so that throughout the coming ages he might display the ever-expanding treasure of his grace, manifested in kindness toward us in Christ Jesus. (Ephesians 1:17-2:7)

There is much in this material that is worthy of comment. Here we have a prayer that Paul prayed for Christians in Western Asia Minor (present-day Turkey), for them to know (1) the enormity of God's power working upon Jesus and (2) how the power of God is "toward/into" those who believe in

Christ. The effect of God's power upon the historical Jesus was just this: He was "crucified, dead, and buried," then "raised" and "seated" far above a host of evil spirit-beings.

Hard on the heels of this material is a vivid description of those who were "energized" by a different spirit than the one which raised Jesus from the dead (2:1-3). This "spirit" caused the so-called "dead" to walk, but their "resurrection" was only the manipulation of a corpse by an outside agency.

Paul remembers that this is what the recipients of the letter were like until God intervened and joined them to the very resurrection of Jesus to co-share the kingly rule of the Messiah above "the powers." Here we have a contrast between the false spirit's power with that of the power of our Lord by an embarrassing comparison. What could be more astonishing to a manipulated corpse than a resurrected Lord? Even more, what could be more upsetting to a demon host that used to "overrule" its "death-walkers" than a whole host of new believers recast into a new people, sharing Jesus' resurrection and His glory forever?

This contrast is startling when it is displayed in parallel columns:

1:19-23	*parallel to*	*2:4-7*
God's power effects		God *joins* believers to
the resurrection, *raising*		the resurrection of Jesus,
and *seating* Jesus "far above"		*co-raising* and *co-seating*
the evil spirits in the heavenlies		us with Christ in the
(1:20-21), contrasting God's		heavenlies (2:6), "far above"
superior power with the		the evil spirits, in
ineffective power of the		order to display to those
unclean spirits, forever.		spirits (3:10) the superior
		kindness and power of
		God forever.

In contrast with

2:1-3

The "power" of the unclean
spirit(s) which "works" upon those
in its domain, but it leaves them
"dead-but-walking" in their sins.

Think of the implications. What happened to Jesus in His resurrection from the dead happens to those who place their trust in Him, to those who ask for God's resurrection power to reshape their situations. The same power that bestowed transforming life upon Jesus' dead body is the same power that flows into and reorders our personal and corporate lives.[41]

When we say, "Yours in the power," we are speaking out in faith. We are saying, "Lord Jesus, move upon our situation so profoundly by the power of Your Spirit that the demonic forces are forever embarrassed by what You do in and through us."

I remember praying that prayer once. I was at an emerging Bible school, just a few short years after the fall of the Iron Curtain and the demise of the former Soviet Union. I had been asked to teach the book of Ephesians to a group of students who, just a few years before, were not allowed to gather for worship, and who, most certainly, were not allowed to acknowledge God in the public forum or to own a Bible. The twenty or so students were all people who had experienced some form of persecution from the days when the Communists banned Christian faith as "the opiate of the masses" and a form of disease. When the Iron Curtain fell, it became possible for faith to be embraced—but many of the same people who had bitterly attacked faith of any kind (whether Christian or something else) were still in positions of power and influence. Even though their worldview was embarrassed, they still lived and believed that faith in God was to be eradicated. (In fact, one student, a recent convert, was shot and killed at the school because he was attending that seminary.)

In 1994 I was in the Ukraine to teach those who were learning about God at great cost to themselves. They would take lessons with a lecturer from Canada, the United States, or Sweden during the day; then in the evenings they would travel to neighboring communities, set up a tent, and share the gospel. I had just given the teaching that Jesus' power is as present to us as it was to Christ, and that the same power that raised our Lord was given to any who call upon Him to embarrass the power of the demons. In fact, I had used the schematic on the opposite page. The students weren't sure what that would look like in ordinary life, but they were eager to put their newfound learning to work.

In a town about twenty miles away (in which they were sharing their faith), there had been a dramatic breakthrough. A sizable number of soldiers from the local army division had committed their lives to Christ; more than this, they were inviting their fellow soldiers and even a number of officers to come to the tent meetings in which the students and an evangelist were sharing their faith in the Lord Jesus and the kingdom of God. At one gathering, an officer told the story of his journey from atheism to believing in Christ; the result was that several of his peers and subordinates committed their lives to follow the Lord. The Bible college students were ecstatic that God had used them to reach members of the formerly atheistic army. We determined to bring Bibles and Christian literature to them the very next evening, after our daily classes were completed. We loaded up the bus with students and literature and were just about to drive out to the tent meeting.

Then it happened.

We learned from a local soldier that the commanding officer overseeing the area, a "true believer" in Communism and a hard-core atheist, heard of the numbers of his soldiers and officers turning to faith in Christ. He issued a direct order that any soldier going to the meetings would be sternly reprimanded, disciplined, and recommended for court-martial. There were enough old party hacks still in positions of power that those charges could destroy the career of many a soldier. This meant that, effectively, about half of our crowd would not be present for the meeting. It also meant that the soldiers who wanted the Scriptures and the literature that we had just loaded onto the bus would not be able to obtain them.

We decided to travel to the meetings anyway, disheartened and discouraged as we were.

Then came the second blow.

Just a few miles into our trip, our bus broke down. Not only did this delay our arrival, but it threatened to shut down the whole event. The meetings couldn't start without us. We had the evangelist and the worship leaders with us. We waited for someone, anyone, to come to our aid—and the wait seemed very, very long.

Finally, after about forty-five minutes or so, a car came by and took a guitar player/singer, the evangelist, and two others to the tent.

But all the rest of us had to wait with the broken-down bus.

The students asked me what to do.

Suddenly it dawned on me. I said, "Pray for God to embarrass the demons—to shame them for this attack on the gospel."

And so we did for about twenty minutes. While the driver tinkered with the engine, these emerging Christian leaders began to weep, pray, and cry out to God to do as His Word said—that the power that raised the Lord would embarrass this attack on the gospel, just like Jesus' resurrection embarrassed the power of death. We prayed for the soldiers who weren't allowed to come, for the new Christians who wouldn't get anything to help them, and for the people waiting at the tent who wouldn't hear the messages that we had planned to bring that evening. It was fervent, believing prayer—in Ukrainian, Russian, and English! We prayed until we received a sense of "lift" in our souls. We knew we were done.

Just as we finished, a military transport stopped beside our bus. After inquiring what had happened (that our bus had broken down and we were supposed to be about a twenty-minute drive down the road) an officer radioed the divisional commander to tell him that there were about thirty people stranded at the side of the road.

Here is what happened. The divisional commander, hearing that local people were stuck, ordered three army transport trucks to take us and our supplies (as it turned out, our supplies of Bibles and gospel literature) down the road.

Later we found out that the divisional officer who gave the order was in fact the very one who had told his soldiers not to go to the gospel meetings. The atheist commander who had stopped his soldiers from going to the meeting wound up issuing a command to his soldiers to take care of us! A number of the soldiers ordered to help us were the very ones who had wanted to receive their Bibles! They were required to accompany us to the very meeting that they had been banned from attending. Some of them gave their lives to Christ that night (sixty people responded to an invitation to accept the Lord, including a handful of the soldiers), and all of those who wanted literature had it carried back to them by their peers!

When the evening was done, the students gathered around in celebration and said, "*Oochichel!—Oochichel!* Teacher! Teacher! Jesus' power over the powers did the job. Jesus' power embarrassed the demons, teacher! He did it!"

It wasn't our power that did that.

When we say, "Yours is the power!" we are asking Jesus to use even the attacks of the powers of darkness as a platform for God's movement to go forward.

Declare it! When the situation is impossible, pray that way and watch to see what the Lord will do.

PEN TO PAPER

1) Nothing is impossible with God. Nothing. Write down the situations that you know you can do nothing about, in which you are "powerless." Then ask for God's power to intervene, to move upon the people, the events, the resources, yourself, whatever is required. Ask for God to embarrass the attack of the forces of darkness. Ask for God to break through in some marvelous way that the human mind cannot even begin to fathom.

PRAYER CHALLENGE

Perhaps you are aware of a challenge that is simply too large for you to handle. Perhaps you face it every day and know that you can do nothing about it. Every time you face it or it comes to mind, offer a prayer to God to demonstrate His power—to embarrass the things that prevent you from living for God. Pray that you be given a gift to see how God will raise something that seems "dead" to life.

DAY 5

To declare "Yours is the glory" is to declare that God's calling on our lives is our mandate.

The Gospel of John is fairly evenly divided into two sections that commentators have come to call "the book of signs" (John 1-11) and "the book of glory" (John 12-21). The first part is filled with signs that point beyond themselves—they point to Jesus' mission, His teaching, His life as, not only the Son of God, but as the preexistent Word, God Himself being revealed in human flesh. In the second, we see Jesus enter into His glory—and in the second half of John, the "glory" that Jesus accomplishes (and that the world beholds) is that He take up the cross and die, and through His resurrection, make God's glory known.

Halfway through the book, some Greeks (representing the non-Jewish world) come seeking Jesus. From this cue, the mission of our Lord shifted into its next phase. It went from the purely Jewish (and introductory) mission to establish a beachhead in Judaism, to the universal mission to save the world. When the Greeks were brought near to where Christ was, His response was a "glory" response. Here God's glory was redefined, filled with new meaning. "Glory" from this point forward was not only magnificent light and wondrous reputation. "Glory" now referred to the accomplishing of God's mission despite the costs:

> Jesus answered them, saying, "The hour has come for the Son of Man to be glorified. Truly, truly I say unto you, unless a grain of wheat falls into the ground and dies, it remains alone; but if it dies, it bears much fruit. He who loves his life loses it, and he who hates his life in this world will keep it to life eternal. If anyone serves Me, he must follow Me; and where I am, there My servant will be also. . . . Father, glorify Your name." (John 12:23-26, 28, NASB)

Here, Jesus knew that for Him to enter His glory, He must pass through the suffering of the cross—and so He would be "glorified."

Did you notice? The text says that we must follow in His footsteps—through suffering as we enter into His mission. So where was Jesus going that we should follow him? He was pursuing the call of God to die, and through this, was beginning His empowerment of the weak and the helpless. That is the "where," and this is where we are to go. That is how we "share His glory." We need to be careful in saying this. The Bible does *not* glorify suffering in and of itself. In fact, much of the ministry of Christ was to alleviate meaningless suffering and through that, to destroy the works of the devil. Rather, we are recognizing that God's glory has a path that we must follow. It is to pass through life, following wherever the Lord sends us—and to celebrate the Lord's presence in the midst of the suffering; this is what produces the glory.

This is not "glorious" as the world sees it. In fact, were it not that we are to receive a glorious inheritance in heaven (and the down payment of God's glorious grace here—His very presence through the Spirit), the suffering would be futile. But we do not live as those whose eyes are focused on this earth alone. We have heard these words before, but they make this point. The apostle tells us about how suffering works together with glory: "For I consider the sufferings of this present time are not worthy to be compared with the glory that is to be revealed to us" (Romans 8:18, NASB).

In fact Jesus redefined glory, right from the very start of His ministry. John's gospel makes that abundantly clear in two places—in the beginning of the gospel where he proclaims that God became a human—and in Jesus' encounter with Pilate, representing the so-called "glory of Rome." Let's listen to them to understand what we mean when we say, "Yours is the glory": "And the Word became flesh, and dwelt among us, and we saw His glory, glory as of the only begotten from the Father, full of grace and truth" (John 1:14, NASB).

When Christ became a vulnerable little babe in a cowshed, taking up residence with humans—and in fact with the poorest of our race—in a conquered, dangerous culture, *this* was the revelation of God's glory. This is glory redefined forever. Here, God's glory consists of Almighty God's absolute identification with human beings forever, and the abandonment of self-focused power; it is full, not of sheer force and brutality—not "God the Overlord." Rather, God's glory is revealed through unity with our weaknesses and vulnerability brimming over with grace and truth. God's glory is revealed in the empowerment of the nobodies living in the "nowheresvilles" of all the dusty corners of creation. It is life from death, hope from despair, beginnings from endings, and empowering presence instead of graceless rejection and abandonment. This is truly a very different kind of kingdom than the ones that claim their own kind of "kingdom, power, and glory forever." Listen to Pilate, representing Rome's glorious kingdom, trying to understand the kingdom of King Jesus:

> Therefore Pilate . . . summoned Jesus and said to Him, "Are you the King of the Jews?"
>
> Jesus answered, "Are you saying this on your own initiative, or did others tell you about Me?"
>
> Pilate answered, "I am not a Jew, am I? Your own nation and the chief priests delivered You to me; what have You done?"
>
> Jesus answered, "My kingdom is not of this world. If my kingdom were of this world, then My servants would be fighting so that I would not be handed over to the Jews; but as it is, My kingdom is not of this realm."
>
> Therefore Pilate said to Him, "So You are a king?"
>
> Jesus answered, "You say correctly that I am a king. For this I have been born, and for this I have come into the world, to testify to the truth. Everyone who is of the truth hears My voice."
>
> Pilate said to Him, "What is truth?" (John 18:33-38, NASB)

Pilate still didn't begin to understand until the chief priests told him that Jesus made Himself out to be the Son of God. Then, as awareness was dawning upon him that this was a unique case, he tried to get answers and found out yet another reality—even his own sheer force, "the power and the glory" of Rome, was in utter submission to the God who was revealing His glory in the abandoning of destructive absolute power:

> Therefore when Pilate heard this statement, he was even more afraid; and he entered into the Praetorium again and said to Jesus, "Where are You from?" But Jesus gave him no answer. So Pilate

said to Him, "You do not speak to me? Do you not know that I have authority to release You and I have authority to crucify You?" Jesus answered, "You would have no authority over Me, unless it had been given you from above; for this reason he who delivered Me to you has the greater sin."

As a result of this, Pilate made efforts to release Him, but the Jews cried out saying, "If you release this Man, you are no friend of Caesar; everyone who makes himself out to be a king opposes Caesar." (John 19:8-12, NASB)

Listen to Tom Wright's comment on these passages about the contrasting types of kingdom, power, and glory:

Caesar's glory is full of brute force and deep ambiguity. God's glory, Jesus' glory is full of grace and truth. . . .

You see the two empires squared off against each other . . . when Pilate confronts Jesus with two questions: don't you know that I have the power to have you killed? And—what is truth? That is the language of kingdom, power and glory that the world knows. Notice how the two halves support each other. In order to be able to say, "Support my kingdom or I'll kill you," pagan empire needs to say that there's no such thing as truth. And if someone not only tells the truth but lives the truth, pagan empire has no alternative but to kill them. Jesus responds by quietly reminding Pilate that all power comes from on high, and by getting on with the job of *being* the truth—living out truly the love of God for the salvation of the world . . . [Jesus invites us] to contemplate the radical and total redefinition of truth, of peace, and above all of kingdom, power and glory.[42]

When we declare "Yours is the glory," we are asserting that we are aligning ourselves with a very different set of values than the world embraces. We are embracing God's empowerment of the weak and the helpless. We are embracing not only truthful living, but living within the "power-sphere" of the person who called His very being "truth": "I am the way, the truth and the life" (John 14:6, KJV). Jesus defined His very existence as truth. We are declaring that to live for and in God's glory is to brim over with grace and graciousness, even when the counterfeit kingdoms of the world offer us only the brutal demand that we bow before sheer force.

Jesus' "kingdom, power, and glory" is countercultural and life-bestowing.

PEN TO PAPER

1) Who is God calling you to love? Write their names in the space below and pray that God's glory be revealed to them through who you are.

2) Pick up a newspaper and record the headlines in this space. Ask if the issues before our society are being reported from the perspective of sheer force to conform, or if they are being addressed from the perspective of God's empowerment of the weak and the helpless. Then pray for God's glory to be revealed. Ask the Lord if you are to align yourself with any of the issues that are current events of our day. If so, pray, "Yours is the glory" and "reveal Your glory in and through me" as you confront the calling God is placing on your heart.

PRAYER CHALLENGE

Today you will meet instances in which you can empower one who is weak or in which you can use your power to "overpower." To be an instrument of God's glory is to choose the former rather than the latter. Choose to raise people up. As you do, sing a song or chorus that speaks to our need to put God's glory first. Or simply declare: "Yours is the glory, forever. Amen."

DAY 6

Jesus did everything for God's glory—
and He gave it to us.

I t only takes a little reading to make certain that it was so, but it was. Jesus did everything so that God could receive "glory." The way the New Testament uses the word "glory" is utterly consistent from author to author. When it is used to describe human activity it always refers to "reputation," "power," and "renown." Beyond these meanings, when it is used of God and God's glory, it has a fluid interchangeability—referring to "divine honor," "divine splendor," "divine power," and "visible divine radiance." All of these meanings and more appear in John's gospel—the place in which Jesus prays another "Lord's Prayer"—prayer having to do with God's glory, Jesus' glory, and the giving of that glory to the disciples and through them to all humanity. It is the high priestly prayer of John 17.

This prayer is packed with depth and power. It cannot be understood in a quick reading. However, one of the principle themes of the gospel comes to light here in this passage—that somehow, some way, God and Jesus are "one"—and this is glorifying. All of the meanings of reputation, light, joy, and radiance come together in the "glory" prayers that our Lord prays in this chapter, revolving around the unity of the Father and the Son, and the magnificent calling that all believers enter into God's glory—through a profound unity that is identical to the Father's and the Son's.

> Father, the hour has come; glorify Your Son that the Son may glorify You. . . . I glorified You on the earth, having accomplished the work which You have given Me to do. Now, Father, glorify Me together with Yourself, with the glory which I had with You before the world was. (John 17:1, 4-5, NASB)

Here it is plain that the phrase "Yours is the glory" was in fact the prayer of Jesus' life. The thrust of the text is that through His joyful obedience to God throughout His earthly life, God's reputation, renown, and power were revealed in and through Him.

Here, to glorify God is to accomplish the things that God wants done. Jesus did that—and so can we.

To glorify God is to know Him intimately. It is to receive "marching orders" from God, and it is to carry them out. It is to look back on our day, our week, our month, or our life and say, "I did what You asked me to do. It is accomplished."

Then it is to take a further step. Jesus could do this like no other. He requested a return to the glory that He had as the preexistent Word of God. In His case, it was a magnificent return to a wondrous reality—to be not only in heaven with God, but to be the center of heaven and to be God. In our case, we ask for the heaven we have never known before.

Our reward will be different in character, though it will be magnificent beyond all human existence. Jesus Christ the Lord is the center and we never can be. But we can be joined to the center and shine with His borrowed radiance forever. We shall share His glory and find ourselves seated in Him and with Him forever.

To obey is to glorify God. This, then, is to receive a heavenly reward as a consequence of following His leading. But the reward is not something akin to what we get for work done on earth (a raise in pay, a kind word of thanks, a promotion, etc.). In heaven we not only obtain heaven, we obtain a "participation in the divine nature." We receive entrance into the life of the Father and the Son themselves. In a way that defies human comprehension, this altered reality begins here on earth.

> The glory which You have given Me I have given to them, that they may be one, just as We are one. I in them and You in Me, that they may be perfected in unity, so that the world may know that You sent Me, and loved them, even as You have loved Me. Father, I desire that they also, whom You have given Me, be with Me where I am, so that they may see My glory which You have given Me, for You loved Me before the foundation of the world. (John 17:22-24, NASB)

This unity cannot be forced into existence by a series of church mergers. This is a unity of different order. This is the unity of those who fully obey the Lord, and through that obedience are brought to others whose very center is the love of God. By divine appointment, God reveals His heart to those who sacrifice to be one with Him. Then by divine appointment we are drawn together around who Jesus is. And this is glorious.

We taste this reality from time to time. This is the glory that comes when someone prays for another, is moved to action, obeys, and then sees God's power break through in a marvelous way. We discover that our actions were in fact the actions that God desired us to do—and they lead to an amazing breakthrough of God's power.

Some years ago, I was in prayer when a burden for a teenager in the youth group came upon me. Let's call the teen "Joe." It was very nearly overwhelming and this burden would not relinquish its hold on my soul. After nearly an hour of prayer, it became clear that I needed to go and visit the teenager at his school immediately. I phoned my wife, who told me that she concurred with the action, and so I began to drive—about forty-five minutes from the church office. All the way, the burden of prayer grew more profound, until I was given a word for the young man. It was such a simple word that I questioned the whole trip. After all, it was something we heard every Sunday. I was to tell him that Jesus loved him!

I walked into the school and there was the very boy standing right by the entrance of the building by the office door. He saw me and very nearly fell over with surprise.

He said, "What are you doing here?"

I walked up to him and told him, "Joe, I need to tell you that you are profoundly loved of the Lord. He has commanded me to find you this morning to tell you that Jesus loves you."

He broke down and began to sob. Joe told me he couldn't believe that I had just said that. Then he started to thank the Lord, right in the hallway.

What I didn't know was his side of the story. Joe went on to tell me that he had been going through a horrible crisis of faith, rooted in the fact that he had suffered some terrible things. It was so very bad that he didn't know if he believed in the love of God at all. And if God wasn't love, he didn't want Him. In fact, he rose that morning and from the depths of despair told

God that he didn't believe He loved him at all. Then he cried out from his soul, asking the Lord to send someone to tell him that He loved him, or he was going to take his life.

That was the moment my prayer burden for Joe began.

We saw the Lord's glory. He heard his prayer. I heard His prompting and obeyed what I was given. The teenager understood that the Lord loved him, and we discovered that we were one, not in all that we thought or said or did. Rather we were one in that we shared the presence and the power of the Lord profoundly.

Joe received the help he needed and he grew into a wonderful man. Yet we tasted this reality called God's glory through a unity that could not be denied.

Heaven will be like that—only there will be no more tears, no more sorrow or sighing—all the former things will end. And insofar as we obey the promptings of the Lord that we are given, we taste a little bit of heaven here on earth and can say, "Yours is the glory, forever!"

PEN TO PAPER

1) Reexamine the first reading from John 17:1, 4-5 above. Paraphrase the point here below.

Is there an action step from the text that you are to take? What is it?

How then are you to pray this text?

2) Now reread John 17:22-24. Pray that the Lord would grant you to see and know the truth of the unity described in that text. Look for any signs of it in your life. Record them here. Then thank God for them.

PRAYER CHALLENGE

Pray that the Father and the Son teach you to glorify God. Say, "Yours is the glory," whenever you meet a situation in which the people of God are not united. Pray for God's glory to be revealed through profound unity.

DAY 7

We await our forever. Amen!

"The kingdom, the power, and the glory forever" has a fulfillment in our present lives—through the presence of the Holy Spirit. But the Holy Spirit with us right now is actually only the down payment—the guarantee of what we are to receive at the end of time:

> While we live in this earthly tent, we groan with a feeling of oppression; it is not that we want to get rid of our earthly body, but that we want to have the heavenly one put on over us, so that what is mortal will be transformed by life. God is the one who has prepared us for this change, and he gave us his Spirit as the guarantee of all that he has in store for us. So we are always full of courage. We know that as long as we are at home in the body, we are away from the Lord's home. . . . More than anything else, however, we want to please him, whether in our home here or there. For all of us must appear before Christ, to be judged by him. (2 Corinthians 5:4-6, 9-10, GNT)

What will we receive at the end? Not just a trinket or two—even if it is a magnificent trinket—like heaven itself. We will receive not only the Holy Spirit's presence in our temporary tent here below. Instead we will receive a permanent home. Better yet, God will too! In a fluid and impossible set of overlapping images, God becomes our home and we become God's.

The point is plain: We will receive God in all His fullness, just like a bride receives her husband on the wedding day. And God gets His bride—the one He has waited for and prepared to marry for eternity.

When a bride marries, she receives all that belongs to the husband, but if she loves him, she doesn't marry to obtain goods. She marries the groom and gets the groom—whether rich or poor. Now this Groom is the author of all things—and we will receive God Himself. There will be God's glory, but even that is a pale and weak side benefit from receiving all of who God is forever. The rest won't matter.

The book of Revelation describes this reality using unearthly language and imagery. Actually, the book has been much misunderstood—and feared. John Calvin the great Reformer wrote a commentary on most every book of the Bible—except this one!

However, the point of the book can be found in the title. The book is "the revelation" or "the unveiling" of Jesus Christ. Jesus is the one revealed—and that is the theme of the entire book from cover to cover. Other things are revealed and unveiled—but the *center* of the material is that Jesus is revealed; the book describes what that "revelation" does.

First, Jesus is revealed to John—but He is revealed only through a kind of veil; the veil is the presence of the church—God's people everywhere. "Then I turned to see the voice that was speaking with me. And having turned I saw seven golden lampstands; and in the middle of the lampstands I saw one like a son of man" (Revelation 1:12-13, NASB).

Did you notice that when John turned to see the voice, he noticed seven golden lampstands before he saw the apocalyptic vision of Jesus. *Through* them, he saw the resurrected Lord. He only saw the Lord as one who was walking through the stands. Jesus Himself told John what the lampstands stood for: "The seven lampstands are the seven churches" (Revelation 1:20, GNT).

Jesus could not be seen by John except *through* the churches!

And Jesus cannot be seen by creation except through the people of God now. That is one of the primary messages of the book.

Secondly, Jesus is revealed to seven churches in perfect symmetry. The churches are either utter disasters and about to perish through losing the presence of God within them (Ephesus and Laodicea); faithful, but weak (Philadelphia and Smyrna); or mixed and in need of repentance (Pergamum, Thyatira, and Sardis). Jesus had longed to be revealed to the cities in which these churches were located, but either weakness or sin prevented His full disclosure. He speaks to them so that Christ be revealed both *to* them, and *through* them, to their cities.

Thirdly, Jesus as the Lamb of God is revealed to the heavenly court, as the Lamb slain from the foundation of the world.

Fourthly, Jesus is revealed to the structures of society, which are infested and infected with systemic evil; in the end, anything that rejects His presence is destroyed.

Fifthly, Jesus is revealed even to the dark powers; they are bound, then destroyed.

Finally, Jesus is revealed to all creation—but this time He is revealed through a purified and glorified church—the corporate community of God's people, which is called "the bride, the wife of the Lamb," and "the holy city, the New Jerusalem."

Here, the bride (us—the people of God) is so completely one with who the Lord is that Jesus cannot be seen unless one looks through the glorified church! This time, though, the view is unobstructed. Opaque things like jasper and gold, precious in their own right, are now so very pure that they too are transparent like glass. Nothing is hidden ever again. The point is not that we go *up* to be with God, but that God *comes down* to dwell in us—and to shine through us so completely that God and God's glory and our existence are forever intertwined, locked together in a joyful union that transfigures both.

> Then I saw a new heaven and a new earth; for the first heaven and the first earth passed away, and there is no longer any sea. And I saw the holy city, New Jerusalem, coming down out of heaven from God, made ready as a bride adorned for her husband. And I heard a loud voice from the throne, saying, "Behold the tabernacle of God is among men, and He will dwell among them, and they shall be His people, and God Himself will be among them, and He will wipe away every tear from their eyes; and there will no longer be any death; there will no longer be any mourning or crying, or pain; the first things have passed away. (Revelation 21:1-4, NASB)

Then all parts of creation everywhere see God—but they don't see God directly. Just as Jesus could not be seen at the beginning of the book except by looking *through* the churches, here creation sees God *by seeing the people of God,* now no longer imperfect, weak, or sinful. Rather they see God by seeing the people of God shining with the glory of God. By gazing through the city (which is the people of God), all creation sees the Lord God Almighty and the

Lamb. They are already so one that they cannot be distinguished. And now the people of God share that destiny . . .

> Then one of the seven angels . . . spoke with me, saying, "Come here, I will show you the bride, the wife of the Lamb." And he carried me away in the Spirit to a great and high mountain, and showed me the holy city, Jerusalem, coming down out of heaven from God, having the glory of God. (Revelation 21:9-11, NASB)

> I saw no temple in it, for the Lord God the Almighty and the Lamb are its temple. And the city has no need of the moon to shine on it, for the glory of God has illumined it, and its lamp is the Lamb. The nations will walk by its light, and the kings of the earth will bring their glory into it. (Revelation 21:22-24, NASB)

Here is the glorious and final hope of the New Testament—that we, the people of God, made into a holy unity by the experience of the Holy Spirit, are brought to the place in which we are forever forged into a magnificent unity through which God shines forever.

When we say, "The kingdom, the power, and the glory are Yours, forever!" we are saying that we are committed to the ultimate ending of all things, in which God becomes the center, and we are in the center with Him, radiating everything that is of Him to all that lives and moves and breathes.

We do that imperfectly now.

But God is calling us to be that forever.

PEN TO PAPER

1) Think for a moment if you know anyone who simply "shines" with the presence of God. It was said of Mother Teresa that anyone who came within sixty feet of her found themselves lifted up into God's presence. Do you know anyone like that? Record here the names that come to mind and thank God for them.

2) By asserting that the kingdom, the power, and the glory belong to God, a wondrous (and paradoxical) interchange takes place. God, as King, receives the praise of His glory. Then in a kingly act of love, He bestows power *upon us* and we discover that *we share His glory*; He makes us shine with His glorious presence to others around us. Anytime we try to obtain that glory for ourselves, we lose His nearness. Anytime we focus on making His glory known, we shine with His grace. Assert that it is so in your life. Assert that God is and shall be the king of your life forever. Speak out loud of each issue in your life, and tell God that it is His, and not yours.

3) Now take this concluding line of the Lord's Prayer and rewrite it into words that make it more real to you. Attempt to capture what it means, rather than to use the exact language.

PRAYER CHALLENGE

Reflect on the reality that we are not just going *to* a city, but that we are (in some way that cannot be understood with our limited capacity for thought), going *to be* the very city of God Himself. Reflect on the truth that we are the temple in which God dwells by the Spirit, and that nations will see God's glory and Jesus' glory only as God shines through us! Pray for those who need the light of Christ to shine on them, and pray to be one through whom the light shines. End your time by declaring, "Yours is the kingdom, the power, and the glory, forever. Amen!"

Endnotes

1. Helen Smith Shoemaker, *The Secret of Effective Prayer* (Westwood, NJ: Fleming H. Revell, 1955), 18.

2. Richard Foster, *Prayer: Finding the Heart's True Home* (New York: Harper Collins, 1992), 6.

3. Cited in J. S. Bonnell, *The Practice and Power of Prayer* (Philadelphia: Westminster Press, 1954), 14.

4. Philip Graham Ryken, *When You Pray* (Wheaton, IL: Crossway Books, 2000), 21.

5. John White, *The Fight* (Downers Grove, IL: InterVarsity Press, 1976), 27.

6. Maxie Dunnam, *The Workbook of Living Prayer* (Nashville, TN: Upper Room Books, 1994), 95-96.

7. R.A. Torrey, *How to Pray* (Chicago: Moody Press, 1902) 13.

8. Torrey, *How to Pray*, 57.

9. Torrey, *How to Pray*, 59-60.

10. A. W. Tozer, "Does God Always Answer Prayer?" *Pray!*, 4 January/February 1998, 37. This article was excerpted from *Man: The Dwelling Place of God* (Camp Hill, PA: Christian Publications, 1966).

11. Cited in Donald T. Williams, *The Disciple's Prayer* (Camp Hill, PA: Christian Publications, 1999), 47-48.

12. William Barclay, *The Lord's Prayer* (Louisville, KY: Westminster John Knox Press, 1964, 1998), 54.

13. Taken from AP wire story, appearing in the Friday, November 14, 1986 edition of the *Edmonton Journal*.

14. Armin Gesswein, cited in Fred Hartley, *Everything by Prayer* (Camp Hill, PA: Christian Publications, 2003), 51.

15. Brother Andrew with Susan DeVore Williams, *And God Changed His Mind* (Tarrytown, NY: Chosen Books, Fleming H. Revell Company, 1990).

16. P.C. Craigie, *The Book of Deuteronomy* (Grand Rapids, MI: Eerdmans, 1976), 185.

17. Dietrich Bonhoeffer, *The Cost of Discipleship* (London: SCM Press, 1959), 155-156.

18. Bonhoeffer, *The Cost of Discipleship*, 158.

19. Adapted from John Maxwell, *Partners in Prayer* (Nashville, TN: Thomas Nelson, 1996), 22-23.

20. Maxwell, *Partners in Prayer,* 65-66.

21. Dietrich Bonhoeffer. Versified by Rev. Walter Farquharson. Taken from *The Hymn Book of the Anglican Church of Canada and the United Church of Canada,* (Anglican church of Canada and the United Church of Canada, 1971) Hymn #105.

22. Bonhoeffer, Hymn #105.

23. N. T. Wright, *The Lord and His Prayer* (Grand Rapids, MI: Eerdmans, 1996), 53-54.

24. Paul Brand and Phil Yancey, *Fearfully and Wonderfully Made* (Grand Rapids, MI: Zondervan, 1987).

25. Corrie ten Boom with John and Elizabeth Sherrill, *The Hiding Place* (Old Tappan, NJ: Fleming Revell, 1971), 217.

26. Ten Boom, *The Hiding Place,* 238.

27. Ten Boom, *The Hiding Place,* 238.

28. Neil T. Anderson and Charles Mylander, *Setting Your Church Free* (Venture, CA: Regal Books, 1994), Appendix C, 339-341.

29. James Houston, *The Transforming Friendship* (Oxford: Lion Publishing, 1989), 294.

30. Dietrich Bonhoeffer, trans. Kathleen Downham, *Temptation* (London: SCM Press, 1953, 1955), 22.

31. Foster, *Prayer,* 14.

32. Charles Durnham, *Temptation* (Downers Grove, IL: Intervarsity Press, 1982), 16.

33. White, *The Fight,* 81.

34. Foster, *Prayer,* 235-237.

35. Foster, *Prayer,* 237.

36. Adapted from Foster, *Prayer,* 237-238.

37. Adapted from George A. Buttrick, *Prayer* (New York: Abingdon Press, 1942), 35.

38. Buttrick, *Prayer,* p. 39.

39. Henry T. Blackaby and Claude V. King, *Experiencing God: Knowing and Doing the Will of God* (Nashville, TN: Lifeway Press, 1990), pp. 18, 32.

40. Taken from Ray C. Stedman, *Talking with My Father* (Grand Rapids, MI: Discovery House, 1997), 75-77.

41. See David R. Chotka, "'Spirit versus spirit'—An Examination of the Nature and Function of the Holy Spirit in the Epistle to the Ephesians" (Unpublished Th.M thesis, Regent College, 1992), 108-132.

42. Wright, *The Lord and His Prayer,* 82-83.

Endorsements

"The litmus test for any book on prayer is two-fold: it should teach you how to pray, and it should make you want to pray. David Chotka's *Power Praying* succeeds brilliantly on both counts. David, using the Lord's Prayer as template, sounds that prayer's depths and, as he does so, serves up a theological and biblical tour de force. But this is no mere theological treatise: in all and through all, David's sheer enthusiasm for praying, and his many stories of prayer in action, leave you hungering and thirsting for God, his righteousness, and his kingdom. There is joy and beauty here to make broken bones dance." —Mark Buchanan, pastor and author of *The Rest of God and Spiritual Rhythm*

"I was quickly arrested by [*Power Praying*]. I was soon struck by David's immersion in Scripture, story-telling ability, skill of clear communication, and passion about prayer. It was difficult for me to put it down. His week about Discernment was superbly helpful to me. Our world would be profoundly blessed if his five points of discernment became the pattern in our churches. Lord, hear our prayer!"—Danny Morris, author of *A Life That Really Matters*

"Stimulating, inspiring, and instructional . . . With insightful revelation David has hit the mark in bringing a refreshing wind to reinvigorate the experienced believer regarding prayer. Simultaneously it is a distinct discipleship tool for the young believer. *Power Praying* is a book for believers at all stages on the journey of cultivating a kingdom heart and intimacy with their Heavenly Father." —Mike Riches, pastor, author, and director of Sycamore Commission

"At first glance the Lord's Prayer is short and seemingly insignificant. Don't let the size fool you. It contains every possible dimension of prayer. When we learn to use it on a regular basis, it will transform our lives. The only problem with the Lord's Prayer pattern is that we have made it religious; Jesus intended it to be relational. David Chotka does a brilliant job unpacking this prayer so that it will have practical and transformational impact in each of our lives. I have been using the Lord's Prayer pattern as a model prayer for 20 years; David Chotka takes it to a new level, exploring its all-encompassing richness. He uniquely shows how every facet of Christ's life and ministry is in one way or another tied to this prayer." —Fred A. Hartley, III, lead pastor, Lilburn Alliance Church, president, College of Prayer International

"Prayer is fundamentally a relationship with God—but even the best of relationships can benefit from professional coaching now and then. David Chotka has taken Jesus' own prayer model and used it as a powerful yet practical foundation for helping anyone develop a vibrant and effective relationship with God through prayer." —Arlyn Lawrence, contributing editor, *Pray!* magazine (NavPress)

"David Chotka has penetrated the Lord's Prayer in a new and refreshing way. His analysis begins with new understanding of our desire for the magnification of the name of the Father through the prayer for the establishment of the Kingdom and the implications of all this for spiritual warfare. He then teaches us to align our own petitions with these desires for the Glory of God. This would be enough, but we are also given carefully constructed guidance for prayer as we pray as Jesus taught us." —Dr. Franklin Pyles, president of the Christian and Missionary Alliance of Canada.

"David Chotka's book is a breakthrough in devotional literature. It anticipates the difficulties many people encounter when they set out to pray. It encourages them to pray without making them feel guilty or inept. It acquaints them with a theology of prayer set in the context of the theology of our Lord's earthly ministry, and all of this within a grand theology that is biblically informed. It provides concrete, how-to-do-it help, without which the best resolve to pray evaporates in two weeks. And not least the book is written in language anyone can understand." —Dr. Victor Shepherd, professor of systematic and historical theology, Tyndale Seminary, Toronto, Ontario.

"My friend and author, David Chotka provides a superb workbook on the Lord's Prayer. It is biblically enriched, contemporary in context and practical in application. This volume is a serious invitation and guide to take an engaging journey of seven weeks to refresh and revitalize your personal life. My personal investment resulted in in much gain. Try it!" —Dr. T.V. Thomas, director, Centre for Evangelism & World Mission.